GUIDED CHANGE OF THE
AMERICAN HEALTH SYSTEM

GUIDED CHANGE OF THE AMERICAN HEALTH SYSTEM

Where the Levers Are

Pamela Doty, Ph.D.

Volume II, Center for Policy Research Monograph Series

Series Editor: Amitai Etzioni, Ph.D

HUMAN SCIENCES PRESS
72 Fifth Avenue   3 Henrietta Street
NEW YORK, NY 10011 ● LONDON, WC2E 8LU

Printed in the United States of America
0123456789   987654321

Library of Congress Cataloging in Publication Data

Doty, Pamela.
  Guided change of the American health system.

  (Center for Policy Research Monograph series ; v. 2)
  Includes index.
  1. Medical policy—United States—Case studies.   2. Social change—Case studies.
  3. United States—Social policy—Case studies   I. Title.
RA395.A3D67   362.1'0973   LC80-12484
ISBN 0-87705-472-X

CONTENTS

5

INTRODUCTION

Alternative approaches to social policy imply alternative underlying conceptual assumptions concerning what and how social factors can most effectively serve as levers for deliberate social change. Some approaches stress the need for increased knowledge about the social problems to be attacked and thus recommend programs of research and development or the establishment of information systems. Some emphasize the key role of more efficient, effective organization, for example, via government or the market. Others give primacy to building societal consensus, or, conversely, the need to bring latent value conflicts to the fore, perhaps by focusing public attention on a problem via media or educational efforts. Still others stress power relations such as the need to redistribute wealth or political power, or, perhaps the need to give government more authority to protect the rights of those who lack wealth or power. Approaches to social policy also differ as to whether they see change as best effected by incremental modifications versus fundamental criticism and reform of the status quo. To explore the implications of alternative theoretical assumptions about the social factors implicated in deliberate social change, four health policy studies and their recommendations are compared. Efforts to implement the studies' recommendations are looked on as natural experiments which allow us to trace the consequences of emphasizing the role of one or two social factors to the comparative neglect of others. The main theme of the book is that deliberate social change tends to be more effective in attaining its aims with fewer problematic side effects to the degree that policymakers and those who advise them work with strategies that acknowledge the interdependence of five main sociological levers for change: knowledge, organization, consensus, power, and decision-making strategy.

To my grandmothers,
Katherine Northrop Doty and
Rose LaForest Sanborn

ACKNOWLEDGMENTS

I wish especially to acknowledge my intellectual debt to Amitai Etzioni, Professor of Sociology at Columbia University and Director of the Center for Policy Research, for his guidance, both his societal guidance theory and the personal guidance he so generously gave me while I was writing this book. I am also grateful for the assistance of the staff of the Center for Policy Research.

The research and writing of this book was supported by NIMH Grant #12 MH27900-07, and its findings are part of a much larger project of which Amitai Etzioni is principal investigator. I owe special thanks to Dr. Howard R. Davis, Chief, Mental Health Services Research, Division of Mental Health Services Program, National Institute of Mental Health, and Ms. Susan Salasin, Chief, Research Diffusion and Utilization Section, Division of Mental Health Services Programs, National Institute of Mental Health, for their intellectual contributions as well as project support. I am also grateful for the intellectual stimulation of NIMH's *Network on Knowledge Transfer.*

Since some of the material and ideas for this research originally came out of my doctoral dissertation research on information systems in the Medicaid program, I would also like to thank the Milbank Memorial Fund which sponsored that project, and, in particular David Willis, as well as Jack Elinson and Edward F. X. Hughes who served on the project's advisory board and Herbert Gans, John Colombotos, and Edwin Winckler who served on my dissertation committee for their helpful comments and suggestions.

Chapter 1

SOCIAL THEORY AND DELIBERATE SOCIAL CHANGE

INTRODUCTION

This book's central theme is the adequacy of the knowledge base—in particular, the intellectual knowledge base—underlying government policies and programs of social regulation. Every proposal for social regulation or regulatory reform is grounded in a set of assumptions about the dynamics of deliberate social change. Alternative approaches to regulation imply alternative theories of deliberate social change. Efforts to implement a new regulatory policy or set of reform recommendations can thus be viewed as "natural experiments" testing the validity of these theoretical assumptions.

The major theoretical issue that a proposal for social regulation must address is: the question of what are the sociopolitical "levers" of deliberate change. It is our thesis, derived from Amitai Etzioni's theory of societal guidance,[1] that societal processes can be guided toward desired goals by deliberately varying the readings on five major sets of variables. These are knowledge, organization, power, consensus, and decision making.

To assess the effectiveness of alternate regulatory strategies we will focus on what social theorist Robert K. Merton has termed the "unanticipated consequences of purposive social action."[2] In this context the concept refers to the fact that efforts to intervene in and guide social processes tend at best to be only partially successful and often produce results that are unintended, unexpected, and undesirable. It is our argument that in any concrete instance many of the problematic consequences of social regulation, although unanticipated by those who advocated the intervention, might well have been predicted on theoretical grounds.

Although a variety of factors can account for the gap between intention and effect so often observed in connection with regulatory intervention, the four case studies we are about to examine will focus specifically on the role played by faulty assumptions concerning the key variables of deliberate social change and their interaction. Thus a regulatory strategy that takes all five sets of "guidance variables" and their interaction into account would be expected to be more effective in achieving its purposes, with fewer "unanticipated consequences." Conversely, a regulatory strategy that emphasizes the importance of one or two sets of factors while paying relatively little attention to the others would be expected to be not only less effective in achieving its goals, but to produce characteristic "unanticipated consequences," depending on which variables have been stressed and which neglected.

We will seek to illustrate this thesis via the qualitative analysis of four case studies involving alternate approaches to regulation in the area of health services. We use the term "social regulation" here in its broadest sense; that is, its meaning is not limited to the standard setting and enforcement activities of a regulatory bureaucracy, but encompasses any attempt to bring about deliberate social change or to intervene in and guide societal processes toward collective goals. Although various terms-may be employed to characterize such efforts—for example, regulation, reform, policymaking—the defining concepts for us are those of "deliberate" and "purposive" social action. The analysis proceeds by classifying the theoretical assumptions underlying each regulatory approach on an analytic grid. The two dimensions of the grid are, first, how critical is regulatory design of existing policy assumptions—that is, does the approach call for relatively incremental versus fundamental changes—and second, does it stress instrumental rationality (i.e., knowledge and organizational variables) or political factors (i.e., power, consensus) as the main levers for effecting deliberate social change. Each of the four case studies represents a different combination of analytic attributes: incremental–rational, incremental–political, fundamental–rational, incremental–political.

FRAMEWORK: SOCIETAL GUIDANCE THEORY

The analytic framework that we will apply to the four cases is based on Amitai Etzioni's theory of societal guidance. Guidance theory differs from most of the more familiar approaches to sociological theory in that it is explicitly active in its orientation toward societal and political processes.[3] Although the aim of any scientific enterprise is to uncover universal laws, classical sociological theory has sought to uncover the laws that determine ongoing societal change, that is, societal processes assumed to proceed according to their own dynamics, outside our control. In contrast, societal guidance theory seeks to specify the laws that condition our ability to choose the kind of society we want to live in. As such, it focuses on what Etzioni terms "malleable variables."[4] Whether or not a variable is malleable and to what degree and by what means it is malleable are central issues, because such attributes are indicative of a variable's usefulness as a lever for deliberate social change. Thus societal guidance theory is to traditional sociological theory what medicine is to physiology, engineering to physical science, or post-Keynesian to classical economics.

Societal guidance theory posits five main variables that societal actors can employ as levers for deliberate social change: power, consensus, knowledge, organization, and decision making. All five have long been basic to sociological and political theory, although decision making has received more attention in political science than in sociology. Again, however, the central theoretical focus up to the present has tended to be the comparative weight or significance of each of these factors in explaining the variance among social phenomena. Thus a fundamental theoretical disagreement between Marx and Weber was over the importance of knowledge as a causal factor of social change; Marx saw knowledge as relatively insignificant; Weber saw it as capable of being quite significant. Contemporary "conflict" and "consensus" theorists disagree over the relative significance of power and shared values in explaining, for example, a society's stratification system.

In contrast, societal guidance theory assumes all five variables have independent causal significance. Rather than attempting to measure how much weight each factor carries, guidance theory focuses on their interaction. Guidance theory is also especially concerned with how societal "actors" (e.g., individual decision makers, organized groups, government) seek to utilize—and often deliberately to vary—the four variables to achieve their purposes as well as the consequences for guided social change of action strategies that stress one variable or set of variables to the exclusion or comparative neglect of the others.

In terms of how these guidance variables relate to the analytic grid, we will be applying to the four cases the "incremental-fundamental" dimension which deals with societal actors' (in this instance, policy researchers') choice between two alternative approaches to decision making.

A leading theoretician of incremental decision making, Charles Lindblom, has provided the following model, intended to be both descriptive and prescriptive, of this approach:

1. Rather than attempt a comprehensive survey and evaluation of all alternatives, the decision maker focuses solely on those policies that differ incrementally—that is, only in a few respects—from existing ones.
2. Only a relatively small number of policy alternatives are considered.
3. For each policy alternative, only a restricted number of "important" consequences are evaluated.
4. The problem confronting the decision maker is continually redefined as conditions change. Incrementalism thus allows for countless ends-means and means-ends adjustments that, in effect, make the problem more manageable.
5. As such, incremental decision making is described as remedial, geared more to the alleviation of concrete present-day social imperfections than to the promotion of future societal goals.[5]

Lindblom has also identified other attributes as characteristic of the incrementalist strategy of decision making. Thus incremental decision making is said to be relatively decentralized and proceeds via "partisan mutual adjustment." As such, it is portrayed as more compatible with the market as opposed to bureaucracy, with negotiation, compromise, give and take, and good old-fashioned political logrolling versus the rationalism of comprehensive planning.

For our purposes, however, the key element is the restriction of decision making or reform alternatives to those that differ only incrementally from existing policies.

In contrast, to open up the decision-making options to include those that are deeply critical of existing policy is to be willing to make fundamental decisions, to undertake fundamental reform. There appears to be no well-elaborated theoretical model of fundamental decision making akin to that provided for incrementalism by Lindblom. Typically, however, fundamental reform may be said to entail a grand design of one sort or another. In the hands of those who espouse a highly rationalistic, systems analytic, comprehensive planning perspective, this grand design may well take the form of a master plan, with clearly specified goals and implementation strategies.

If, however, it comes from more politically inclined reformers, a grand design for fundamental reform may be expressed with the simplicity of a slogan or rallying cry.

The contrast between incremental and fundamental reform can perhaps be best characterized by an analogy to Thomas Kuhn's conceptualization of scientific progress. According to Kuhn, "normal science" evolves step by step or incrementally, by making new applications and relatively minor modifications, additions, and deletions in an existing theoretical "paradigm." At some point, however, scientists begin to experience the existing theoretical paradigm as no longer viable in some fundamental sense. After a difficult period of growing criticism and futile attempts to deal with the problem via the incrementalist means of normal science, a "paradigm shift" occurs in which crucial underlying assumptions of the old paradigm are discredited and replaced. Even though the new paradigm may incorporate some sizable elements of the old, its core is thus regarded as fundamentally different.[6]

Viewed from a historical perspective, incremental reforms often prepare the ground for fundamental ones, whereas follow-through on a fundamental reform often necessitates a series of incremental elaborations; but though over time history may favor both incremental and fundamental reforms, policy researchers and policymakers are in each instance largely forced to choose. This is because to call existing policy into question on different levels of generality requires at each level acceptance of a different set of mutually contradictory "givens." For policy researchers and policymakers, the adoption of a critical stance that is relatively more incremental or fundamental involves making both a diagnosis as to the seriousness of the problems afflicting current policy and a prognosis concerning the feasibility of effecting the needed reforms. It is our contention that here policy researchers and policymakers confront a range of choices, entailing trade-offs between specifiable risks and bene fits.

The second dimension of the analytic grid distinguishes between approaches to reform that stress as levers for deliberate social change either the rational guidance variables (knowledge and organization) or the political variables (power, consensus). We use the term "rational" here in the sense Max Weber used it. Thus when Weber referred to the dominant historical trend of modernity as the "rationalization" of social phenomena, he was referring to (a) the expansion and growing societal significance of knowledge—in particular, science and technology, professional and bureaucratic expertise—and (b) the proliferation of complex organizational structures (bureaucracies, markets, corporations) which, unlike premodern communities and kinship networks, were not "naturally" evolved and all encompassing but were deliberately created to serve particular, limited purposes. From this perspective, knowledge and organization in modern societies are first and foremost rational instrumentalities for achieving collective goals.

Unlike incremental and fundamental decision making, which are to a high degree contradictory (hence mutually exclusive approaches) confronting policy researchers and policymakers with a clear-cut choice, there is no similar necessity to focus *either* on rational or political variables. Indeed, our argument is that policy researchers and policy reformers who seek to implement their reform proposals are less likely to generate crippling unintended consequences in the course of their reform efforts if they attend to all four guidance variables, both rational and political.

REGULATORY ISSUES IN HEALTH SERVICES

As we see it, an analysis of the underlying intellectual assumptions concerning deliberate social change and how it can be effected may be usefully applied, and much the same analytic framework employed, with respect to any substantive policy area. We have decided to focus here on regulation of health services, because this area poses problems of particular theoretical interest.

Until quite recently the medical profession and the health services sector as a whole were comparatively free from government regulation. Reliance was on professional ethics and voluntary self-regulation via professional peer review. Moreover, the prevailing social science perspective during the 1950s and early 1960s was that outside regulation of the medical profession was ill advised. Talcott Parsons held professional autonomy to be a "functional prerequisite" of quality in medical care due to the differential distribution of knowledge between the individual physician and his patient as well as between the medical profession and the lay public, including government officials.[7] Analytically this means that for many years it was taken for granted—by the health professions, the public, government officials, and social scientists alike—that a particular reading on knowledge (i.e., the knowledge differential between professional and client) was (a) a nonmalleable variable, a constant, not subject to being altered, overcome, or circumvented, and (b) that this knowledge reading therefore dictated particular readings on organization, consensus, and power. Since the mid-1960s, however, this view has been increasingly challenged both in theory (e.g., Elliot Freidson's critique of "professional dominance")[8] and practice (i.e., the growing involvement of government in regulating the quality, cost, and distribution of medical services via such programs as Medicare and Medicaid, neighborhood health centers, and comprehensive health planning, to name but a few). Thus beginning in the late 1960s the issue was no longer *whether* government could or should regulate medical care, but *how* and *for what* purposes it should do so.

In contrast to the view of those who see the barriers to health care reform as almost exclusively ones of ideology and vested interest,[9] this book accepts Parson's premise that health care as a professional, knowledge-based activity poses special regulatory problems. Unlike Parsons, however, we do not see these problems as necessarily precluding outside regulation nor do we perceive them as unique to medicine or other traditionally autonomous professions.

Similar problems increasingly affect regulation of business and industry as industrial products and processes become more and more scientifically and technologically sophisticated and as our regulatory concerns as a society become less and less exclusively economic and more oriented toward quality of life issues. Regulation of health services is in this respect neither unique nor unusual, but, in fact, prototypical. Many of our most pressing national social problems involve a similar knowledge differential between the lay public and professionals or experts, by which we mean that the public, without the help of those who possess the technical knowledge, is often unable to understand the nature, gauge the size, or in some instances even perceive the existence of the problem. Examples include environmental pollution, the energy crisis, occupational and consumer product safety, and such white-collar crimes as computerized theft. (Not all social problems, it is important to note, are of this sort. Racial discrimination and its effects, as well as classical crimes of violence, are social problems whose detection, measurement, and attempted solution entail a much lower quotient of scientifically based expertise.)

Daniel Bell has suggested that two of the most salient characteristics of the emerging postindustrial society are the "knowledge revolution" and the increasing importance of the services sector of the economy.[10] Health care can readily serve as an illustration of both these trends. Long an art of rather dubious reliability, medicine has become in the twentieth century an applied science, involving considerable technology, with a success rate high enough to cause its practitioners to lament the unrealistic expectations of perfection thereby created. As a service industry, the gross national product that goes to pay for health services has risen from 3.5% in 1929, to 4.5% in 1950, to 8.6% in 1977.[11]

Thus, regulatory issues in health care and innovative approaches to dealing with them may well have wider relevance than might at first appear.

THE FOUR CASES

In each of the four cases to be analyzed, the proposed regulatory strategy was the recommendation of a policy study. As such, the four cases are representative of growing societal efforts to bring knowledge and research to bear more directly on social policy decision making. The studies and their principal recommendations follow.

1. The Medicaid Task Force appointed in 1969 by the Secretary of the Department of Health, Education and Welfare (HEW). The *Task Force on Medicaid and Related Programs Final Report,*[12] issued in 1970, called for improving the efficiency and effectiveness of the Medicaid program through the introduction of an "integrated Medicaid management information system" (MMIS), the setting and monitoring of uniform federal "performance standards" for state Medicaid administration, allocation of 5% of the total Medicaid budget for research on improving health services delivery, reorganization of the federal Medicaid agency so as to align more rationally management structure and function, and increased staffing to ensure adequate federal oversight of state Medicaid programs.

2. "Health Maintenance Strategy,"[13] a position paper, written for the Nixon Administration in 1970 by a team of health services researchers at Interstudy, an independent Minneapolis-based research institute. The position paper advocated that the federal government take several steps to promote the growth of a highly diversified and competitive, self-regulatory pri-

vate industry that would provide prepaid health care via "health maintenance organizations" (HMOs). A follow-up series of conferences, working papers and a volume entitled *Assuring the Quality of Health Care*[14] called for the establishment of an independent regulatory agency, known as the "health outcomes commission," to encourage, assist, and monitor the development of internal peer review quality assurance systems in health maintenance organizations.

3. The New York State Moreland Act Commission on Nursing Homes and Residential Facilities, appointed by the governor in 1975 to investigate the causes and and correctives of recent nursing home scandals. The commission held public hearings, issued 7 staff reports, and drafted 17 legislative proposals.[15] The main thrust of the commission's recommendations was legal: more legal rights for nursing home patients (e.g., class action suits), clarification and some strengthening of the state's regulatory inspection and enforcement authority vis-a-vis nursing homes, and attempted elimination of a main source of political corruption (i.e., state legislators and legislative employees acting as legal counsel to private clients in state agency proceedings).

4. *Heal Yourself,* the *Report of the Citizens' Board of Inquiry into Health Services for Americans,* first published in 1970.[16] Funded by private foundation grants and organized by C. Arden Miller, M.D. of the University of North Carolina, the citizens' board was a self-appointed 31-member panel whose participants include business executives and labor leaders; academics; federal, state, and local government officials; physicians and other health professionals; well-known representatives of minority groups; and welfare recipients. Their recommendations called for egalitarian reform of the health services delivery system and for

replacement of professional dominance by consumer control of health system decision making at all levels —that is, facility, service system, or program, and neighborhood, city, state, and local.

We now turn to the analysis.

Chapter 2

AN INCREMENTAL–RATIONAL APPROACH:

The Medicaid Task Force

INTRODUCTION

The analysis and recommendations of the Medicaid Task Force exemplify an approach to social regulation grounded intellectually in the administrative science tradition. Such a managerial approach places primary emphasis on the attributes of the regulatory apparatus itself, rather than on what or whom is being regulated. The main aim is to "rationalize," that is, to improve the efficiency and effectiveness of administrative structures and processes—in this instance, of Medicaid, a government program financing health services for the poor.

The Medicaid Task Force recommendations identify knowledge—in particular, improved "management information" and increased attention to research and development—as the principle lever for Medicaid management reform. Implicit in the Task Force's emphasis on information processing, communication, and feedback is a cybernetic model of government similar to that advanced theoretically by political scientist Karl

Deutsch. According to Deutsch, the cybernetic viewpoint suggests that "every organization is held together by communication."[1] Communication transmits messages that contain quantities of information and it is this ability to transmit messages and react to them (i.e., learn from the information they contain) that "makes organizations."[2] As we shall see, this conceptualization of the regulatory process in terms of what Deutsch calls a "self-modifying communications network or learning net"[3] is quite different from one that perceives a regulatory bureaucracy as a structure of power and government regulation as a tool for exercising power, that is, overcoming resistance.

Properties of formal organization, for example, rational realignment of organizational structure and managerial function, as well as adequacy of fit between a unit's resources and its functional requirements constitute a secondary emphasis in the Medicaid Task Force analysis. The intellectual roots of these task force recommendations can be traced to classical organizational theory, known in sociology as the Weberian model of bureaucracy and in public administration as the "scientific management school."[4]

ORIGINS OF THE REFORM PROPOSAL

The Task Force on Medicaid and Related Programs (also known as the McNerney Commission) was appointed by the secretary of the Department of Health, Education and Welfare (HEW) in July 1969, just a few months after the new Republican (Nixon) Administration took office. Composed of 27 members drawn from health services' administrations, state welfare administrations, academia, and industry, the Medicaid Task Force was co-chaired by Walter McNerney, President of the Blue Cross Association and Undersecretary of HEW, John Veneman. Its staff director was Arthur Hess, Deputy Commissioner of Social Security. Staff were drawn mainly from within HEW.

According to the HEW secretary, Robert Finch, the purpose of the Medicaid Task Force was to "deal immediately with the crisis in that program."[5] For most policymakers at HEW and in Congress, the "Medicaid crisis" was how to put a lid on costs that had greatly exceeded original estimates.[6] Although it is likely that the costs of virtually all new social programs are optimistically underplayed in order to sell the legislation to Congress, the subsequent backlash in Medicaid's case was especially rapid and severe. First, Medicaid had been a legislative sleeper. As a late addition to the Medicare compromise, it was passed with little debate or understanding, hence little opportunity to evolve a solid congressional consensus as to its goals, strategies, and scope. In effect, many in Congress who voted for Medicaid had not realized they were granting their approval to another new initiative of the War on Poverty.[7] Indeed, the Medicaid cost crisis reflected even more deeply a societywide turning away from the social activism of the Great Society era, which was soon to bring a conservative Republican administration into the White House.

Initially Congress sought to control costs via cutbacks in eligibility and services that could be accomplished with the rapid stroke of a legislative pen. By one of those ironies common to policymaking, however, a major source of new Medicaid eligibles turned out to be liberalized welfare reform for which Congress itself was in large measure responsible.[8] Thus unless Congress wanted to rescind liberalized welfare eligibility or virtually repeal Medicaid, those eligibility cutbacks that could be introduced would economize little.[9] Accordingly, the emphasis shifted more and more toward effecting savings via more efficient program administration, and a number of studies were launched.

The first, carried out in the fall of 1967 and published in June 1968, was a questionnaire survey of state administrators undertaken by the New York-based, nonprofit Tax Foundation.[10] In December 1967, a request from the National Conference of State Legislative Leaders led to a study by the Advisory Commission on Intergovernmental Relations.[11] That same year President Johnson set up the State–Federal Task Force on the Costs of Medical Assistance and Public Assistance. Its report, released in October 1968, foreshadowed the 1970 Medicaid Task Force report in proposing an information system that would include regular sampling studies in each state.[12] In the spring of 1969, the Senate Finance Committee held hearings on the fiscal and administrative problems of Medicaid. The Committee staff's preliminary findings, which appeared just as the Medicaid Task Force was beginning its work, offered the following diagnosis:

> Federal officials have been lax in not seeing to it that States establish and employ effective controls on utilization and costs, and States have been unwilling to assume the responsibility on their own. The Federal Medicaid administrators have not provided states with the expert assistance necessary to implement proper controls. Also, they have not developed mechanisms for coordination and communication among the States about methods of identifying and solving Medicaid problems.[13]

Finally, in August 1969, the HEW audit agency released a summary of its management review of Medicaid programs in 16 states where 85% of program monies were spent. The report documented "widespread administrative problems which require prompt action to achieve program objectives efficiently and economically and to retain public confidence."[14]

The cumulative effect of these less-encompassing studies and investigations was to create, according to Medicaid historians Robert and Rosemary Stevens, a politically "hot" climate from which the McNerney Task Force greatly benefited.[15] Moreover, the Task Force was able to rely heavily on the fact finding and analysis already accomplished by the previous studies and place greater emphasis on drawing interpretative conclusions and making policy recommendations.

Positioning the Medicaid Task Force on the Analytic Grid

Managerial Reform: A "Rationalist" Approach

The Medicaid Task Force recommendations exemplify a rationalistic approach because they stress knowledge and organizational variables as the levers for deliberate social change. Though analytically we see the main Task Force focus as being on knowledge variables, with organizational variables taking second place, most of the Task Force's specific recommendations are best characterized as dealing with aspects of the interaction between knowledge and organizational variables. Thus the Medicaid Task Force did not concern itself with medical knowledge in the scientific or professional sense, but with the "management information" required by government agencies to regulate the distribution cost, cost effectiveness and, to a lesser extent, the quality and health impact of medical services financed under the Medicaid program.

Medicaid Task Force recommendations considered as having a primary focus on knowledge variables include development and implementation nationwide of a computerized Medicaid management informative system, allocation of 5% of the Medicaid budget for research on improving the delivery of health services, and the setting and monitoring of performance standards—that is, output measures—for state Medicaid programs. Medicaid Task Force recommendations that stress organizational variables include an internal reorganization of the federal Medicaid agency to produce a more rational alignment of organizational structure and function, creation of new organizational units to perform previously neglected functions—

such as the proposed new Office of Program Innovation—and, finally, authorizing what we will term an appropriate "cybernetic ratio"; that is, allotting to organizational units of the federal Medicaid agency sufficient resources to carry out their assigned tasks properly, in particular, assuring sufficient personnel to units charged with making periodic evaluations of state Medicaid programs.

Although the importance of deliberately manipulating knowledge and organizational variables in order to improve the efficiency and effectiveness of the Medicaid program was thus stressed, the Task Force accorded virtually no explicit attention to the role of the "political variables," power and consensus. As we shall see, however, the Task Force's recommendations focusing on knowledge and organization had latent consequences for and conflicts with prevailing power relations and values.

Opting for Incremental Improvements

The recommendations advocated by the Medicaid Task Force represented relatively incremental departures from the existing approach to Medicaid management. It is worth noting, however, that in the process of arriving at their recommendations, the Task Force members faced some difficult decisions concerning how critical of existing Medicaid policy and administration their analysis and recommendations should be. The problem was posed in terms of identifying Medicaid's basic goals and the knowledge needs and organizational forms congruent with those goals.

Thus although the Task Force members readily accepted the rationalization of Medicaid management as their prime mission, the question arose: rationalize it for what? It was their classical "scientific management" approach to public administration, in fact, that led them to want to specify the goals and program priorities to which particular types of management informative as well as particular organizational structures and functions would relate.

Few members of the Medicaid Task Force were content to pursue the HEW–congressional emphasis on administrative efficiency and cost consciousness as goals unto themselves. During the War on Poverty era, Medicaid's goals had been defined principally in terms of social justice: expanding the medical services available to the poor, expanding eligibility to cover not only those on welfare but the "medically needy," doing away with the two-class system of medical care, and integrating the poor into "mainstream medicine." According to Robert and Rosemary Stevens, many of those who served on the Medicaid Task Force were still personally committed to these goals.[16] By 1969–1970, however, it was obvious that economic contraction and a shift toward a more conservative political consensus in the nation at large necessitated that such redistributive goals at least be indefinitely deferred, if not abandoned.

Much of the Medicaid Task Force staff was drawn from parts of HEW having a "quality of care" orientation. Initially their inclination was to marry the concern of Congress and the Administration for cost control with their own professional focus on public health and quality of care issues; that is, the Task Force was most inclined toward advocacy of managerial reforms that would not simply curb Medicaid expenditures but would make Medicaid more cost effective by paying for those services and only those services that were medically necessary and appropriate and further—the Task Force ambitiously hoped—that could be demonstrated to have a clear payoff in terms of measurable improvements in the health of the poor.

Moreover, according to the *Task Force on Medicaid and Related Programs Interim Report,* Medicaid and related programs such as Medicare "should not be merely conduits for funds which reinforce the inadequacies of the existing health care system, but should be used as instruments to improve the system."[17] Behind this lay the conviction of many Medicaid

Task Force members that the real need was for a major reorganization of the health care delivery system—chiefly along the lines of prepaid health plans—and that the administration of government programs such as Medicaid could provide the leverage to accomplish this aim.

Both these aims, had they remained central to the Medicaid Task Force final report and recommendations, would have implied fundamental reform of the existing Medicaid program. Medicaid, as a health care financing mechanism linked to welfare eligibility, was not designed to ensure that the health needs of the poor were being met. Most especially, Medicaid was not designed to give government such a direct role in determining whether particular types of medical services were or were not effective or appropriate to particular health problems—this being a prerogative traditionally reserved to the individual physician or to the medical community and considered to be a vital element of "professional autonomy."

Rather, Medicaid was a specific form of income supplement for the poor, enabling them to purchase particular types of health services which, taken together, might or might not constitute an adequate or appropriate response to the health problems afflicting the poor. At the time of the Medicaid Task Force report, little effort had been made to evaluate the impact of access to Medicaid-financed health services on improving the actual health status of poor people. Nor had there been much assessment of patterns of utilization of Medicaid services to determine whether they were necessary, appropriate, or beneficial with respect to the types of health problems for which Medicaid clients sought treatment.

By the same token, the existing Medicaid program was not meant to give government a means to promote reorganization of the American health care system. Indeed, quite the opposite: It was intended to give the poor greater access to the prevailing solo, fee-for-service private practice system of primary care used by middle- and upper-income Americans.

In the Medicaid Task Force final report, however, these two themes—movement toward linking government financing of health services to measurable criteria of health need and effectiveness on the one hand and reorganization of the health care delivery system on the other—appear only in cautious, muted form. Moreover, the Task Force recommendations for Medicaid management reform were far too weak, that is, represented much too little change from the preexisting situation—to bring about any such major reorientation in program goals. (Where these themes are expressed in ringing tones deeply critical of prevailing policy assumptions, they come across as almost pure disembodied rhetoric.) Thus although the Task Force contained many ardent proponents of prepaid, comprehensive health care delivery systems, their final report did not suggest that Medicaid be reoriented toward prepaid care, but merely that within the federal agency responsible for administering Medicaid, a "Division of Program Innovation" be set up and monies allocated to research, among other things, prepaid plans. The "incremental" character of the Task Force reform recommendations is also clearly evident in the group's decision, after considerable heated debate, not to urge that the Medicaid administration be transferred from the "welfare" to the "health" side of HEW. Clearly such a bureaucratic rearrangement could scarcely be considered a fundamental reform in and of itself. It would, however, have been a vital component in the context of a strategic reorientation of Medicaid away from the "welfare" goal of subsidizing access to existing medical services toward the "health" goal of promoting high-quality care leading to measurable improvements in the health of poor people.

We will now analyze in greater detail the Medicaid Task Force's main knowledge and organizational recommendations as well as the latent conflicts between these recommendations and the "political variables," power and value consensus.

Knowledge and Organization as the Key Levers for Deliberate Social Change

Management Information

According to the Medicaid Task Force's final report, what the Medicaid administration most needed to promote the quality of care more effectively, while also curbing costs, was more and better management information. In the language of societal guidance theory, the organizational units administering Medicaid were seen as deficient in "reality-testing" mechanisms.[18] Put more colloquially, the McNerney Task Force diagnosis of Medicaid's major problem was that its administrators were "flying blind" like pilots over unfamiliar terrain, in bad weather, with incomplete maps, and faulty instruments. As a result, Medicaid administrators did not know enough about the health care delivery system whose behavior they sought to guide to take appropriate rational action to further program goals. Moreover, once they took action, they did not receive enough information feedback to know whether or not their actions had had the intended results, or if not, what consequences they did have and why, so that appropriate adjustments could be made.

Sociologist Harold Wilensky has characterized the cognitive maps policymakers and administrators require to guide their actions as "organizational intelligence."

> Intelligence denotes the information—questions, insights, hypotheses, evidence relevant to policy. It includes both scientific knowledge and political or ideological information; scientific or not, this definition is broad enough to encompass general pictures of social and natural order as well as specific messages (significant sequences of symbols) about immediate issues.[19]

It is worth noting, however, that whereas Wilensky's definition of "organizational intelligence" includes both what he terms "scientific" and "political" knowledge, the McNerney

Task Force, true to its rationalistic orientation, held a concept of "management information" that stressed technical forms of knowledge almost exclusively. Again, drawing on societal guidance theory, policy-relevant knowledge may be seen as serving two policymaking functions: (a) it provides a relation to reality by containing information about the environment, (b) it provides meaning by interpreting facts cognitively and by evaluating them in normative terms.[20] The McNerney Task Force was almost solely concerned with the reality testing function as opposed to that of evaluative interpretation. The result was a technocratic focus on "management information" as data— that is, on data collection, data analysis, data feedback, and the hardware that goes with it.

Accordingly, the principle lever for improving Medicaid's effectiveness as the Task Force saw it was to design and implement a computerized information system. The final report stated:

> The Task Force is convinced that the immediate need is for an integrated Medicaid information system. The integrated system must provide for the organized and systematic collection of data in the states, for the timely flow of information to SRS [Social and Rehabilitation Service] and MSA [Medical Services Administration], and for the return of useful comprehensive information to the states. This system must be dynamic and have a high degree of flexibility to accommodate continuing change. Since increased efficiency and effectiveness hinge on the development of an integrated information system, the Task Force is especially concerned that top priority be given this key area.[21]

The McNerney Task Force identified several different types of information required at different organizational levels to fulfill a variety of managerial functions.

LOWER-ORDER MANAGEMENT INFORMATION NEEDS. A main emphasis was on how to obtain the information needed to curb costs and promote quality of care at the lowest administrative level, that of the interface between program administrators and providers of services via claims processing. Collection, analysis, and evaluation of claims data would focus on ensuring that provider charges did not exceed the "reasonable and customary" and on eliminating all duplicate, disallowable, or ineligible claims. The Medicaid Task Force stressed that the most important aim here was not cost control per se or even elimination of fraud and abuse, but redirecting otherwise wasted resources toward advancing the program's basic health goals. Even more important, the information generated via computerized claims processing could be utilized for curbing inappropriate utilization of services. Here again, the Task Force emphasized that cost cutting was really only a secondary aim; the main objectives were to eliminate unnecessary services that could be potentially harmful to recipients' health and to redirect these resources to pay for needed services.

In connection with these latter—specifically medical— functions of utilization review, the Task Force stressed the need to incorporate professional review bodies into the Medicaid administrative structure.[22] The Task Force's specific suggestions foreshadowed the 1972 legislation creating professional standards review organizations (PSRO) to perform utilization and quality of care reviews for Medicare and Medicaid. In contrast to the way in which the professional standards review program actually evolved (in which each local PSRO largely developed its own information base), however, the McNerney Task Force recommendations emphasized the development of an integrated management information system based on claims data that would meet both administrative and professional information needs.

In documenting the need to develop information systems in connection with claims processing, the Task Force relied greatly on the HEW audit agency's 1969 review of Medicaid administration in 16 states. Among its findings, in 12 states,

> The agencies responsible for Medicaid did not make systematic utilization reviews of services provided to recipients, either because the necessary data were not available or because the agen-

cies did not use data that were available. Without such management reviews of program expenditures, neither the state nor SRS can be assured that there are not abuses in the Medicaid program resulting from (a) overutilization of services by recipients, (b) overservicing by medical providers, (c) duplicate payments, (d) fraudulent claims, and (e) other undesirable practices.[23]

Thirteen states were found to have inadequate procedures for preventing, identifying, and recovering duplicate payments, overpayment, and alternate liability for payment by Medicare or private insurance. "As a result, substantial amounts of Federal funds which could have been used for other worthy purposes in the Medicaid program were spent unnecessarily."[24]

An approach to regulation with different theoretical assumptions might not have seen in such findings a "knowledge" deficiency—that is, lack of management information—but mainly a "power" deficit: either a failure of political will (e.g., a politically motivated reluctance to place strict controls on the powerful medical profession) or, at the very least, an inadequate intrabureaucratic control system.

The Medicaid Task Force noted that claims processing and utilization review lend themselves well to "state of the art" techniques in computerized data processing. Indeed, medical information systems utilizing such techniques were already in use in the nongovernmental sector (for example, the computerized patterns of care profiles of the Professional Activity Study, a voluntary information system for subscribing hospitals). In other words, it was not a question of major new breakthroughs in medical or other scientific knowledge or information technology being required before such information systems could be implemented. The chief obstacle was rather the high costs entailed (prohibitively high for small states) if each state had to develop its own system. The McNerney Task Force could see no rational reason why each state should spend enormous sums to, in effect, "reinvent the wheel" 54 separate times. The recommendation that the federal government research and develop a computerized information system that could be used by all states was thus the centerpiece of the final Medicaid Task Force report.

HIGHER-ORDER MANAGEMENT INFORMATION NEEDS. The Medicaid Task Force also accorded considerable attention to the information needs of higher-order, more encompassing policy-implementing and policymaking functions. Again the Task Force relied on the 1969 HEW audit agency review to establish that the appropriate information needs were not being met on the state level. Thus the HEW audits had found that high-level decision makers within the "single state agencies" in charge of Medicaid in the states typically lacked adequate mechanisms for monitoring the performance of other state agencies to which particular managerial functions were delegated or even the performance of the various departments and local level units ostensibly under more direct hierarchical control. For example, in New York,

> The State Department of Social Services did not make adequate audits of Medicaid operations at local agencies. During the period May 1, 1967, to December 31, 1968, only 31 audits were started, of which only 16 were completed at the 64 local agencies in New York State. In the New York City area, only three audits had been started, and none completed, since the inception of the program.[25]

Concomitant with a lack of effective supervision was the virtual absence of any capacity to undertake policy-level reviews. In Pennsylvania the HEW auditors noted

> Weaknesses in administration of Medicaid in the State Welfare agency were generally attributed to (a) failure to comply with prescribed procedures, (b) poor internal controls, and (c) lack of effective supervision and review. There was reason to believe that top management was not always aware of these conditions. We recommended that the State agency establish an internal review

section to determine that its policies and procedures are accomplishing their objectives and to evaluate the effectiveness of administration. There should be a regularly programmed procedure for periodic reviews, evaluations, and appraisals of all ongoing operations of the agency. This could result in (a) a more timely remedial action, (b) improved safeguards and stronger administration, and (c) significant reductions in program costs to the state and federal governments.[26]

In other words, ineffective supervision was perceived by both the HEW audit agency and, subsequently, the Medicaid Task Force, as largely a matter of inadequate information feedback.

The final report of the Task Force went on to stress the importance of generating information for longer-range management purposes as well. Thus

Evaluation in Medicaid must include more than ordinary program monitoring and surveillance; it must also include many other aspects normally associated with both performance and planning. In order to carry out on a continuing basis the requisite evaluations, objective techniques of measurement and assessment need to be developed and applied. This evaluation process should encompass administrative agency operations (state, local, and fiscal agents), state Medicaid programs, quality of effectiveness of provider institutions, program economics and, most importantly of all, actual changes in the health of the target population.[27]

At the federal level the task force was particularly concerned that the federal Medicaid agency lacked adequate information about each state's administrative performance and the impact of Medicaid, by state and nationwide, on recipients.

With, however, a single, standardized Medicaid Management Information System (MMIS) in place in each state, the Task Force assumed that the federal Medicaid agency would be able to generate an integrated data base for national Medicaid management purposes.

CONSTRAINTS ON THE MALLEABILITY OF KNOWLEDGE AND ORGANIZATION

The Legally Prescribed Organizational Linkage of Medicaid and Welfare

Earlier we noted that the *Task Force on Medicaid and Related Programs Final Report* represented a retreat from earlier more fundamental criticisms of the Medicaid program. The reform recommendations that the Task Force ended up advocating were characterized as "incrementalist" because they accepted certain basic features of the existing Medicaid program as, for the time being, not readily subject to change. Thus as the Task Force final report put it,

> In formulating short-range management recommendations, we have accepted as short-term "givens" the basic character of Title XIX as a state-administered program; the tying of eligibility to public assistance categories, and the financing of the program through federal, state and local general tax revenues.[28]

Many Task Force members apparently hoped and expected that these attributes, which from their viewpoint were highly dysfunctional to the goals of a health program, could soon be eliminated in the context of a national health insurance program that would supersede Medicaid.

These "givens" posed serious limitations on the character and scope of the organizational reforms the Task Force could propose and concomitantly on the kinds of "knowledge" recommendations that could be made as well.

For example, the Medicaid Task Force was greatly concerned that more attention ought to be given to evaluating Medicaid's performance with respect to health "outcome" indicators; that is, the Task Force wanted Medicaid program management to include ongoing assessment of Medicaid's effectiveness in meeting the previously unmet health needs of the poor and in bringing about measurable improvement in their health.

Measuring health outcomes and setting performance standards accordingly were, however, not as amenable to "state of the art" techniques as utilization review—a problem that the McNerney Task Force glossed over. The Task Force did recognize that a great deal of research and development would be needed in this and other areas and recommended that 5% of the total annual Medicaid budget be set aside for the purpose of researching improvements in the delivery and organization of health care under the program.[29]

Medicaid was being administered, however, by the Medical Services Administration of the Social and Rehabilitation Services, an agency located in the "welfare" side of HEW, which lacked professional health expertise. The question arose: Would a welfare agency have either the interest in or the capability of pursuing the difficult tasks of developing outcome indicators of Medicaid's health impact and researching improvements in organization and delivery of health care? It is clear that many members of the Medicaid Task Force believed that the reorientation of Medicaid from a welfare to a health program could not be accomplished without transferring Medicaid's administration from a welfare to a health agency. At the same time, such a recommendation would transgress the structural "givens" the Task Force was supposed to work within. Such a transfer was not a simple matter of reshuffling organizational charts; it probably could not be accomplished without a thorough overhaul of Medicaid's eligibility and financing arrangements which were tied to welfare. To accomplish this would require not only major new legislation but would also raise many difficult questions about welfare reform. Accordingly, the Task Force final report noted

> The Task Force gave early and intensive consideration to the proper organizational context for the agency administering Title XIX, since major difficulties in managing the program were assumed to grow out of location. We considered the fact that a health program was being managed by an agency more traditionally concerned with social services and payment mechanisms. We considered whether continued vesting of responsibility for

program operations in MSA was compatible with the fact that
responsibility for health policy rests in a different part of HEW.
In spite of strongly held opposite views by some members, the
Task Force concluded that a fundamental change in the Medical
Services Administration's location at this moment would not
justify the high cost in time and possible resulting confusion
unless it were made in response to simultaneous changes in the
basic structure of the program—that is, in one or more of the
"givens."[30]

In addition to the ongoing linkage between Medicaid and
welfare, it will be recalled that the Task Force also accepted as
a structural "given" the continued joint financing and administration of Medicaid by federal, state, and, in some instances,
local government. We saw in the earlier section on management
information that the McNerney Task Force dealt with relations
both among and within the three levels of government largely
in terms of a cybernetic model of information processing, communication, and feedback. Levels and units of government were
thus defined in the final report of the Task Force in terms either
of their management information needs or their role in producing the various types of management information needed by
other units.

This approach is in marked contrast to the more typical
and traditional "political" approach to intra- and intergovern-
mental relations which focuses on power or authority (legalized
power) relations among levels and units of government. The
American Constitution is a classic example of such a focus on
organizational power relations. Its main organizational concern
is with specifying the legitimate scope and limits of the government's power vis-a-vis the citizenry, of the federal government
vis-a-vis the states, and the executive, legislative, and judicial
branches vis-a-vis each other.

In the Medicaid Task Force's final report, however, questions of power and authority were all but ignored. Indeed, as
noted earlier, standard issues of bureaucratic authority—for
example, supervision and accountability—were treated almost

entirely as matters of inadequate information processing and feedback.

The specification of organizational units' management information needs assumes that these units have particular management functions for which the information is required. In this respect, the Task Force final report reads like a textbook example of the application of scientific management principles. "Management" is subdivided into rational functions—for example, policy, planning, and evaluation—and these functions are in turn assigned to particular formal organizational structures—for example, a particular department of the Medical Services Administration (MSA)—to perform. No important function is left without a structure on which to fulfill it; all structures must justify their existence in terms of the functions they perform.

Implicit in the assignment of particular management functions and corresponding information needs to an organizational unit is a concept of that unit's scope of authority to make or carry out decisions. Classical public administration theory takes as "given" both a hierarchical authority structure and a structure in which each unit's scope of authority is clearly and specifically delineated with relatively little overlap. As we shall see, however, these assumptions do not hold for "federalism," the pattern of authority relations that has evolved historically among the national, state, and local governments in the United States. It is not only that the hierarchically superior authority of the federal government cannot be taken for granted under the American federal system, but the lines of authority—that is, which level and which unit has what authority—are often overlapping or uncertain.

In the following section we will explore the latent conflicts that the actual authority relations characteristic of American government—and the place of "federalism" as a revered value in American political ideology—posed for the knowledge and organizational reforms recommended by the Medicaid Task Force.

Power: Hierarchical versus Feudal Authority Relations in Bureaucracy

As a help to understanding the nature of the conflict, it is useful to consider two contrasting theoretical models for federal–state authority relations. One is the classic model of bureaucratic authority set forth by Max Weber. For our purposes its most salient characteristic is the emphasis on a hierarchical chain of command. Here final authority over all aspects of the organization's mission is vested in the positions at the top. The headquarters or central office can divide up and delegate or withdraw authority to subordinate organizational units as it sees fit, in line with its conception of efficient, effective functioning and contingent on satisfactory performance. The federal Medicare program, run by the Social Security Administration, conforms, in theory at least, to the Weberian bureaucratic model. Thus whenever Medicare, in order to avoid wasteful duplication of personnel, contracts with state agencies to perform certain regulatory functions at the local level (such as hospital and nursing home inspections), state personnel temporarily become federal employees and must implement federal not state policy. Concomitantly, if the federal Medicare agency should become dissatisfied with a state agency's performance, it has the legal authority to make alternative arrangements.

The Medicaid program, however, was initially designed according to a quite different model which we will term "bureaucratic feudalism." Metaphorically, each state Medicaid program can be looked on as a separate fiefdom unto itself. The "barons" at the state level owe a certain allegiance to their HEW "lord," but it is by the same token the strictly limited deference a feudal vassal owes to a feudal overlord; that is, the authority relations between the central headquarters and local units (in this context, the federal government and the states) are defined by a set of reciprocal rights and duties, analogous to those between feudal lords and vassals, which being few in number and strictly delimited, serve mainly to circumscribe the authority of the central government and preserve a high degree of local autonomy. Thus according to the 1965 Medicaid legislation, states were given the right to federal matching funds so long as they fulfilled the corresponding duty of using the funds for the agreed on purpose (financing individual health services for the poor) and so long as their Medicaid plans satisfied a handful of federal requirements concerning client eligibility and service coverage. Needless to say, "bureaucratic feudalism" is not the name by which Americans know such an administrative structure. In the context of federal–state relations, this relationship has usually been termed "grants in aid."[31]

At this point an administrative rationalist might be inclined to suppose that policymakers seeking to design new social programs have a free choice as to which of these two bureaucratic models they would like the program to conform, based on a weighing of each type's advantages and disadvantages relative to the purpose at hand. Actually it is perhaps more a question of alternative political values. Bureaucratic feudalism is compatible with a normative preference for (comparatively) weaker government and local variability in rules, regulations, and policy. The disadvantages of these advantages are relatively greater vulnerability to pressure groups and a bias against social redistribution and egalitarianism.[32] The advantages of a "Weberian" hierarchical bureaucracy are, as Weber pointed out, relatively greater "rationalism" (efficient, effective control) and greater fairness and egalitarianism (in the sense that all are subjected to the same rules). The disadvantages, of course, are the possibilities that the central government may become too powerful and overbearing and that a certain rigidity (refusal to bend rules or make exceptions even when these are well warranted) may develop.[33]

In practice, however, as those more sensitive to political considerations will immediately recognize, policymakers do not have quite so much choice. For a number of reasons American social programs almost never fully conform to the hierarchical model—even in terms of formal, let alone informal, organizational structure. One major reason is that historically health, welfare, and other social services were a local or state responsibility, or else a nongovernmental function performed by private, for-profit, or voluntary organizations. Federal social programs must, hence, grow by replacing the local, state, and private sector or, more commonly, by incorporating and building on them. Thus even the Medicare program, which we earlier characterized as hierarchical in the context of federal–state authority relations, is "feudalistic" in its relations with the voluntary sector. (As a political trade-off to the for-profit and not-for-profit insurance companies which lost business as a result of Medicare, these private-sector organizations were incorporated into the program's administrative structure as "fiscal intermediaries" and "carriers.")

The pull toward "feudal" authority relations in American social programs reflects even more deeply the characteristically American balance of power between the society and the government. Despite the growth of the latter, "private power," particularly that of business and industry, remains by far the stronger.[34] On the other hand, as Weber pointed out, a main current of modernity is the tendency toward "rationalization." Feudal bureaucracies tend to be deeply inefficient and structurally resistant to purposive control; hence the desire for government to "get things done" will militate in favor of the hierarchical model. In designing or seeking to reform the administrative structure of a social program, policymakers may choose to ride with either current, but then they must fight the other.

Because of their different functional attributes, these two types of authority structure, hierarchical and feudal bureaucracy, clearly have quite different management information requirements. A hierarchical bureaucracy requires an information system for "compliance monitoring"—that is, to ensure that subordinate organizational units implement the central office's overall policies as well as its specific directives efficiently and effectively. Such an information system is particularly necessary if the aim is to run a decentralized administration with authority over most day-to-day operational decision making delegated to subordinate units that are widely dispersed geographically. The ability to know that day-to-day administrative functions are being taken care of and to intervene only when a serious problem arises frees the headquarters to focus on long-range policy issues related to overall goal attainment. Accordingly, the headquarters also requires organizational intelligence for purposes of planning and evaluation.

In contrast, the central office of a feudal bureaucracy has comparatively few organizational intelligence needs. Its compliance monitoring information needs are few because its authority to require compliance is so limited. Similarly, the central office of a feudal bureaucracy has little need for information for planning and evaluation because it has only very limited authority to direct its nominally subordinate units to conform to systemwide policies and goals. Instead it is the subordinate units (the states, in the case of Medicaid) who have the greatest organizational intelligence needs because it is they who have the greatest decision-making authority. At best, the central office can seek to persuade the states that in order to avoid needless duplication of effort, it should meet these information needs for all of them. In doing so, however, the central office clearly agrees to define its mission as that of an advisory "staff" serving the "line" decision makers in the states. Providing technical assistance to the states, calling conferences where state program directors can share problems and experience, and otherwise serving as an information exchange, as well as researching and developing administrative innovations for the states are the intelligence functions of a federal agency, compatible with bureaucratic feudalism.

From the standpoint of logic the two bureaucratic models, hierarchical and feudal, are mutually exclusive, because the former places the locus of authority in the "headquarters," the latter in the "field" units. A mixed structure would be fundamentally unworkable because it would posit two loci of authority between which there would be a constant tug of war.

By 1970, however, Medicaid had in fact evolved just such a mixed structure and its corresponding struggle for power between state and federal government. This evolution resulted from a characteristic process of congressional decision making, which itself reflected an ambivalence within the American political consensus concerning those two warring tendencies discussed earlier: resistance to growing governmental power, especially federal government power, on the one hand; and a desire to rationalize administrative structure so as to make it more efficient and purposeful, on the other. Thus though the initial Medicaid legislation clearly enshrined the principle of each state's essential autonomy to set policy for and administer its own program, Congress rapidly grew dissatisfied with state performance (in particular, the fiscal inefficiency and wastefulness of so many state programs) and impatient with the federal government's lack of ability to assert corrective controls. Thus, from 1967 on, Congress increasingly directed the federal bureaucracy in HEW to set standards for state performance in ever more areas—from fire safety in nursing homes, to utilization review of hospital services, to family planning—all, however, without challenging the basic structure of a state-run program. Not insignificantly, then, although Congress did greatly increase the authority of HEW over the state Medicaid programs, it did so not by granting HEW a general mandate to require more efficient, effective management from the states through whatever administrative means it judged necessary and appropriate, but via an ever-lengthening "laundry list" of specific areas for federal standard setting, frequently specific even in what the standards were to be and how they were to be enforced. In other words, Congress has not made the state agencies hierarchically subordinate to HEW, but merely increased the number of their feudal obligations. This practice of strengthening the federal bureaucracy's authority by issuing highly specific, limited mandates was to leave HEW with no, or at best a highly ambiguous, authority to assert control outside these narrowly circumscribed areas. It also made HEW highly vulnerable to legalistic resistance by the states or by medical providers based on claims that HEW was exceeding its authority or not exercising it precisely within the limits prescribed by Congress.

The Medicaid Task Force recommendations neglected to take into account these important power variables. Rather than seeking a resolution of the federal–state power struggle in one direction or another, they merely reflected its continuing lack of resolution. Thus the Task Force's recommendation for a workable division of labor between HEW and the states was that the Medical Services Administration should provide "clear statements of overall mission, goals, and objectives" while at the same time relying on the states for "initial problem definition." In fact, the first half of the recommendation was incompatible with the second. The idea that the Medical Services Administration should provide clear statements of overall mission, goals, and objectives implied that the federal agency should play an activist, national policymaking role. Most important, it suggested that states would have to tailor their programs to fit in with HEW's definition of national directions. The second half of the recommendation implied the traditional relationship of HEW vis-a-vis the states: the "by invitation only" arrangement whereby HEW gave advice and technical assistance when states requested help in solving a particular problem.

Because it did not give explicit consideration to the issue of the balance of power between federal and state government, the Medicaid Task Force failed to perceive that the inadequate communication, processing, and feedback of information between the state and federal Medicaid agencies was integrally related to the "feudal" authority structure designed into the original Medicaid legislation. The intent of this authority structure had been, in fact, to preserve state autonomy from federal control. For the federal government to increase its management information capabilities and, most especially, to employ management information for the purpose of demanding compliance with uniform national standards of management performance would require changes in federal–state authority relations, which would give the federal government a legal right to exert such control.

The Task Force critiqued the Medical Services Administration's relationship to the states as overly crisis oriented, but failed to recognize that this attribute was a function not only of inadequate numbers of personnel to perform frequent, in-depth "PREP" (Program Review and Evaluation Project) review and lack of an integrated information system but also flowed logically from the congressional practice of granting HEW authority to set standards and develop an information system to monitor performance crisis by crisis.

We will now look at how the inadequacy with which power (especially federal, state, and local authority relations) and consensus (in particular the role of "federalism" in American political ideology) were taken into account largely precluded implementation of some Task Force recommendations, thus producing "unanticipated consequences" that hindered the effective implementation of others.

IMPLEMENTATION OF THE TASK FORCE RECOMMENDATIONS: THE UNINTENDED CONSEQUENCES OF LEAVING POWER AND CONSENSUS UNCHANGED

We have seen that many of the reforms proposed by the Medicaid Task Force to improve the efficiency and effectiveness of Medicaid management were logically incompatible with the program's prevailing patterns of organizational authority (i.e., the administration of a health program by a welfare bureaucracy and, especially, the "feudal" authority relations between the states and federal government characteristic of American federalism). In part, the Task Force had consciously decided to adopt an "incrementalist" approach to decision making that would leave unchallenged certain basic structural givens of Medicaid program administration. Because it failed to give explicit consideration to power and consensus variables, how-ever, the Task Force also failed to perceive the logical incom-patibilities between certain of its recommendations and the structural givens it had decided not to attempt to change. Not surprisingly then, the implementation and effectiveness of each Task Force recommendation depended on the size and severity of its latent conflict with the unaltered political variables, that is, the constraints imposed by the existing structure of authority and by the continued allegiance to federalism as a political value. As we shall see, the more incremental the proposed recommendation, the better it accommodated to the constraints imposed by the political variables. More ambitious reforms posed greater incompatibilities, hence resulted in greater and more serious unanticipated consequences.

Conflicts Between the Power and Consensus Assumptions of American Federalism and Task Force Recommendations for Improving Organizational Knowledge

PERFORMANCE MONITORING. A potentially far-reaching Task Force recommendation was the idea that the Medical Services Administration should develop "specific performance stan-dards for state administrative and program management func-tions;" that is, not input or process but actual output indicators of administrative efficiency and effectiveness.[35] Moreover, the Task Force went on to suggest that if states failed to measure up, they should be penalized financially. The Task Force proposed that HEW be granted broad discretionary authority to determine the size and nature of the financial sanctions to be applied against noncompliant states as well as the forms of noncompliance that justified their use. In particular, the Task Force suggested penalizing state bureaucracies by withholding *some administrative* rather than *all program* funds. Exactly what percentage of administrative funds would be withheld would depend on which standards were being violated. (This recommendation went quite counter to the prevailing legal interpretation of HEW's general authority under the Medicaid statute, which was that HEW must cut off *all* federal funds— but only if a state program was in *total* noncompliance with federal standards—otherwise it could cut off none.)

> The Task Force believes that by viewing the State Plan as a contractual agreement between the Federal Government and the States which is reviewed periodically for progress toward conformity with goals, rather than as a prospectus for gaining entry into the program, the Federal management and the program can be strengthened. Specifically, the Federal Government should view the States as violating parts of the contract where they are out of conformance with only parts of the Federally-established standards.[36]

In brief, the Task Force was suggesting that the federal government treat the states as a business firm would a subcontractor: A subcontractor must meet specifications; if not, the material will not be purchased. The recommendation had a lot in common with, and may perhaps have been inspired by, the then highly popular idea of performance contracting in education. In 1970 the Office of Economic Opportunity funded experiments in 54 school districts in which private firms were retained to improve students' standardized test scores. The companies could use whatever means they wished, from teaching machines and special course material to cash incentives for teachers and students to attain the goal, but it was agreed that the companies would only be paid if students did achieve higher test scores.[37]

The concept of a "performance contract" between the states and federal government worked best as a politically acceptable formula for asserting greater federal control of Medicaid without directly advocating federalization. The latter would not only have been a red flag to opponents of big government and hardly likely to be embraced by a Republican administration, but also almost certainly could not have been achieved without the federal government agreeing to nationalize the full costs of the program. Nonetheless, the idea of such a contractual relationship was fundamentally incompatible with the existing legal authority on several counts. First, it ignored the fact that HEW did not possess the kind of broad authority that would allow it to set performance goals for the entire Medicaid program and then operationalize these in terms of specific administrative performance standards for state programs. Insofar as Medicaid's authority structure was still feudalistic, each state retained the right to enshrine its own political values and goals in its state plan.[38] At best, it would seem that the Medical Services Administration could suggest to each state how that state's goals could be expressed in terms of administrative performance standards, which the states themselves would then enforce if they so chose. From its rationalistic perspective, the Task Force did not seem to recognize—or perhaps did not fully understand—that because of the historical and statutory limits on the federal role, HEW could not claim authority to set performance standards merely because better administration would result. Congress would first have to give it a legislative mandate and that would require a political fight. Even assuming Congress did grant the authority, however, the Task Force recommendations still failed to come to grips with one other crucial problem: How could HEW penalize a state Medicaid program without simultaneously penalizing the program's clients?

The Task Force recommendation, as noted earlier, was to penalize administrative rather than service payment funds. In truth, the distinction is rather artificial, since administrative funds pay the costs of getting payments for services to the hospitals, doctors, nursing homes, and so forth, who may cease to see Medicaid patients if their payment is chronically delayed.

It can be argued, moreover, that much of the power a business firm wields over a subcontractor lies not in its power to withhold payment until specifications are met, but the further right to drop a contractor whose performance is persistently problematic and take its business elsewhere. The issue is how to penalize poor performance but also to get the job done. Because Medicaid is statutorily designated a state-run program, HEW is in a poor position to threaten to cut off funds to a state because it lacks the authority to take over administration of the state's program itself or to designate some other unit (such as a private fiscal agent) to do so. Thus medical providers and program beneficiaries who depend on Medicaid may become in effect the "legal hostages" of a noncompliant state.

STRENGTHENING FEDERAL RESEARCH AND DEVELOPMENT CAPACITIES. The Task Force recommendation that 5% of the total Medicaid budget each year be set aside for research on more effective delivery of health care services was not adopted. Indeed, according to National Planning Association figures, between 1968 and 1974, funds available to the Social and Rehabilitation Service (the Medical Services Administration's parent agency) for research on improving the organization and delivery of health services fell in absolute terms from $3,253,000 to $1,847,000 and as a percentage of total Medicaid funds from .002 to .0003.[39] In addition, the negative impact of "bureaucratic feudalism" on federal research and development capacities is especially evident when one looks at Social and Rehabilitation Service-supported research and development. Because Social and Rehabilitation's research and development funds were tied to the matching formulas of the Social Security Act, Social Rehabilitation Service supported research took the form of cooperative research and demonstration projects with individual states. A 1977 General Accounting Office evaluation of Social and Rehabilitation Service research efforts in social services, health services, and income maintenance concluded

> These projects are primarily focused on the administrative aspects of social programs and are limited to experiences within a single state. Although projects of this nature may be useful to the

state and local officials and SRS personnel, we believe that the scope of project results without additional research limits their usefulness to national policymakers.[40]

Moreover, just as the Task Force foresaw, the continued location of Medicaid on the "welfare" side of HEW meant that research efforts were directed toward issues of cost control and more efficient administrative mechanisms, not quality of care. Insofar as there was Social and Rehabilitation Service–Medical Services Administration-supported research directed toward ascertaining Medicaid's impact on recipients, it was focused mainly on Medicaid's value to recipients as an income supplement. As one indicator the Medical Services Administration *Commissioner's Status Book* for November 1975 lists a total of 16 ongoing evaluation projects. All involved short-term contracts with private management consulting firms concerning rather narrowly defined "applied research" topics. One study, for example, aimed to develop a Medicaid management control system whose purposes were described as "identifying exemplary practices in state procedures to eliminate erroneous expenditures and capture third-party liability." Perhaps the most quality oriented study on the list was one entitled "Impact of SNF/ICF Standards" which sought to arrive at a mathematical model to measure the cost impact of SNF/ICF standards and develop recommendations for changing reimbursement levels to reflect the higher costs of compliance with standards.

Unable to effectuate a transfer of Medicaid to the health side of HEW, the Task Force recommended greater coordination with HEW health agencies to make up for lack of health expertise in the Social and Rehabilitation Service, Medical Services Administration. Sharing organizational knowledge between and among subunits is, however, a classic problem in bureaucracies[41] and one that Medicaid has had no special success in overcoming. In the 5 years following the Task Force report, only one major cooperative effort seems to have been undertaken: A Medical Services Administration–Public Health

Service project begun in 1975 to develop area-wide health care systems for underserved rural areas.[42]

In an effort to stimulate attention to program planning and evaluation over and above the prevailing preoccupation with administrative mechanics, the Task Force recommended an internal reorganization of the Medical Services Administration to include among a number of principal elements: (a) "a Deputy Commissioner for Program (in addition to a deputy for administration) to provide high-level leadership in defining program goals and influencing program content,"[43] and (b) "a Program Planning and Evaluation Unit, reporting to the Deputy Commissioner for Program."[44] In March 1970, HEW did in fact adopt a reorganization plan for the Medical Services Administration substantially similar to the one proposed by the Task Force.[45] Again, however, bureaucratic feudalism operated to orient the newly created Department of Planning and Program Evaluation away from the kind of national policy research the Task Force envisioned toward serving the information needs of state administrators. Thus as of 1975, the Department of Planning and Progress Evaluation project that Medical Services Administration officials seemed most enthusiastic about was the effort to identify "exemplary practices" in state program operations and then seek to disseminate these to other states by "circulating brief write-ups and through a series of workshops tailored to the needs of states."[46]

CYBERNETIC RATIOS: THE RELATIONSHIP OF ORGANIZATIONAL RESOURCES TO FUNCTIONAL RESPONSIBILITIES. "Cybernetic ratio" is an analytic term we have coined to refer to the amount of resources (funds, manpower, etc.) an organizational unit *qua* "societal guidance mechanism" has available to carry out the guidance functions assigned to it. A unit with insufficient resources will perform poorly due to a condition of persistent structural overload.

In evaluating the poor performance of HEW in the surveillance of the implementation of Medicaid in the states, and in the planning, recommending innovations, and setting of goals for the program nationwide, the McNerney Task Force paid considerable attention to the HEW Audit Agency's findings that the Medical Services Administration was greatly understaffed. As of 1970 the Medical Services Administration central office in Washington had a staff of 50 professional and 35 support personnel; Medical Services Administration staff in the six regional offices comprised 2 to 3 persons. Because the regional offices were understaffed, the HEW Audit Agency reported that staff tended to operate mainly on the "exception theory of management, with attention being devoted essentially to problems as they arose, rather than under a positive ongoing management concept." Instead of assuming an active leadership role Medical Services Administration personnel acted mainly as liaison between the central office and the state agencies.[47]

In theory, the main source of management information at the federal level concerning the administrative performance of state Medicaid programs was supposed to be program review and evaluation project (PREP) reviews carried out by central office Medical Services Administration staff with the cooperation and assistance of regional personnel. The audit agency concluded, however, that the program and evaluation reviews were not made often enough to identify on a timely basis those aspects of state programs in need of improvement. Thus it was noted

> During August 1967, MSA instituted an internal policy providing for one PREP review to be made each month. At this rate, almost 4 years will be required to review all States and jurisdictions participating in the program. Although 24 PREP reviews had been made as of May 1969, 16 states and 3 other juridsictions had not been reviewed. MSA stated that with only seven professionals available in the Medical Program Evaluation Division, not more than one PREP review can be made each month. These seven cannot devote full-time to the PREP activity because of their other responsibilities.[48]

The HEW Audit Agency review further noted that regional office personnel were in charge of discussing Program Review and Evaluation Project recommendations with the state agencies, ascertaining whether or not the state agencies were implementing the recommendations, and reporting back to Washington on this. Yet, characteristically, 3 to 9 months would elapse between transmission of the Program and Evaluation Project report to the states and regional office follow-up, which was then often ineffectual.[49]

On the basis of these and similar findings, the McNerney Task Force recommended that a minimum of 125 additional Medical Services Administration staff positions be created. As of the publication of its final report, the Task Force was able to note that 86 additional positions had, in fact, been authorized by Congress, although it reiterated that more positions of a higher grade (enabling better qualified, more experienced personnel to be hired) were needed.[50]

Within 2 years, however, these gains had been more than wiped out by the 1972 Social Security Act amendments which added considerably to the surveillance functions of the Medical Services Administration vis-a-vis the states without proportional increase in its manpower authorization. Moreover, in keeping with the Nixon Administration's antibig government thrust (i.e., the "New Federalism") most of the new personnel were assigned to the regions, not to the central office as the Task Force recommended.

The earlier discussed tension between Congress' philosophical stance in favor of highly autonomous state programs and its pragmatic frustration with states' poor performance expressed itself during the next 5 years in Congress' continually requiring HEW to take on new regulatory functions but remaining antibig government by keeping the units charged with performing these functions small. As the 1975 Medical Services Administration "Forward Plan" notes,

> The constraints on the Federal role grew out of Medicaid's historical antecedents and the political reality of 1965. Medicaid was passed as an add-on to the welfare system; the states had

always maintained responsibility for providing and managing their own welfare services. A bill with a strong Federal management presence would probably not have passed Congress.

The minimum staff resources assigned to MSA reflect the intended federal role. At no time has the central office exceeded 200 positions; and, in fact, is currently operating at a strength of 135 with 190 positions. Medical Services staff in the Regional offices totals less than 100.[51]

The Forward Plan report goes on to note that as federal Medicaid expenditures rose from 2.6 billion in fiscal year 1970 to 6.5 billion in fiscal year 1975, there was a corresponding rise in federal concern over how well this money was being spent; and in a number of high priority areas, the Medical Services Administration was mandated by the HEW leadership or, more often, by Congress to undertake much greater oversight of state programs.[52] According to the *Forward Plan*, to carry this increased regulatory load, the Medical Services Administration "would require an estimated total new staff for the Federal Medicaid program of 720 people, in addition to the current slots of 190 in the Central Office and 130 in the Regional Offices, and the 108 slots which have been requested in the FY1976 budget."[53] Although the Medical Services Administration did receive the added personnel requested in the 1976 budget (mainly for fraud and abuse control, which was *the* crisis issue that year), the agency did not receive adequate added personnel to carry out its less newsworthy missions.

THE MEDICAID MANAGEMENT INFORMATION SYSTEM.   We noted earlier that the Medicaid Task Force recommended "top priority" be given to the development of an integrated Medicaid management information system (MMIS). As such, the Task Force's success in instigating the Social and Rehabilitation Service to research and develop a prototype Medicaid management information system which could be implemented by state Medicaid programs could well be considered its most important accomplishment. It is also, however, in the development of the Medicaid Management information system that the failure to take fully into account the power and consensus variables that some of the most crippling unanticipated consequences were produced.

The "MMIS" developed by the federal agency for the states, has two components. The Surveillance and Utilization Review (S/UR) Subsystem is designed to overlay claims processing to identify patterns of inappropriate care and services. The Management and Administrative Reporting Subsystem (MARS) is described in the MARS manual as

> Intended to provide to State Title XIX Program timely and meaningful information, reflecting the key areas of program activity. The 26 MARS reports are designed to help in the difficult task of effectively planning, directing and controlling a State Medicaid Program by providing information to support the decision-making process. These reports should assist program management positively to plan program activity and to avoid undesirable situations rather than being forced to react to situations as they arise.[54]

It will be recalled that the McNerney Task Force envisioned an integrated management information system for the entire Medicaid program. As such, the capacity of the federal government to obtain the management information required to carry out federal surveillance and policymaking functions was contingent on *all* states adopting the same prototypical standardized management information system. Such a system would give all states an equal capacity to generate quickly comparable information useful to the federal government.

The McNerney Task Force assumed that if the federal government developed the "MMIS" prototype and agreed to pay most of the costs entailed both in initial adoption and subsequent operation in the states, the states would welcome this opportunity to improve their administrative efficiency and effectiveness. That states might refuse or balk at the Medicaid Management informantion system seems not to have occurred to the Task Force. Yet this is precisely what occurred.

It was not until 1975 that the first Medicaid management information system was certified. As of April 21, 1976, six states had approved operational systems (New Hampshire, Minnesota, Arkansas, New Mexico, Montana, and Utah). Four states (Georgia, Michigan, Ohio, and Texas) were awaiting ceritification review. Medicaid management information systems in California and Hawaii had been reviewed and some modifications requested. Thus, by 1976, 12 states did have operational or near operational systems. However, 17 states (nearly a third of all Medicaid programs) were described in Medical Services Administration documents as "inactive" or "no interest shown." Most of the rest were in the very early stages of developing a proposal or letting a contract with no guarantee that they would proceed further.[55] As of mid 1979 nearly ten years after the Medicaid Task Force recommended the development of an integrated Medicaid management information system, 15 states were operating certified MMISs. Eleven states were awaiting certification and 23 states were said to be developing or to have partially implemented a Medicaid management information system.[56]

It might be thought that the process of adopting the Medicaid management information system in a particular state program was simply fraught with complex debugging problems. Indeed, there have been many such problems. The data suggest, however, that once a state made a definitive decision to implement the Medicaid system, implementation took 1 or 2 years; much longer delays were associated with making the decision to implement the Medicaid system in the first place. The New York State Department of Social Services, for example, contracted for no fewer than four feasibility and design studies for Medicaid management information systems in 1973, and another in 1974. In 1975, a special study commission of state legislators recommended "MMIS" adoption.[57] Yet the required legislation consistently went nowhere until the late fall of 1976. (Even then, the main push seems to have come from a year and a half of front-page Medicaid scandals.)

Why did states hesitate to adopt the MMIS? One federal Medicaid official interviewed for this study suggested as the main reason for state reluctance that state administrators did not understand why they needed such a sophisticated information system and had to be educated—a process that took time. Although he did not put it quite this way, the implication was that Medical Services Administration technical assistance personnel were akin to Peace Corps volunteers bringing shiny new tractors to the backward peoples of underdeveloped countries who up to that point had been using water buffalo. It was understandable that as they were being asked to skip over several stages of technological development, they did not at first quite know what the machinery was to be used for and all the marvelous things it could do.

It is true that in many states administration was rather primitive. (As one local social services commissioner told the 1975 New York State legislative commission studying Medicaid administration, "Utilization review in my district consists of two elderly women with an adding machine."[58]) Yet "backward" peoples have been known to embrace modern methods with unexpected alacrity when to do so has suited *their* purposes. The question is, did adopting the Medicaid management information system suit state purposes?

From the viewpoint of an administrative rationalist, it should have. All the states had an urgent need to gain control over rapidly rising Medicaid expenditures. However, if one also views administration in terms of the balance of power (a) between Medicaid administrators and providers and (b) among units and levels of government, the political rationale behind state ambivalence becomes clear. The MMIS threatened to renegotiate the prevailing balance of power, strengthening the states vis-a-vis Medicaid providers and local government while at the same time weakening the states vis-a-vis the federal government.

Some states appear to have been primarily concerned with the balance of power between levels of government. In New

York State, the main political obstacle to the introduction of the Medicaid management information system was the fact that the 58 counties enjoyed a tradition of considerable autonomy from state government in running both welfare and medical assistance programs. In return for a high level of local control, the counties shared the costs equally with the state.[59] The introduction of MMIS would allow the state greater administrative control without, however, a correspondingly higher share of the financing load. A handful of states developed and implemented (and, of course, paid for) their own computerized management information systems. As of the beginning of 1976, however, none of the states that had developed what federal officials considered[60] efficient, effective information systems on their own initiative (New Jersey, California, Texas, Mississippi, Michigan, and Oklahoma) had yet received federal "MMIS" certification, despite the incentive to qualify in order to obtain federal funds. In California's case, at least, the lack of certification of the state's system as of April 1976 was clearly the result of the state's refusal to modify certain of its administrative procedures in line with federal requirements.[61] Those states, however, that showed little or only sluggish interest in developing a computerized information system seemed to have been mainly concerned with the balance of power between government and Medicaid providers.

Theodore Lowi has characterized policy outputs as distributive, redistributive, or regulatory.[62] Medicaid encompasses all three types: It is redistributive with respect to taxpayers and the poor who qualify as program beneficiaries; it is distributive and regulatory with respect to relations between government and Medicaid providers. From the program's inception, however, state governments were inclined to stress the distributive functions of Medicaid to the neglect of the regulatory ones. That this should be so is scarcely surprising since the distributive function (i.e., that of allocating resources to someone or some group) is one that is responsive to powerful societal interests, whereas the regulatory function (i.e., defining and enforcing behaviors that are required versus impermissible) is one that calls for governmental resistance to those very same forces. (One measure of the discrepancy in state performance vis-a-vis these two functions is to compare the enormous nursing home building boom and rise in per diem patient rates sparked by Medicaid as against the much lesser degree of improvement in quality of nursing home care.)

From the inception of the Medicaid program, the primary relationship of the states to Medicaid providers was that of a distributor of resources. The states' power vis-a-vis providers and the power of providers vis-a-vis states were expressed in terms of power to grant or obtain a more-or-less favorable share of resources as measured by rate setting and other financial arrangements. Many of these arrangements reflected a power balance that objective observers would be likely to judge as neither to the advantage nor to the credit of the states that had negotiated them. The Medicaid management information system would render these arrangements, which had been relatively "invisible" sociologically, much more visible.[63] In more colloquial terminology, adopting a centralized information system such as "MMIS" would be administratively analogous to shining a light into a dark corner or picking up a rock: A lot of dirt was likely to be exposed.

Moreover, the argument that they lacked the necessary informational and administrative capacities had historically provided the states with a credible excuse not to attempt to assert more than a weak, negligible regulatory power vis-a-vis Medicaid providers. The MMIS, by providing the previously lacking information gathering and processing capabilities, would either pressure weak state welfare or health departments into taking on politically powerful Medicaid providers *or* make it apparent to federal reviewers that the states were evading, or performing ineffectually, their regulatory responsibilities.

Finally, the states had historically used federal ignorance about the details of state Medicaid programs and their management as a means of safeguarding state autonomy in decision making. We already noted that federal reviewers have been greatly hampered in their efforts to evaluate state administration by the necessity of devoting so much time to first learning the basic facts of what is going on. State officials, for their part, perennially complain about the burden of having to shepherd inexperienced federal personnel. In fact this has been an important socializing mechanism, giving states considerable influence over the picture both in terms of factual "bits" and contextual interpretation federal evaluators gain of a state's program. (Thus state officials' complaints are reminiscent of the military's complaints about the burden of having to respond to congressional committees' requests for budget information or having to deal with congressional fact-finding visits to military bases when, in fact, these constitute major opportunities to indoctrinate congressmen in promilitary views.) With the Medicaid management information system in place, state officials would lose not all but a significant part of their current capacity to keep the federal government at bay through selective information—or pleading of ignorance—about various aspects of the state program.

CONCLUSION

The analysis, conclusions, and recommendations contained in the Medicaid Task Force's Final Report were predominantly rationalistic, first, in their almost exclusive concern with program administration and, second, in their focus on the "rational" variables, knowledge and organization, as the main levers for effecting change. The Task Force's main recommendation was for the development of an integrated management information system. Other recommendations centered around better alignment of organizational structure and function and strengthening organizational resources.

In large measure, the Task Force's rationalistic orientation was preset: in the definition of the problem given to the Task

Force by its "client" (HEW), by the prevailing assumptions concerning the nature of the Medicaid crisis (among congressional and executive policymakers), and by the cumulative weight of previous fact-finding studies that had stressed defects in program administration. Those who served on the Medicaid Task Force, however—most of whom were either professors of health administration or, most often, administrators by profession (whether they came from within HEW or the private bureaucracies of the health insurance industry)—seem to have found the focus on management information and organization compatible with their experience and training.

There is little doubt that Medicaid administration would have been made more efficient and effective through implementation nationwide of an integrated management information system such as that proposed by the Task Force and subsequently developed in prototype by HEW. Nearly a decade after the Task Force report, however, the system had as yet to be fully implemented in all states.

With its rationalistic blinders on, the Task Force failed to take sufficiently into account the political implications of and barriers to effective implementation of such an information system. The Task Force did not understand that implementation of a nationwide integrated information system would alter the existing balance of power between state administrators and Medicaid providers and clients, and between federal and state administrators. Those who favored the existing power balance would thus resist the information system. Because the Task Force failed to perceive the likelihood of such politically motivated resistance, it did not formulate recommendations for dealing with it.

The recommendations of the Medicaid Task Force reflect an incrementalist approach to reform in that each recommendation represents a relatively minor departure from previous policy and program administration. (The introduction of a computerized Medicaid management information system was the greatest single change proposed.) This was not, however, because the Task Force perceived only minor defects in the Medicaid program. Indeed because the Task Force's diagnosis was of more serious problems, the Task Force recommendations, as incremental reforms, were too weak to accomplish the Task Force's ostensible goals. Thus the Task Force analysis implied that efficiency and effectiveness required federalization of Medicaid administration; yet the Task Force did not recommend it. Also, despite the Task Force members' conviction that Medicaid should be reoriented away from "welfare" (providing an "in kind" income supplement) toward health (ensuring high-quality services, necessary and appropriate to bringing about improvements in recipients' health status), the Task Force declined in the end even to recommend that Medicaid be administered at the federal level by a health rather than a welfare bureaucracy.

How is it that the Task Force, many of whose members were deeply critical of the Medicaid program's basic philosophy, produced a final report so "incrementalist" in its analysis and especially its reform recommendations? Although a number of factors no doubt entered in, one important one appears to have been the Task Force's sense of timing. Thus, although it was probably evident to the Task Force that a slow, evolutionary "creeping" federalization was a clear historical trend in Medicaid administration, the Task Force may well have been reluctant to propose making an explicit policy decision to federalize Medicaid since this would have been seriously at odds with the Republican administration's announced desire to return authority over social policy and programs to the states (Nixon's "New Federalism").

In addition, more basic Medicaid reforms were seen as deeply tied to basic welfare reforms, and Congress was then (1969–1970) considering President Nixon's proposed "Family Assistance Plan" (a federally guaranteed minimum income program). The Task Force members appear to have been persuaded that only after the enactment of the family assistance plan or some other basic welfare reform could Medicaid be administratively disengaged from public assistance and redirected from welfare to health goals. Finally, and perhaps most important, however, the Task Force seems to have reconciled itself to incrementalist tinkering on the basis of the widely held belief (especially prevalent among the health administration experts and political liberals who predominated on the Task Force) that national health insurance was just around the corner. Had national health insurance actually been imminent, the Task Force's sense that more fundamental Medicaid reforms would be too expensive if they would almost immediately have to be undone and redone in the context of national health insurance would have made a good deal of sense. Little did the Task Force suspect that nearly 10 years after their report, national health insurance would still seem as close to—*and* as far away from—enactment as ever.

Chapter 3

A FUNDAMENTAL–RATIONAL APPROACH
The InterStudy Health Maintenance Strategy

INTRODUCTION

The InterStudy "health maintenance strategy" is grounded in classical capitalist economic theory. The aim was to create a self-regulating market mechanism to keep the cost of health services under control while assuring consumers sufficient access to high-quality care—especially preventive care—to maintain good health. The InterStudy proposal sought to accomplish this by building into the organizational structure of the "health maintenance organization" rational incentives—primarily economic rewards and santions—for health care providers to curb costs, avoid unnecessary or inappropriate overutilization of services, and stress preventive medicine.

As with classical capitalist market theory, the intellectual roots of the health maintenance strategy lay in utilitarian social philosophy and in the Enlightenment concept of a social contract rationally designed to further the economic self-interest of both parties to the exchange.

73

Market organization was thus to be the principal lever for effecting deliberate social change. Professional knowledge, specifically measurement of health care quality with special emphasis on measurement of health outcomes via government-supervised internal peer review, received secondary emphasis.

The InterStudy health maintenance strategy aimed for a fundamental reorganization of the American health care delivery system. This was a task the InterStudy researchers likened to an "industrial revolution" in health care since it would involve bringing modern corporate organizational rationality to a service "industry" hitherto composed largely of independent, highly individualistic "craftsmen."

ORIGINS OF THE REFORM PROPOSAL

What is a "health maintenance organization?" As we shall see, the concept has had somewhat different meaning and appeal to different groups of supporters. However, in a 1971 HEW white paper—which signaled the Nixon Administration's decision to make health maintenance organizations a major policy initiative—"health maintenance organizations" were defined as "organized *systems* of health care, providing comprehensive services for enrolled members, for a fixed prepaid annual fee. No matter how each health maintenance organization may choose to organize itself (and there are various models), from the consumer's viewpoint they all provide a mix of outpatient and inpatient services through a single payment mechanism."[1]

The basic idea had for some years had a following among specialists in public health and health administration (especially those in academia). It was, however, a team of researchers, under the leadership of Dr. Paul Ellwood, Jr., at InterStudy, an independent Minneapolis-based research institute, who coined the term "health maintenance organizations" and spearheaded efforts to make promoting these organizations an object of national policy.

A number of organizations of this type—generally known as "prepaid health plans"—had been in existence for many years, chiefly in the West. The oldest, largest, and best-known was the Kaiser Foundation Health Plan, originally organized in the 1930s under the auspices of industrialist Henry J. Kaiser to meet the medical needs of Kaiser Industries employees working in remote areas. Following World War II, the Kaiser Plan opened its rolls to non-Kaiser employees and expanded to many localities in California and in three other states. By the early 1970s "Kaiser-Permanente," as it came to be called, had a total of 2 million subscribers, only a small percentage of whom were Kaiser Industries employees. The Health Insurance Plan of Greater New York (HIP), founded in 1946, had ¾ million enrollees (mainly New York City municipal employees) by the early 1970s. At the opposite extreme in size, many small, rural, prepaid health clinics were organized by consumers as an outgrowth of the farmers' cooperative movement during the 1930s. The first of these was organized in 1929 by Dr. Michael Shadid in Elk City, Oklahoma, a farming community of 6,000. Other long-established prepaid plans include the Group Health Association, of Washington, D.C., founded in 1937 by the Home Owners Loan Corporation for its employees and later opened to all government employees; the Community Health Association of Detroit, initially sponsored by the United Auto Workers; and the Group Health Cooperative of Seattle, an urban and suburban medical co-op started in 1959, which was inspired by the rural co-op movement. Still other prepaid health plans were set up as physician-owned, for-profit businesses, the best known being the Ross-Loos Clinic in California.

Finally, there had also evolved what came to be called "independent practice associations" or "medical foundations." These were set up by physicians who opposed the group practice, salaried reimbursement features of the original prepaid plans. "IPAs" or "medical foundations"—of which the San Joaquin Foundation in California and the Physician's Association of Clackamas County in Oregon are two of the best known —offered consumers a prepaid plan, but physicians could continue solo practice in their own offices and be reimbursed on a fee-for-service basis.

Since these prototypes have been in existence, a number of them 25 and 30 years, the question arises, why, specifically in 1969–1970, the idea of prepaid health care should be put forward as national policy. Many factors are responsible, but two in particular deserve attention. First, the interdisciplinary team at InterStudy decided to research and formulate a health maintenance organization policy and then campaign for it. Second, and equally important, the political climate seems to have been ripe for such an effort. The Nixon Administration was just getting underway and high-level policymakers in the White House and HEW were looking for new ideas that would exemplify Republican political values: reliance on the private sector versus government, market mechanisms versus bureaucratic regulation, the profit motive, decentralization, and "localism."

POSITIONING THE INTERSTUDY PROPOSAL ON THE ANALYTIC GRID

Health Maintenance Organizations: A Rationalist Approach

The InterStudy position paper entitled *A Health Maintenance Strategy* was originally presented to the Nixon Administration in March 1970.[2] Analytically, it focused on organizational variables.

The central element of the health maintenance policy according to the InterStudy team was the alignment of positive economic incentives on the side of cost control and preventive medicine (i.e., health maintenance). According to the position paper,

> The operation of health maintenance organizations is contingent upon the health maintenance contract—the key feature which assures that these organizations will deliver health services more efficiently and effectively than conventional providers. By this contract, the health maintenance organization (HMO) agrees to provide comprehensive health maintenance services to its enrollees in exchange for a fixed annual fee. The consequences of this contract to both the consumer and the provider are vital to this strategy. The economic incentives of both the provider and the consumer are aligned by means of their contractual agreement, which assures that the financial risk of ill health with the consumer. Since the economic incentives of the contracting parties are identical, both would have an interest in maintaining health.[3]

Once the Nixon Administration had decided to adopt the health maintenance strategy, the InterStudy team shifted its attention and efforts to helping the Administration get legislation to assist health maintenance organization (HMO) growth through Congress. Almost immediately, they encountered skepticism concerning the ability of such organizations to assure quality of care. To respond to these concerns, the Inter-Study team turned its attention to knowledge—specifically, the professional knowledge required to measure quality of care. According to a subsequent InterStudy publication,

> As we at Interstudy began to dig into the issue, we began to realize several important points. First, HMO care did not appear to be of any lower quality than the care of other providers. In fact, most comparative studies showed that, if anything, the quality of HMO care was somewhat higher. Nevertheless, a number of members of Congress made it clear that if the legal boundaries to HMOs were to be removed, some measures of quality assurance had to be put in their place and that the most probable means would be standards based on traditional professional standards such as how many of what kinds of people worked in the HMO. Second, most studies did, however, show

that the quality of medical care, irrespective of provider, was at times highly variable and in most instances lower than had been anticipated by those providing the care. Third, it became apparent that important and perhaps far-reaching developments in quality assessment technology had occurred during the last several years, especially in the area of assessing the outcomes of episodes of care.[4]

InterStudy decided in the fall of 1971 to embark on a major policy research effort devoted to analyzing different approaches to assuring quality of care. InterStudy staff reviewed the existing quality assurance literature, ascertained through personal contact the results of recent, as yet unpublished, research as well as work in progress, and wrote a number of monographs on such topics as the latest developments in quality assurance technology, research on the quality of care in different institutional settings, analysis of the effectiveness of current regulatory mechanisms, and the experiences of regulatory bodies attempting to control quality in industries other than health, health maintenance organizations, and the law.[5]

In December 1971, InterStudy held a small conference which brought together nine experts in the technical assessment of the quality of health care. In January, 1972, preliminary findings and conclusions were drawn together into a draft monograph that served as the principal discussion document for a much larger conference on quality assurance sponsored by InterStudy in New Orleans in mid-January, 1972. Participants included experts in the technical assessment of the quality of health care; managers of health maintenance organizations; practicing physicians; experts in regulatory theory and technique, including economists, political scientists, and other analysts; lawyers familiar with administrative law and regulatory agencies; and representatives from the Administration and the Health subcommittees of the U.S. Senate and House.[6]

There were two main results from the New Orleans conference. First, many respected and influential health care experts were mobilized by their participation to join the political campaign on behalf of HMOs and, in particular, on behalf of the quality assurance proposal as it evolved out of the conference. The second result was that InterStudy was led to modify its original thinking in response to the criticisms and suggestions of the conference participants.[7]

There were two key features to the InterStudy quality assurance proposal. One pertained to the knowledge needed to regulate health care quality, the other to the organizational structures through which quality regulation ought to be implemented.

Concerning knowledge, the InterStudy team proposed that HMO performance with respect to quality assurance be measured via outcome (rather than the more traditional input or process) indicators.[8] They were convinced that recent and continuing breakthroughs in medical science and in information technology made such outcome assessment technically feasible, at least in so far as it focused on medically attainable or preventable outcomes among groups.

> The outcomes definition of quality is based on maximizing desired outcomes over a population and not necessarily for each individual patient. However, the desired population results are not going to be achieved unless the health system commits itself to serving each individual in an effective manner.[9]

Such population-based measures would entail a shift in emphasis away from "super care for a minority" toward "acceptable care for the many." Given limitations on financial, professional, and technical resources, a focus on overall population outcomes was also recommended as more cost effective. Moreover, the InterStudy researchers argued that although such a focus on the statistical probabilities of various outcomes among patient populations would ensure *more* quality regulation, physicians would actually find the increased regulation *less* burdensome:

Our present medical malpractice system, what Fuchs has called the "technological imperative in health," imperfectly recognizes this fundamental concept of acceptable quality for a defined population group. The performance of a physician, with respect to *all* of his patients seldom allows accommodation of a chance bad result.[10]

Concerning the organizational mechanisms through which quality assurance should be implemented, the InterStudy proposal called for the creation of a federal Quality Assurance Commission. Patterned after the independent regulatory commissions for other industries (the FCC, FTC, FPC, etc.), the Quality Assurance Commission was to concern itself with three major related functions: (a) quality of assurance, (b) monitoring of the provision of information to consumers, and (c) research and development in both areas.

The Quality Assurance Commission would be concerned with promoting the health care industry, controlling costs, planning, and distribution of health care resources on third-party payment plans. Unlike the traditional regulatory commissions, however, the Quality Assurance Commission would not actually engage in the day-to-day regulation of quality of care, but would delegate this to "peer review" committees within the health maintenance organizations and focus its own efforts mainly on monitoring these internal self-regulatory mechanisms.

Health Maintenance Organizations: A Fundamental Reform

InterStudy's health maintenance strategy constituted a fundamental critique of the prevailing American system for delivering health care, in particular, primary care. Like many health administration experts, the InterStudy team viewed the solo practice, fee-for-service system as a sort of premodern "cottage industry." Hence their design for health care reform was to be above all a process of economic modernization. As they saw it,

> The emergence of a free market economy could stimulate a course of change in the health industry that would have some of the classical aspects of the industrial revolution—conversion to larger units of production, technological innovation, vigorous competition and profitability as the mandatory condition of survival. . . .[11]

Although the organizational transformation posited might not entail the total replacement of solo practice, fee-for-service medicine, the InterStudy team did envision a "projected transition from 200,000 small unintegrated fee-for-service health firms to perhaps 5,000 vertically integrated HMOs, plus other providers."[12] This was to be accomplished via a series of five steps that the federal government could undertake over a period of 5 to 10 years. The steps were (a) for the federal government to employ its exhortational and convening powers to call on private enterprise, public agencies, and the health industry to cooperate in implementing the national objective of health maintenance; (b) provide incentives for the creation of health maintenance organizations; (c) foster the elimination of any legal barriers blocking creation of such organizations; (d) begin purchasing services under Medicare, Medicaid, and other federal reimbursement programs by health maintenance contracts rather than by the existing method of paying for individual medical services; (e) build into these contracts a sufficient return to support necessary investments in manpower, facilities, and health services research by the contracting health maintenance organizations; (f) review government activities in the health field to determine how they currently contribute to or frustrate the health maintenance strategy, and initiate necessary modifications to support it.[13]

We will now turn to examine elements of the health maintenance strategy in greater detail.

HEALTH MAINTENANCE ORGANIZATIONS IN THEORY: ORGANIZATION AND KNOWLEDGE AS THE KEY LEVERS FOR DELIBERATE SOCIAL CHANGE

Organization: Market versus Bureaucracy

A familiar theme in American political ideology is that "market" and "bureaucracy" are two utterly opposite organizational principles, and that a choice of one *or* the other must be made. In addition, bureaucracy is typically associated with government intervention, whereas the market is associated with free enterprise, competitive capitalism.

The InterStudy position paper on health maintenance strategy posed this choice in the following terms:

> The Nixon Administration must make a major decision on its strategy for dealing with the much proclaimed health crisis in America. It can either
> —Rely on continued or increased federal intervention through regulation, investment and planning, or
> —Promote a health maintenance industry that is largely self-regulatory and makes its own investment decisions regarding resources such as facilities and manpower.[14]

The InterStudy proposal stressed the HMO as a market-oriented approach, and portrayed its virtues as those of classical competitive capitalism. "Under this system a new medical economics for both providers and consumer emerges, where the pressure is on providers to provide the most economical combination of health services and the consumer has the opportunity to shop for the most convenient and economical health plan." Furthermore, reliance on a competitive market in which the producer–sellers are HMOs and the buyers are the general public "should develop more efficient ways to allocate resources and services in accordance with both consumer and provider preferences."[15]

Yet it is one of the curiously chameleonlike qualities of the HMO concept that it may just as readily be characterized as the embodiment of bureaucratic *or* market rationality, depending on which aspects are focused on.[16] Although the InterStudy team chose rhetorically to emphasize HMO as a market mechanism, their proposal actually had many bureaucratic features. We refer not only to the later addition of some government regulation in the form of the Quality Assurance Commission, but to elements much more central to the HMO concept: first, the bureaucratic structure of the HMO plan itself and, second, the notion of vertical integration of health services, defined as a "situation in which one entity (the HMO) assumes continuing responsibility for, and control over, most of its enrollees' medical care, including physicians services and hospitalization."[17]

To proponents of classical market theory, the market is competitive to the extent that it is atomized; that is, both buyers and sellers are typically characterized as individuals or, at the most, "organized" as small entrepreneurial, family, or partnership businesses. For example, Harry Schwartz, a conservative proponent of market reform in health care, is scathingly critical of those who would "eliminate the private practice of medicine by individuals or small groups and replace them by 'medical systems' of the Health Maintenance Organization type."[18] He goes on to compare the integration of American hospitals and physicians into health maintenance organizations to Stalin's collectivization of Soviet agriculture in the early 1930s. If, however, such organizations do resemble Soviet collective farms because doctors practice in groups according to a specialized division of labor, then so do the large business corporations that have to such a considerable extent replaced the small businesses of the 19th century in the 20th-century American industrial economy.

The point is that much traditional American ideology regarding such concepts as the "market," "free enterprise," and "capitalism" is based on individualistic antibureaucratic principles which, logically, are as hostile to modern *corporate, bureaucratic* capitalism as to any foreign organizational forms more conventionally labeled "socialistic."

To those for whom economic individualism is an essential element of what they mean by the competitive market, corporate bureaucracy would appear to have inherently monopolistic tendencies because economic concentration by definition means fewer competitors. Moreover, "vertical integration" (which is the organizational principle whereby General Motors rationalizes the entire process of auto production and sales by owning most of the myriad small firms that supply particular auto parts as well as car dealerships) is regarded by many free enterprise purists as a form of monopoly only slightly less evil than the "horizontal" integration practiced by John D. Rockefeller, and one that should be made equally subject to trust-busting efforts.

The point is that the diametric opposition of market versus bureaucracy and government intervention versus private enterprise as organizing principles is no longer an accurate description of reality, although we continue to debate the pros and cons of each alternative as though it were. Many, if not most, American organizations are actually hybrids, combining various elements of market and bureaucracy, government intervention and private (both for-profit and not-for-profit) enterprise. Although the InterStudy researchers chose to characterize the HMO concept as a "private market" approach, it is clearly a hybrid organizational form. This particular hybrid form favors corporate rather than government bureaucracy and requires government intervention in order to set up a competitive market in which government (via its various health care financing programs for the poor, the aged, and other specialized populations) is a major purchaser of services.

KNOWLEDGE: THE LIMITS OF CONSUMER ABILITY TO JUDGE QUALITY OF CARE. The original InterStudy proposal stressed as one of the greatest strengths of the HMO approach that economic rationality would be organizationally built in. Critics in Congress and elsewhere lost no time, however, in pointing out that the same economic incentives to curb excessive utilization of unnecessary or inappropriate services might also operate to promote underservicing: the withholding of necessary and appropriate, but expensive, care. As conservative economist Harry Schwartz observed, for the purely profit motivated health maintenance organization "Death is the ultimate economy."[19] According to Schwartz,

> It has been argued by HMO proponents that . . . a prepaid group is an incentive to keep patients healthy. But looked at purely from a bookkeeping point of view, an HMO has an equally strong interest in having its seriously ill patients die quickly and inexpensively.[20]

A less extreme version of the same principle is that a purely profit-seeking health maintenance organization would seek to limit consumer demand through such devices as long waiting lists, surly appointments secretaries, and impersonal, insensitive treatment. Consumers would be driven to obtain much of their care outside the health maintenance organization, while the organization nonetheless kept all of the prepaid fee.

Harry Schwartz and some others saw this as an argument for retaining the traditional fee-for-service system. The InterStudy researchers pointed out that most studies of existing health maintenance organizations suggested their quality of care was at least as high and often higher than that of traditional medicine. They had to concede nonetheless that a potential for profit-motivated underservicing did exist. The main reason was that the classic market maxim *caveat emptor* (let the buyer beware) could scarcely be applied to a product as complex and technical as medical care. As InterStudy's Walter McClure put it, "Concerning quality, we [meaning medical care consumers] are in much the position of buying a car for $5,000, not knowing whether it is a Cadillac or a Pinto."[21]

KNOWLEDGE AND ORGANIZATION: HEALTH OUTCOMES ASSESSMENT VIA REGULATED PEER REVIEW. According to the InterStudy researchers, if individual medical care consumers are unable to judge whether or not they are getting their money's worth, then a case could be made for quality regulation by government—or some outside agency. The issue is, however, would a regulatory agency's judgments be any better informed than those of the individual consumer?

The root problem as identified by the InterStudy team was that traditional measures of medical care quality did not measure outcomes—that is, actual improvements in health—but only poorly correlated inputs having to do with the qualifications of medical staff and facilities. The researchers went on to note the paucity not just in health maintenance organizations but in the health system generally of systematic follow-up concerning the results of clinical interventions. Practicing physicians (as opposed to medical researchers)—particularly by those involved in primary care—seldom sought to ascertain according to scientifically reliable (as opposed to ad hoc, impressionistic, or intuitive) methods whether their diagnostic judgments, choice, and implementation of particular courses of treatment yielded the expected health outcomes, not just in particular cases, but on a statistical basis. Nor were physicians, again primary-care physicians especially, inclined to measure their own performance in achieving expected patient outcomes against that of other doctors, on a statistical basis.

Although ostensibly a response to the problem of how to control economically motivated underservicing in health maintenance organizations, the InterStudy analysis actually raised some rather different, much broader issues in quality of care. In addition, their approach posited poor quality medical care as less a function of "greed" than of "ignorance."

The new, modified "HMO" proposal the InterStudy team brought before the Congress in 1972 thus differed from the original in stressing knowledge as well as organization as a lever for health care reform. Like the Medicaid Task Force before it, the InterStudy team now stressed the need for an information system. Also like the Medicaid Task Force, the InterStudy researchers stressed the need for outcome or performance indicators:

> It is not necessary to design a perfect system, usually an impossible, rapidly outmoded endeavor. But it is necessary to design a system that is self-correcting. A system is self-correcting when it knows its goals, can measure how far its performance is from its goals, and has incentives to apply this information to improving its performance. The Apollo moon flights are the classic modern example of intricately controlled feedback systems. No system can correct itself if it cannot measure its performance against goals. If the goal of quality is improved outcomes, then the gravest defect in the health care system is its continued inability to measure or regulate itself systematically and continuously on the basis of outcomes performance.[22]

Whereas the Medicaid Task Force had, in fact, focused on the information technology of "process" measures (e.g., utilization review), the InterStudy researchers set about ascertaining whether or not outcomes measurement of medical care quality was technically feasible. They found that

> A technology of outcomes assessment has been slow to develop; indeed substantial progress has been so recent (the last decade or so) that many professionals still regard outcomes assessment as infeasible or problematic.[23]

The InterStudy team's review of the literature and research in progress and their discussions with leading experts in the field led them to conclude, however, that "While far from perfected, a sufficient outcomes technology is immediately available and can have a large and constructive impact on health care performance."[24] The most serious obstacles to ongoing outcomes assessment of medical care are quality did not result from an insufficiency of scientific knowledge but from "structural," that is, organizational barriers.

One major organizational barrier was the fragmentation of the prevailing medical care delivery system in which the average solo, primary provider, care practitioner provides care to only about 2,000 patients (much too small a number to constitute a scientific sample) and is neither responsible for nor even has access to data about the whole patient. The health maintenance organization, however, overcomes both these difficulties:

> As a provider of long-term and comprehensive care, it is easier for an HMO to keep continuous medical records. One file, containing a consumer's past use of all facets of the HMO and present episodic details allows the provider to carry out the additional managerial task of observing and directing each person's care. It is upon this coordinated tracking that a quality assurance system could be built, with these records becoming the means to find out exactly what happened to the patient and the quality of that experience. Coupled with this, the vertical integrating and centralized management aspect of the HMOs should facilitate the institution of effective internal professional supervision of provider performance.[25]

In addition, the HMO provider has the capability of assessing the quality of care by comparing the health status of the active patient group with that of the nonactive patient group and attempting actively to uncover the unmet health needs of the enrolled population.[26]

HEALTH MAINTENANCE ORGANIZATIONS IN PRACTICE: THE UNINTENDED CONSEQUENCES OF INADEQUATE ATTENTION TO CONSENSUS AND POWER

We have seen that InterStudy's recommendations focused on organizational and knowledge factors (in particular, self-regulating organizational forms and professional knowledge regarding outcome indicators of health care quality) as the main requirements for reforming and "rationalizing" the American health services delivery system. In contrast, what we refer to as the political variables, power, and value consensus were left almost entirely out of account. The following sections will now explore some of the unintended consequences that resulted during the implementation of the health maintenance strategy from insufficient attention to these factors. We will look particularly at two separate efforts to implement steps in the five-point program that InterStudy had proposed to encourage the growth of health maintenance organizations over a 10-year period. These are the Health Maintenance Organization Assistance Act of 1973 which sought to remove legal barriers and create incentives for development of such organizations and the encouragement of Medicaid-financed HMO programs in California. The analysis will seek to show that the severe and largely unforeseen problems in implementing the Health Maintenance Organization Assistance Act were primarily due to an inadequate process of consensus building. In the case of the California Medicaid organizations, the unexpected scandals involving financial fraud and abuse, poor quality care, and political corruption will be traced to two factors: first, a program in which a highly unequal power distribution was inherent in the design, leaving a constituency both politically weak and stigmatized in public opinion (i.e., welfare recipients) in a position to be exploited for economic profit by politically powerful business interests and, second, failure to recognize and provide for professional ethics as an important (though not the only important) check against the excesses of the profit motive.

Inadequate Consensus Building: The Health Maintenance Organization Assistance Act

BACKGROUND TO THE ANALYSIS.   One of the main points in the original position paper was that the federal government should create incentives for the development of health maintenance organizations. In 1973, Congress passed the Health Maintenance Organization Assistance Act to do just that. Three years after its passage, however, the act was widely viewed as a failure. Thus, as of May 1976, only 12 such organizations were "federally qualified" under the act.[27] Moreover, although the total number of operational health maintenance organizations in the nation had increased since the act's passage, the rate of their growth had actually declined. Between 1971 and 1972, the percentage increase in the number of operational organizations was 52%: between 1972 and 1973, the percentage increase was 68%. Between 1973 and 1974, however, the growth rate dropped to 38%, and then to virtually zero between 1974 and 1975. In July 1976 there were 175 operational health maintenance organizations in the nation—down from 871 in July 1974.[28] This was a far cry from the Nixon Administration's initial 1971 goal of 1,600 by 1980[29] or even HEW's much more modest aim as of 1974 for the legislation to spark directly some 170 new organizations in 5 years.[30] So few health maintenance organizations were able to meet the stiff qualifying regulations that in the first full year of the HMO assistance program, HEW had available $40 million in grants, but made use of only $22 million. As a result, Congress appropriated only $15 million for the following year.[31]

Members of the InterStudy team and others argued that health maintenance organizations had not been given a fair market test under the act. Indeed they argued that in certain respects the Health Maintenance Organization Assistance Act had probably retarded their spontaneous growth.[32] This critique was widely shared. As of 1977–1978, the prevailing explanation for the poor growth of the organizations was that HMO development had been crippled by undercapitalization and, most especially, overregulation.

We do not dispute either of these points. They do not by themselves, however, constitute a sociological explanation for the "unintended consequences" of the HMO Assistance Act because the sociopolitical forces that produced these defects are left shrouded in mystery.

It is our contention that the HMO act with all its defects was the product of a typically American process of political consensus building in which conservative "market" advocates (including the InterStudy researchers) and liberal "government interventionists" each championed different social values. Though not incompatible in the abstract, these values could not each be maximized in practice without coming into conflict. On the level of implementation strategy, the conflicting ideologies were, of course, market versus bureaucracy, private sector versus government. Above and beyond these procedural disputes, however, and, in part, responsible for them was conflict concerning the "higher" values implicated in the goals of the HMO program: cost control, quality of care, and social justice.

THE VALUE CONFLICT: COST CONTROL FOR THE MIDDLE CLASS VERSUS EQUALITY FOR THE POOR.   The principal value conflict that was to paralyze the implementation of the HMO act was mainly one pitting the champions of cost control—and the market as the best organizational structure to implement this value—against the champions of greater social justice, best implemented via government regulation.

The original InterStudy paper for the Nixon Administration concerned itself almost exclusively with the health maintenance organization as a mechanism for controlling the spiraling costs of health care. A main selling point was the argument that spiraling health care costs could be controlled via such classical business methods as market competition, contracts, and economic incentives favoring greater efficiency and cost effectiveness. Emphasis was placed, in particular, on eliminating the inflationary aspects of existing private health insurance as the motivating factor behind introduction of universal, government financed, government-run national health insurance. The position paper was not concerned with such social justice goals as increasing or redistributing access to health services, of eliminating class-associated distinctions in access or ensuring equal access to HMO coverage by all citizens. In this respect the original InterStudy proposal could be said to favor the economic interests of those already covered by some form of health insurance as against those without such coverage and to reflect conservative, Republican values.

It is important to note, however, that the HMO concept itself is not intrinsically conservative. It is malleable enough to be made a carrier of liberal values as well.

Medicaid historians, Robert and Rosemary Stevens, took note of the extraordinary appeal the HMO concept had circa 1969–1970 to both political liberals and conservatives, stating, "As with similar programs for the use of 'vouchers' in education, the old liberals appear to have been overtaken in radicalism by the new conservatives."[33] Indeed, they point out that virtually every national health insurance plan proposed to the 91st Congress (except the AMA plan) by both Republicans and Democrats alike included a version of the HMO concept.

What attracted liberals such as Senator Edward Kennedy to health maintenance organizations or, as Kennedy preferred to call them, "comprehensive health service organizations"?[34] It was mainly the potential of these organizations to introduce a much greater degree of social justice into the health care system. If the entire health care delivery system were eventually reorganized into health maintenance organizations—or if they at least came to dominate the system as proponents envisioned, this would tend toward reduction of "two-class" medical care. Instead of the well-off receiving their primary care from office-based physicians while the poor relied primarily on hospital emergency rooms and outpatient clinics, all would receive their care from the same type of facility, often the same facility (although some class segregation based on residential patterns would persist). Liberals also favored health maintenance organizations because under such an organizational arrangement, it would be possible to give all Americans—including the poor—equal access to the same package of comprehensive services. The prepayment mechanism would also be an equalizer, since there would no longer be financial incentives to cater to wealthy patients and neglect poorer ones. Finally, these organizations would also overcome the fragmentation of the existing care system. Patients, again including the poor, would receive continuity of care in the deepest sense that one provider (the HMO) would be responsible for the "whole patient." This would also make it much easier to build in the kind of "outreach" health care mechanisms thought to be an essential feature of public efforts to improve the health of poor Americans.

Now we come to the question: Why did the values of cost control and social justice, and with them the conservative and liberal design for health maintenance organizations, tend to conflict?

The "conservative" HMO plan called for reliance on the private sector—the competitive "free market." This meant that developing health maintenance organizations would have to win clients (both individual and institutional, such as corporations and unions) away from existing insurance plans. Most insurance plans cut costs via consumer cost-sharing devices (e.g., deductibles and co-insurance) and provide only "basic" services. In contrast, an HMO plan patterned after the Kaiser-Permanente prototype of prepaid care would charge an annual, per capita fixed fee (providing "first dollar" coverage and no additional costs to the consumer) for a much more comprehensive package of services. The result would be, of course, that standard insurance premiums would tend to be lower than HMO capitation fees. If the HMO subscriber became seriously ill and needed expensive medical care, however, he would receive more than his money's worth, whereas the average person covered by a standard health insurance plan would probably incur high, additional out-of-pocket expenses.

From the HMO provider's viewpoint the ability to offer more comprehensive benefits at a price still low enough to be competitive with traditional health insurance depends in part on more efficient management and more effective utilization review; but it also depends on an ability to screen out as much as possible the type of consumer likely to make heavy use of expensive services.

For the consumer the choice between enrolling in an HMO

plan or purchasing a standard health insurance policy clearly involves a weighing of risks against benefits. The risk-to-benefit ratio may in turn vary from individual to individual, group to group. In particular, middle-income working persons between the ages of 21 and 65 are statistically a health population requiring few medical services. They may thus prefer to gamble that they will not need the more comprehensive protection of the HMO coverage and retain whatever cost differential there is between standard insurance premiums and the HMO capitation fee as disposable income. The risk-to-benefit ratio is likely to appear more favorable to health maintenance organizations in the case of those consumers more likely to use many services and having less ability to pay extra out-of-pocket expenses: the elderly, the poor, the chronically ill, families with several young children. Finally, health maintenance organizations would be expected to appeal to corporate and union consumers mainly insofar as these find themselves under pressure to furnish ever more comprehensive health benefits (as opposed, say, to fatter paychecks).

Thus, depending on the expectations, wants, and needs of different types of consumers, health maintenance organizations might well have to provide a less than "comprehensive" package of services or incorporate some form of consumer cost sharing in order to compete with traditional health insurance in many parts of the country.

Such pluralism can, of course, be seen as a virtue: the market accommodates differential consumer preferences by providing a range of HMO plans, varying in cost and comprehensiveness; but it also poses serious problems if a main aim of HMO coverage is to promote greater egalitarianism in health care. (Although free-market HMO proponents have generally expressed faith that, "eventually," under "mature" market conditions HMO plans would tend to provide ever more comprehensive services and these differences would even out.)

Under the competitive market model, government involvement would be limited to "buying into" health maintenance organizations on behalf of disadvantaged groups—such as Medicare and Medicaid eligibles. As a practical matter, however, government officials faced with a range of HMO plans offering variable benefits at variable costs would be hard pressed to offer standardized coverage to all program eligibles. (To allow those enrolled in less comprehensive HMO plans to purchase additional services on a fee-for-service basis would produce administrative chaos since each plan would need its own set of rules. Moreover, this would remove one of the main appeals of prepaid care to a government agency: the ability to avoid having to make individual claims payment decisions, with all the costly, cumbersome, and usually not very effective policing that entails.)

Additionally, in an unregulated market the natural tendency of HMO operators, as hard-headed businessmen, would be to favor the enrollment of young middle- and upper-income persons, since they constitute the healthiest, hence the most profitable, HMO clientele. This practice is often referred to perjoratively by those who oppose it as "cream skimming." Like the related "redlining" practiced by property insurers, it is standard insurance industry practice when not explicitly prohibited by government regulation. Thus the more profit-motivated the HMO plan, the more it would be expected to reject poor, elderly, or other bad-risk clients—or else to demand much higher than average fees to include them. The natural tendency, given both of these sets of circumstances, would be for government programs such as Medicaid or Medicare to let contracts for HMO plans serving only or mainly their beneficiaries. The enrollment fees for these would, however, be quite high because, in effect, they would be providing a kind of group insurance for a group solely composed of "bad risks."

At first glance this result may seem paradoxical: we said the conservative market proposal stressed cost control. Note, however, that if the government undertook to pay the per-capita premiums for all or most high-risk groups such as the elderly, the poor, the disabled, and the unemployed in separate health maintenance organizations, the net result would be that the average healthy, middle-class American enrolling in a free-market HMO plan—or a union or business corporation purchasing HMO coverage for a group of workers—would pay lower rates because they would not have to share in paying the extra costs these high-risk populations would impose on them if they belonged to the same HMO plan. Health maintenance organizations serving the general population would thus be more competitive with traditional insurance plans, which also largely exclude the poor, the elderly, the chronically ill, and so on. Of course, if middle-class and poor people belonged to and received their care from more or less completely separate HMO plans, this would recreate (perhaps even intensify) the prevailing class structure in medical services.

"Conservative" proponents hoped that health maintenance organizations would make national health insurance unnecessary. This was not an unreasonable expectation since as we have seen that the cost-control benefits would go to middle-class consumers, as well as to unions and businesses offering insurance coverage, thereby reducing their financial incentive to push politically for national health insurance. (At the same time, the extremely high costs of health maintenance organizations, whose enrollees are all or mainly poor or elderly—although due actually to the economics of insuring groups composed wholly of bad risks—would likely be interpreted as proof that government involvement naturally breeds waste and inefficiency).

Liberal HMO proponents, in contrast, saw the HMO concept as the vehicle for introducing a truly comprehensive and egalitarian national health insurance. With government paying the *per capita* premiums for all Americans, all citizens would have access to the same comprehensive care. Liberal HMO proponents knew that such a program was, for the time being, not politically feasible. In order, however, to prepare the ground for eventual victory, they insisted on incorporating the following social justice oriented requirements in the HMO assistance act. First, in order to qualify for federal financial assistance with starting up costs, health maintenance organizations were required to provide a broad range of services, including not only hospitalization, physicians' services, but also mental health care (up to 20 visits), home health services, family planning, preventive dental care for children, and medical treatment and referral services for alcohol and drug abuse. In addition, to be federally "qualified," health maintenance organizations were required to charge *all* subscribers the same "community rate" instead of charging higher "experience rates" for higher-risk groups, as regular insurance plans generally do. Finally, "qualified" organizations were required to allow open enrollment of individuals for at least 30 days per year, regardless of their health. That is, unlike conventional insurance, HMO coverage would not be permitted to exclude anyone as a bad risk during this 30-day period each year. Although this requirement could be waived if such an organization could show it jeopardized the plan's fiscal integrity, the burden of proof was on the health maintenance organization to convince federal officials. Needless to say, these requirements raised the cost of premiums considerably. (Ironically, they also had antisocial justice consequences in the short run—preuniversal national health insurance— since the higher costs tended to discriminate against lower middle- and working-class consumers not covered by company or union insurance plans and not eligible for government programs.) After the Health Maintenance Organization Assistance Act incorporating these provisions was passed and signed by the President in late 1973, HEW officials estimated the average monthly cost for HMO membership could be about $25 an individual, or $70 per family, compared with $45 to $60 a family for the most expensive group plans currently in operation.[35]

Understandably, "market" proponents of health maintenance organizations fought the requirements on the grounds that HMO plans could not be competitive with conventional insurance. Shortly after the HMO act passed the Congress,

Richard Burke of InterStudy told the *American Medical News,* "This whole benefit issue is something that could easily be determined by the marketplace. But that is a tough piece of logic to sell to some legislators. There's a school of thought in Congress that includes basic mistrust of the free market system."[36] Several years after the HMO act's passage, Walter J. McClure of InterStudy characterized the economic efforts of the social justice requirements as follows: "The law says we'll give you $11 to sell Kool-Aid, but you'll have to sell it for $5 per glass."[37]

In defense of the provisions, Dr. Philip Caper, a member of Edward Kennedy's staff, explained, "We are trying to get away from the antisocial practices in health insurance," which he defined as refusing sick people insurance because they are bad insurance risks. "The private sector has not assumed their social responsibility. They are in it to make money. The government should get involved to do what private industry has not done."[38] Moreover, the Kennedy forces were willing for government to pay the price of social justice. The original Kennedy legislation would have authorized $5 billion over 3 years.[39] Dr. Caper pointed out also that the original Kennedy legislation would have supplemented operating deficits caused by providing care to persons who would normally be considered "bad insurance risks," but that funds for this purpose had been removed from the compromise bill.[40]

Market proponents were against such subsidizing in principle, because if health maintenance organizations were not designed to make a profit, and indeed were allowed to charge their operating deficits to the government, the rationale of a self-regulating market mechanism with built-in economic incentives would be seriously undercut. In the question of the subsidies it appears to have been the views of the HMO opposition, however, which proved decisive. Organized medicine had long opposed prepaid health plans. In general, physicians groups championed solo, fee-for-service medical practice against group, salaried practice, because the former organizational structure gave the individual doctor considerably more autonomy with respect to his professional judgment as well as his income. Dr. Thomas Dorrity, past president of the Association of American Physicians and Surgeons, expressed this outlook when in a 1972 speech entitled "HMOs versus Ethical Medicine," he stated

> It is easy to overlook how well off we are now and underestimate how badly off we would be under medical care foundations acting as HMOs. . . . For example, today, as far as government is concerned, a physician has freedom to do all of the following things: select patients; prescribe by brand names; control how much or how little he will practice; use independent ethical judgment; admit patients to the hospital of their choice; follow patients into hospitals and continue care; keep patients in hospitals as long as deemed wise; locate offices where desired; treat patients at home, in office, clinic, or hospital; test, diagnose, and treat patients according to the dictates of his own conscience and medical ethics. Also, except for the Price and Wage Control Regulations, compensation can be based upon mutually agreeing with the patient regarding fees. Under the Health Maintenance Organization schemes, all of these freedoms would be lost. . . ."[41]

Not all the opposition to HMO plans by organized medicine was based, however, on physicians' self-interest—some clearly did involve concern for the patients' welfare. Thus the AMA has repeatedly characterized HMO "profit-sharing" schemes (in which physicians are given a year-end bonus out of the HMO "profit" for holding down costs) as contrary to professional ethics because they ally not only the physician's own motivation for personal profit, but peer group pressure on the side of underservicing HMO patients.

When federal assistance to HMO plans was put up for consideration by Congress, opposition by organized medicine was blunted by including, under the rubric of the "HMO," medical care foundations organized by local physicians' groups (usually county medical societies) to provide a prepaid option to consumers but within the context of solo, fee-for-service medicine. Nonetheless, physicians' groups drew the line at massive subsidies.

In March 1972, HEW Secretary Elliot Richardson told an AMA council meeting that the administration's projections were for 1,210 operative health maintenance organizations by 1980, giving 90% of Americans an HMO option. Council members of AMA complained that for the federal government to subsidize "the competition" was unfair. Richardson replied that if organized medicine insisted on all-out opposition to the idea, Congress probably would shape the system on its own.

According to the *National Journal's* account of the meeting,

> The talk was too much for the doctors, most of whom are Republicans who believe that their past support for the party entitles them to better treatment from the Administration than creation of a competing health-care delivery system.
> One physician council member said privately in an interview: "I absolutely blew my damn lid, after Richardson's comments at that meeting. I told Todd (Dr. Malcolm C. Todd, chairman) I would quit the Physicians Committee (for the reelection of the President) if this was all we could expect from the Nixon administration.[42]

As a result, although, the AMA engaged in an impressive amount and range of anti-HMO lobbying activities, its main efforts were directed at making the Nixon Administration defer to its financial leverage in an election year. As one association official told a *National Journal* interviewer privately,

> We're in the driver's seat now, but once the election is over, it will be a different story. Any commitment we get from the White House to curb HMOs must be made before Nov. 7.[43]

Accordingly Dr. Malcolm C. Todd, chairman of the Physicians' Committee to Re-Elect the President (a personal and political friend of Nixon's since his Senate campaign against

Helen Gahagan Douglas in 1950 and one-time physician to him when he was vice-president) informed the President that he was having a difficult time raising funds for the campaign due to the Administration's stand on the proposed HMO legislation. The effort was successful. Gracious in victory, Todd later explained that the President had from the start only meant for HEW to run some pilot HMO plans, not finance a whole new delivery system—but that the "Wilbur Cohens" (referring to Lyndon Johnson's HEW secretary during the heyday of the Great Society) in the bureaucracy had temporarily gotten out of control.[44] Although Nixon's February 1971 message to the Congress had in fact referred to launching health maintenance organizations "in all states" and Elliot Richardson was obviously no Democratic holdover, the administration indeed began acting as if all it had ever intended was a small-scale demonstration project.

Thus instead of the $5 billion over 3 years proposed by Senator Kennedy or even the $1 billion approved by the Senate, the authorization was lowered to $345 million over 5 years when the Health Maintenance Organization Assistance Act finally passed the Congress.[45]

It is equally important to note, however, that although organized medicine opposed the extensive subsidies that would have enabled the fledgling HMO programs to fly despite the heavy load of social redistribution they were being required to carry, it favored the social justice requirements themselves. Thus Dr. James H. Sammons, executive president of the AMA, wrote to Rep. Paul Rogers arguing that the HMO plans should be required to have open enrollment and community rating provisions on the grounds that since the organizations could dispense medical care more cheaply than the individual doctor could, they should repay the system out of their efficiencies.[46]

The fate of the Health Maintenance Organization Assistance Act of 1973 thus offers some insights into those features of the American political consensus-building and interest-articulation processes that are responsible for allowing minority opposition to exercise veto power over the preferences of the majority. "Liberal" and "conservative" social values of different groups of HMO proponents were in conflict. The failure of the two camps of proponents to concede sufficient legitimacy to the other's values or to recognize the political muscle of each other's supporters led to a refusal to make the necessary trade-offs to arrive at a workable compromise bill. Organized medicine was thus able to èxercise a kind of veto power over HMO development, in part via direct opposition but even more by playing liberal and conservative HMO proponents off against each other and by throwing its support behind a crippling pseudo-compromise of liberal social justice values and conservative concern for cost control and opportunities for profit-making.

Unequal Power and Low Allegiance to Professional Service Ethics

BACKGROUND TO THE ANALYSIS: THE MEDI-CAL PREPAID HEALTH PLAN SCANDALS.   It will be recalled that, in addition to recommending federal financial aid for HMO development, the original InterStudy proposal also called for the government to redirect Medicare and Medicaid financing via the HMO program. Although little was ever done to encourage health maintenance organizations under Medicare, steps were taken early on to promote them under Medicaid, especially via California's "Medi-Cal" program.

The major spurt in Medicaid HMO growth took place during 1971–1973. As of September 1, 1973, 12 states had negotiated HMO contracts with 67 prepaid plans.[47] Thus at that time about half of the health maintenance organizations in the United States were partly or wholly composed of Medicaid clients. All but 17 of these organizations were in California.

Medi-Cal was the leader for several reasons. One important one was that the state had been the nurturing ground for the oldest, largest, and most successful of the original prepaid plans, Kaiser Permanente, as well as the prestigious medical society–sponsored San Joaquin and Sacramento Medical Foundations. With such impressive prototypes before their eyes, California officials were probably much more convinced than officials in other states that the HMO concept had been tested and proved.

The Medi-Cal HMO initiative was launched in January, 1971. At its peak, in late 1974, Medi-Cal had contracts with 54 prepaid health plans, covering roughly 300,000 Medicaid enrollees. By this time, however, a cloud of scandal hung over the "second-generation" plans; that is, those HMO plans that had been organized specifically to serve Medi-Cal clients.[48] In late 1973 a California assembly investigating committee had concluded that only a handful of the 48 plans then under contract were providing a quality of care commensurate with the tax dollars they were receiving. The committee focused its attention on reviews that the California Health Department was required by law to conduct biannually on all Medi-Cal prepaid health plans. Recent reviews of 12 of the prepaid plans were scrutinized in detail. Of the 14 categories on which these plans were rated (from adequacy of facilities, to completeness of records, to peer review of quality control) only two of the plans emerged with no deficiencies. The average was 5 deficiencies, but one prepaid health plan was rated as deficient in 11 categories, another in 10 categories. What particularly outraged the legislators, however, was that the latter prepaid plan had been allowed to renew its Medi-Cal contract without any indication that the deficiencies had been corrected.[49] In addition, evidence of financial abuses began to accumulate.

In April 1974, an audit of 15 Medi-Cal prepaid health plans by the California Auditor General's office revealed excessive profits and overhead:

> Of the $56.5 million payments made by the California Department of Health to 15 PHP contractors, only an estimated $27.1 million or 48%, was expended for health care services for Medicaid recipients. the balance of $29.4 million of the California Department of Health payments, or 52% of such payments was expended by the PHP contractors and their affiliated subcontractors for administrative costs or resulted in net profits.[50]

An October, 1975, U.S. General Accounting Office audit of one of these prepaid health plans verified the findings and further recommended that the federal government recover up to $4.6 million in federal Medicaid monies overpaid to that plan.[51] In March, 1975, the U.S. Senate's Permanent Subcommittee on Investigations held hearings on the Medi-Cal HMO scandals at which staff investigator David Vienna charged that profiteering was going on with the knowledge of state and federal officials.[52]

Following these hearings and other press exposés, the number of prepaid health plans fell to 45 and enrollment dropped by 30,000 over 6 months. In June, 1975, Governor Jerry Brown (newly elected in November 1974) announced the cancellation of Reagan's prepaid health plan program to be replaced by "Institutes of Medical Services"—actually prepaid plans by another name but subject to tougher regulatory standards.[53a] A massive regulatory crackdown did occur during the next year that resulted in 23 health maintenance organizations dropping out of Medi-Cal rather than face cancellation of their contracts for failure to meet standards.[53b]

In April, 1976, however, a new scandal erupted that threatened to taint the Democrats and reformer Brown's administration with corruption as well as the Republican Reaganites.[54] Thomas H. Moore, acting deputy director of the California Department of Health and leader within the department of health of the regulatory effort, was dismissed from office when he asked for HEW assistance in investigating irregularities in the operations of Omni-Rx Health Care, Inc., a nonprofit prepaid health plan in Hawthorne, California, and its for-profit management group, Omni-Rx Health Systems, Inc. The investigatory unit in the health department responsible for looking into Omni-Rx was also disbanded.

According to the investigative journalists' reports, the profit-making arm of Omni-Rx had on two occasions employed the legal services of Charles T. Manatt, the Democratic state chairman in California and one of Governor Brown's chief backers in his presidential bid. In documents filed with the health department, Omni-Rx listed such personal references as Governor Brown's chief aide Grey Davis and Leo T. McCarthy, speaker of the California State Assembly as well as Mr. Manatt and Mervyn Dymally, the lieutenant governor. In addition, Omni-Rx employed as its chief of marketing William Burke, the husband of Rep. Yvonne Braithwaite Burke. Mr. Burke had formerly been a business associate of Mervyn Dymally, the lieutenant governor, in another private health care operation.

Governor Brown stated that Moore was dismissed for incompetence; Moore claimed he was fired because of political influence brought to bear on Brown. Dr. Jerome Lackner, director of the California Department of Health, a Brown appointee and the man who dismissed Moore, told reporters that Moore had been dismissed because he "rubbed people the wrong way"—in particular, members of the state legislature and members of the prepaid health plan industry—and that he had received many complaints about Mr. Moore. However, Lackner said he regarded Moore as "brilliant" and had offered him an advisory position at his same salary. David F. Chavkin, a San Francisco-based lawyer with the Neighborhood Legal Assistance Foundation who had been a member of the reform panel that studied the health maintenance organizations at the start of the Brown administration, said he believed Moore had been dismissed because the governor had entered into "political deals" with opponents of the Omni-Rx investigation. Dr. Paul O'Rourke, a medical doctor in charge of research for the California Senate and a member of a panel that studied California's health department, said, "My diagnosis is that he (Mr. Moore) was removed by political pressure exerted by legislators who themselves were under pressure from the prepaid health plans. . . ."[55]

In December 1976, a U.S. General Accounting Office investigation was released detailing fiscal improprieties in Omni-Rx and four other Medi-Cal prepaid health plans. Federal officials warned Governor Brown that California could lose some $80 million dollars in federal funds if the program was not cleaned up by February.[56] In late December, Omni-Rx lost its Medi-Cal contract, and its profit-making subsidiary was placed into receivership by a state court.[57] After a year of legal maneuvering, this was made possible by a new federal law denying Medicaid funds to any state prepaid health plans that could not be certified as a federally qualified health maintenance organization (under the 1973 HMO assistance act).[58] In addition, the company's president and four other directors were accused in state civil suits of illegally diverting more than $1 million of the nonprofit Omni-Rx plan's funds into their own profit-making corporate subsidiaries.[59]

Thus, as a result of the scandals and cleanup campaign, by the spring of 1976, the number of Medi-Cal prepaid health plans had dropped to 25 with less than 188,000 enrollees. By the spring of 1977, there were only 13, with 110,000 enrollees.[60]

What went wrong? Analytically, we shall argue that the California prepaid health plan scandals resulted from failure to design a policy for providing Medicaid coverage via the HMO program that adequately took into account the two nonrational, or political guidance variables, consensus and power. Concretely, it is crucial to note that throughout the entire period of scandals, the older established prepaid health plan prototypes such as Kaiser Permanente, the San Joaquin, and the Sacramento Medical foundations remained untainted by scandal, despite their becoming involved in Medi-Cal. It would appear then that these established prepaid health plans possessed something akin to sociological antibodies that immunized them against the fraud and corruption that afflicted so many of the newer plans started under Medi-Cal auspices.

HEALTH MAINTENANCE ORGANIZATIONS—THE BALANCE OF POWER: DIFFERENCES BETWEEN HEALTH MAINTENANCE ORGANIZATIONS SERVING MOSTLY POOR VERSUS MIDDLE-CLASS CLIENTELE. One major set of characteristics that differentiated the established prepaid health plan prototypes from the second-generation Medi-Cal plans had to do with power relations, both lateral (i.e., between HMO consumers and providers) and vertical (i.e., HMO provider and consumer political interest groups vis-a-vis government). The established prepaid plans such as Kaiser had a mostly middle-class clientele. This remained the case even after these plans obtained Medi-Cal contracts; that is, Medicaid clients remained a minority integrated into a basically middle-class subscriber population. In contrast, most of the other prepaid plans with Medi-Cal contracts served only Medicaid clients (37 out of 48 in December, 1973).[61] A General Research Corporation evaluation of quality of care in the Medi-Cal plans supported by HEW's Office of the Assistant Secretary for Planning and Evaluation later concluded that "those plans which had significant numbers of non-Medicaid enrollees gave better care, with greater enrollee satisfaction and financial viability."[62]

Integrating Medicaid clients into an otherwise mostly middle-class clientele affords protection for several reasons. First, unscrupulous prepaid health plan businessmen and physicians find it easier to exploit the poor and minorities because these are not people with whom they identify and whose good opinion they care about either as friends and neighbors or as members of "better" social circles to which they aspire. In addition, such "social predators" tend to group together and to be attracted to settings where large numbers of their prey will be concentrated, such as, in this instance, health maintenance organizations serving an exclusively Medicaid clientele. Nor do the poor and minorities possess a sense of "civic competence" or the material and political resources to defend themselves against exploitation to the same degree as middle-class whites.

Second, some of the original prepaid health plan prototypes provide mechanisms for direct consumer participation on grievance committees, boards of directors, and so on—again a role that middle-class consumers are more activist and confident about fulfilling. As we see it, however, the single most important factor explaining the relative immunity to scandal of the established prepaid health plans is that their middle-class clients generally subscribe not as individuals but as organized collectivities—for example, as employees of a corporation, as members of a labor union, or, more rarely, a consumer union. It is the power of these organized collectivities—both as collective bargaining agents and, potentially at least, as political interest groups—that protects the middle-class client from exploitation by unscrupulous health plan providers. Medicaid clients who subscribe to prepaid health plans serving mainly a clientele of union members, corporation employees, and so on, are similarly protected because they "piggyback" on the consumer power of these organized collectivities.

Of course, Medicaid clients also join the prepaid health plans as members of a group, that is, as beneficiaries of a government program. It may thus be asked why the Medicaid agency cannot serve as the functional equivalent of a corporation or union, representing its clients' interest collectively. A basic problem is that under a program such as Medicaid, the taxpayers who pay for the services and thus have a strong interest in curbing costs are an almost completely separate group from those who receive services and hence have an interest in services of an appropriate quantity and quality—which are likely to be expensive. A corporate management, by contrast, has an interest in saving the corporation money, but not to the point of conflict with the availability and quality of medical care which the managers and their families will rely on. Moreover, although Medicaid clients interested in obtaining a high quantity and quality of service are politically weak, both the taxpayers who demand cost controls on welfare programs and the unscrupulous providers interested in profiteering from Medicaid are politically strong.

The particular form that prepaid health plan profiteering took under Medi-Cal clearly reflects these power vectors; that is, "fast buck" operators were able to bilk the program because they took care to hide their illegitimate profits behind a public facade of cost control. They did this by agreeing to provide services at bargain rates. Unscrupulous health plan providers were able to reap large illegitimate profits despite these low—

indeed often quite unrealistically low—capitation fees through a variety of techniques, including (a) making it so difficult or unpleasant for enrollees to obtain services that they would be driven to seek them outside the plan; (b) providing fewer services than appropriate, or lower-quality services, or both; (c) selective enrollment, that is, refusing to enroll Medi-Cal clients with any existing health problems; and (d) forging the enrollments of Medi-Cal subscribers. (A Medi-Cal subscriber who is fraudulently enrolled without his or her knowledge will not use any services, so the capitation fee no matter how low is all profit and no loss.)[63] In a number of instances, prepaid health plan operators reaped handsome profits through financial or real-estate manipulations, without ever even getting into the actual business of providing health services. In one case, three doctors and their accountant obtained a contract from the state of California to provide care for a maximum of 10,000 poor persons in northeastern Los Angeles, at approximately $22 per person per month, or a maximum of $216 million yearly. Instead of starting a prepaid health plan, however, the three partners held onto the contract for a year, then sold it for $50,000 to a fourth doctor who had previously been denied a contract of his own by the state.[64] Still another technique for putting a legitimate appearing public facade on illegitimate private profiteering was to have the prepaid plan incorporated as a not-for-profit entity, in order to benefit from the aura of public trust that has traditionally surrounded charities and other voluntary service organizations. In fact, however, these not-for-profit organizations are often mere shells for a variety of privately owned, profit-making subsidiary corporations. In October, 1975, two officials of the California State Auditor General's office told a joint Senate/House of Representatives committee hearing that

> The complex relationship created by the use of these interlocking
> firms makes it more difficult to determine how much of the
> California Department of Health's payments to the PHP con-

tractor actually is expended for health care services for Medicaid recipients and how much results in net profits or is expended on executive salaries and other costs of administration.[65]

The two officials went on to point out that existing statutes permitted extensive subcontracting, but did not require adequate audit trails. Indeed, what was later to hinder not only the bringing of criminal charges but even successful civil suits was that under the weak or ambiguous laws governing not-for-profit corporations, much of the profiteering engaged in by unscrupulous prepaid health plan operators was not illegal.[66]

Some investigators blamed state incompetence in regulating prepaid plans.[67] Such a critique overlooks our basic sociological premise: that wherever a government program provides services to a target population composed only of persons who are impoverished, politically weak, and socially stigmatized by purchasing the services from wealthy, well-connected, politically powerful businessmen, this gross inequality of power makes a situation ripe for profiteering. Incompetent and probably corrupt regulation has, in effect, been designed into the system.

VALUES: THE IMPORTANCE OF PROFESSIONAL ETHICS AS A CHECK ON THE PROFIT MOTIVE. A second set of factors that differentiated the original prototype prepaid health plans and medical foundations such as Kaiser and San Joaquin from the second-generation Medi-Cal plans was the attitudes, motivations, and values that characterized the prepaid health plan providers.

As we saw earlier, the InterStudy research team, in characterizing the health maintenance organization as a self-regulating market mechanism, stressed its built-in economic incentives to control costs by keeping patients healthy and by curbing excessive or inappropriate utilization of services.

In the initial InterStudy position paper, it is ambiguous whether the researchers mean by "economic incentives" simply that a health maintenance organization that fails to stress pre-

ventive care and appropriate utilization of services will probably not be able to balance its books and hence have to fold; or
whether they are actually seeking to suggest that by keeping
patients healthy and curbing excessive services, a health maintenance organization could be made profitable. Whatever the
intent of the InterStudy team, however, many of those who
became HMO advocates in the early 1970s clearly were attracted by what they thought to be the HMOs potential to
develop into a profitable industry. Thus according to a 1973
article in *Fortune,* the business magazine,

> By far the most important advantage of HMO's is that their fixed
> annual fees hitch the profit motive toward a new goal in medi-
> cine: keeping the cost down.

The article went on to state that,

> All the serious studies so far support the conclusion that when
> well managed and properly financed, HMO's can sharply reduce
> the cost of care at a level of quality at least equal to that of the
> fee-for-service system, while earning a decent return for lenders
> and investors.[68]

The Medi-Cal "PHP" boom of the early 1970s was
launched on the basis of these premises. That is, whether organized as actual for-profit corporations or as not-for-profits subcontracting to multiple for-profit affiliates or subsidiaries,
nearly all the new Medi-Cal prepaid health plans were established by profit-motivated businessmen. This set them quite
apart from almost all the original, much admired prepaid plan
prototypes in which the financial motivation was not to make
money for owners or investors but to cut costs to consumers.
Industrialist H. J. Kaiser's interest in prepaid care, for example,
was not as a profit-motivated businessman but as a purchaser
of health services for his shipping industry's employees. For the
rest, the physicians, managers, and sponsoring organizations
involved in the original prepaid plans were recruited mainly on

the basis of ideological rather than material motivations. As earlier noted, many of the first generation prepaid care plans had social movement origins, either in the labor or farm co-op movements. In the case of the medical society–sponsored "medical care foundations," the ideological aim was to show that prepayment could serve to lower costs to consumers in the traditional solo, fee-for-service, practice setting that most doctors prefer just as well as in a group, salaried, practice setting. The original medical society–sponsored foundations were also established to prove the value of locally based professional peer review, and hence became leaders in developing sophisticated quality assurance programs. Finally, attitude surveys comparing the attitudes of physicians generally with those of physicians practicing in prepaid plan settings (especially those set up on the group, salaried, practice model) indicate that the latter are drawn to practice in an organized prepaid plan setting mainly on the basis of political and philosophical orientations. These studies indicate that from a purely economic standpoint physicians view practice in an organized, prepaid plan setting as unattractive. Rather, to the degree that practice in organized prepaid plan setting appeals to the physician's self-interest, it is in terms of such nonmaterial "quality of life" values as collegiality, less paperwork, more leisure time, and release from the kinds of financial management chores and concerns that burden the solo-practicing physician.[69]

The idea that prepaid health care could be a profit-making business just like any other ran counter not only to most of the existing plans' past experience, but to traditional sociological wisdom as well. In his classical work on the sociology of medicine, Talcott Parsons stressed a *moral* dimension in the doctor-patient relationship which he believed to be largely missing from other buyer-seller relationships;[70] that is, by virtue of the knowledge differential between doctor and patient, the patient is unable to judge the quality of the services he receives. Moreover, unlike the typical purchaser of goods and services, the purchaser of medical care is at the mercy of the seller to tell him how many services, of what type, he should buy. The patient must be able to trust that the physician makes this determination based on his expert judgment as to the patient's needs and not on the basis of a businessman's desire to maximize profit. Accordingly, Parsons characterizes the normative pattern of the medical profession as "collectivity orientation," in contrast to the self-orientation of businessmen.[71] Unlike profit-oriented business, the profession of medicine is thus said to emphasize the physician's obligation to place the patient's welfare above his own personal interests, particularly economic interests. Parsons further observed that strong sanctions had arisen within the medical profession to restrict commercialism and the profit motive.

By 1970, however, a number of leading medical sociologists had come to repudiate the Parsonian view that physicians actually could be differentiated from profit-motivated businessmen on the basis of a value orientation alternatively characterized as "collectivity orientation," the "professional complex" or the "service ethic."

Elliot Freidson argued, for example, that

> The "collectivity or service orientation" usually refers to the orientation of individual members of an occupation rather than to organizations. But clearly, the attitudes of individuals constitute an entirely different kind of criterion than the attributes of occupational institutions. . . . But curiously enough, there appears to be no reliable information which actually demonstrates that a service orientation is in fact strong and widespread among professionals. . . .
>
> Parsons does not specify performance at all, but only expectation. Furthermore, those expectations are part of the broad institutional norms connected with professions as officially organized occupations. They are, in fact, the normative segment of the formal organization of professions, expressed by codes of ethics, public statements of spokesmen for the profession, and the like. They are quite distinct, analytically and empirically, from the actual norms of individual professionals. . . . More concrete norms seem necessary for the analysis of medical work.[72]

In our view, the Medi-Cal prepaid health plan experience rather strongly supports Parsons over Freidson; that is, it suggests that professionalism as a value orientation is far more than the sometimes self-serving codes of ethics of the professional associations. It is behaviorally real in that one can clearly differentiate individual conformers and deviants. Moreover, where there is a genuine internalized commitment and not just lip service, subordination of the profit motive to professional values and attitudes toward one's work actually does serve to protect patient and public from medical exploitation, or, more precisely, from economically motivated fraud, abuse, and poor quality care.

Where we do differ with Parsons, however, is in not accepting his implication that between the physician and the businessman only the physician is morally required to subordinate economic self-interest to higher altruistic values. It is our contention that the subordination of personal profit to professional ethics is a useful criterion not only for differentiating ethical from exploitative physicians, but also ethical from exploitative businessmen and, on the organizational level, ethical from exploitative corporations.

As we see it, the California Auditor General's and General Accounting Office reports suggest that the relative balance of "professionalism" to profit motive in corporations—in this instance health care corporations—is not only behaviorally measurable, it is quantifiable in monetary terms. This indicator is the percentage of total corporate revenues that actually constitutes profit, with "profit" being defined as personal, private gain to individuals.

The central issue here is what happens to the corporation's surplus income, that is, all revenues over and above what it costs in terms of labor and material resources actually to produce products or provide services—in this instance, health services. As we see it, the stronger the "collectivity" or "professional" value orientation among those in control of the corporation, the greater will be the percentage of surplus income that is reinvested in the corporation itself toward such purposes as expansion or upgrading of services; subsidization of those services or aspects of service considered worthwhile but that do not earn or may actually lose money for the corporation; support for research and development; quality assurance programs; and the like. Conversely, the stronger the self-orientation among those who control the corporation, the greater will be the share of surplus income that goes toward the personal, private enrichment of individuals. The extreme of self-oriented profit motivation is that of the "fast buck operator" who not only declines to reinvest surplus income in the corporation but actually cuts corners with respect to those costs necessary to provide quality service in order to reap personal profits.

Our behavioral measure of professional versus profit orientation should not be confused with whether or not the organization has the legal status of a profit or a not-for-profit corporation. That is, although only a "for-profit" corporation is legally permitted to distribute surplus income to individuals (a "not-for-profit," to the degree that it is permitted to make or to retain surplus income, is required to reinvest such income in the corporation), the "for-profit" is not required to distribute all or even most of its surplus income as individual profits. In other words, we would expect a for-profit corporation with a strong professional as opposed to profit orientation to keep profits distributed to investors to the bare minimum necessary to secure investment capital. Similarly, we would expect employee profit-sharing within a predominantly professionally oriented for-profit corporation to be of a rather limited and mainly symbolic character. By "symbolic" we mean that close inspection would reveal that its real purpose is not to enrich the employee (whose main source of remuneration is, in fact, salary or wages) but to provide the employee with a visible measure of how his individual job performance contributes to or detracts from the corporation's goals.

Moreover audits of the scandal-tainted Medi-Cal prepaid health plans clearly indicate that where the overarching interest of those in control of a corporation is their own economic gain, they will soon discover that the most lucrative method of drawing personal profits from the corporation is by disguising such profit as administrative overhead. Disguising personal profits as administrative expenses may, at times, enable the individuals to avoid paying taxes on such gains and, often, to conceal from outsiders the actual extent of the personal profit taking that is going on.

An example of disguising as administrative overhead or legitimate business expense what is in truth individual gain is provided in the *Fortune* magazine article referred to earlier. The article noted approvingly that HMO international of Los Angeles recruited physicians by offering them free use of corporation-leased Cadillacs and Mercedes. Although there are no doubt some legitimate business expenses that also happen to benefit particular individuals, and the line between these and disguised personal profit may at times be a fuzzy one, it should be obvious that making available company-leased luxury cars for employees' personal use is not part of the legitimate cost of providing health care, but a way to augment personal, private income without either the corporation or the individual having to pay the associated taxes. The California Auditor General and General Accounting Office audits of Medi-Cal prepaid health plans indicate that profit disguised as legitimate business expense was a favored method of profit taking in supposedly not-for-profit corporations. Thus a 1976 GAO audit revealed that HMO International (the for-profit firm that provided its physicians with Mercedes) received 41% of its income from Consolidated Medical Systems, an ostensibly not-for-profit firm established to obtain Medicaid funds of HMO international when the state denied the company a Medi-Cal contract in its own right. The General Accounting Office also found that Family Health Program, Inc., a "nonprofit" firm and its for-profit subsidiaries charged off to administration the costs of a rented boat and mountain cabin for use by the doctors and directors of the company. Moreover, the rent on the boat and cabin was paid to Leisure Facilities, Inc., a for-profit firm wholly owned by a man who was both a trustee of the not-for-profit corporation and a major stockholder in at least 10 of the 12 for-profit subsidiaries.[73]

In sum, not only can sociologists distinguish conceptually between behavior that is genuinely professional and collectivity oriented and behavior that is disguised economic self-interest, but the concepts are precise enough to be operationalized and applied by accountants.

CONCLUSION

We have characterized the InterStudy "health maintenance strategy" analytically as based on rationalistic assumptions concerning how to effect deliberate social change in the American health care system. Thus the main focus was on organizational factors as the levers for reform. Central to the InterStudy proposal was the concept of economic rationality designed into the organizational structure of the health maintenance organization. A prepaid comprehensive care contract between HMO providers and consumers sought to align the economic self-interest of both parties in such a way as to promote the objectives of maintaining good health via preventive care and curbing the cost and overutilization of services. As such the health maintenance organization was expected to be a self-regulating market mechanism and to provide a private sector alternative to government financing and regulation. At the same time, however, that the health maintenance organization provided an alternative to government bureaucracy, it also sought rationalization of the market via what the InterStudy team referred to as "vertical integration"—in other words, corporate bureaucracy.

Critics of the original InterStudy position paper point out that consumers in the health care market lacked the equality of knowledge with providers that would enable them to assess the quality of the services they received and to protect themselves against profit-motivating underservicing or poor quality care. In other words, the traditional maxim of the free, unregulated market, *caveat emptor* or "let the buyer beware," was ill suited to something so complex and so increasingly science and technology based as medical care. In response, the InterStudy team turned its attention to researching techniques of quality assurance. Their research persuaded them that the state of the art of quality assurance was sufficiently advanced that measurement of medical care quality via outcome indicators—that is, in terms of actual improvement in patients' health—was technically feasible. Here again, however, the main stress was actually on organizational variables. It was the health maintenance organization's large, well-defined, and relatively stable patient population along with the organization's responsibility to provide continuous comprehensive health-maintaining care that were credited with making meaningful quality assessment possible. The InterStudy team's recommendations for HMO quality assurance programs thus centered around organized professional peer review within the organizations themselves, supervised by an independent federal regulatory commission.

It is important to recognize, however, that the kinds of quality assurance measures and mechanisms InterStudy proposed were akin to the Medicaid management information system advocated by the McNerney Task Force in that they stressed information processing, communication, and feedback to promote greater organizational self-awareness. The tacit assumption behind such an approach is that health care providers and consumers share the same values—in particular, that both accord the same high priority to quality of care. It is thus further assumed that if and when poor quality care occurs, it is not deliberate and intentional but a result of ignorance and error that can be remedied through the cybernetic use of knowledge for organizational self-monitoring and self-correction. Philosophically the InterStudy approach to quality assurance is thus allied with the movement from within the medical profession for continuing education, voluntary periodic recertification, and so on.

Many of the original prepaid health plans, in particular those of the medical society–sponsored foundation type, have instituted sophisticated quality assurance peer review and, indeed, have pioneered in developing quality assurance programs for ambulatory care. As the California Medicaid HMO scandals illustrate, however, such an approach to quality assurance is not equipped to deal with profit-motivated underservicing and poor quality care. Those unscrupulous providers who are, in fact, motivated almost entirely by desire for personal economic gain and who have little or no internalized normative commitment to uphold professional standards of quality or to serve the public can scarcely be trusted to introduce and utilize such peer review information systems, except as a lip-service activity or a self-protective "cover."

The original InterStudy proposal had implied that health maintenance organizations could be made to function in the public interest solely on the basis of the economic incentives organizationally designed into the system, plus a measure of government-monitored peer review. By neglecting the role of power relations and shared values, the InterStudy researchers failed to perceive and to alert policymakers to the kinds of conditions that would protect these organizations from, rather than make them more vulnerable to, economic exploitation. Thus the Medicaid experience illustrates the naivete of theorizing that market mechanisms can so perfectly align opportunities for personal gain with pursuit of the public good that neither consumer power nor professional values will be needed to retrain the negative consequences of the profit motive.

Insufficient attention to consensus—in this instance, the need to build consensus between two groups of HMO proponents—also produced unintended consequences with respect to Health Maintenance Organization Assistance Act of 1973; that is, the contradictions inherent in the HMO act reflect the inadequate resolution of an underlying value conflict between conservative and liberal HMO advocates.

This basic conflict between provisions of the HMO act intended to serve liberal social justice goals and those "conservative" provisions meant to encourage opportunities for business and keep down the costs to the middle class—both as private purchasers of prepaid health care and as taxpayers subsidizing HMO development—has yet to be fully faced up to and overcome. Indeed discussion of remedies has continued to focus on the symptoms, such as underfinancing and especially overregulation, as if they rather than the underlying value conflict concerning program goals were the root problem.[74]

In other areas, however, subsequent changes in HMO policy indicate a tacit recognition by policymakers of the need to adapt the original HMO concept to ensure sufficient commitment to professional values on the part of HMO providers as well as a relatively equal balance of power between HMO providers and consumers. Thus, in the wake of the Medicaid scandals, a new regulation was passed prohibiting federally qualified health maintenance organizations from having more than 50% Medicaid clientele.[75] The current thrust is no longer toward stimulating virtually anyone and everyone, especially small businessmen, to become HMO entrepreneurs. Rather the idea is to encourage established, reputable HMO programs to expand and to have them integrate Medicaid clients and other politically weak and vulnerable groups into their predominantly middle-class clientele. In New York City, for example, Medicaid clients are being given the option of joining the Health Insurance Plan of Greater New York (HIP), the HMO plan that serves New York City municipal employees.[76] Similarly, Massachusetts has enrolled Medicaid clients in the Harvard Community Health Plan, which includes among its 65,000 non-Medicaid subscribers Harvard University employees as well as 4,000 Massachusetts state employees.[77]

In addition, federal efforts have focused more strongly on

implementing the "dual option" provision of the HMO Assistance Act which requires all business corporations and unions that provide health insurance coverage to give their employees or members a choice between a traditional insurance plan and an HMO plan. Also HEW has sought to encourage business corporations and unions to voluntarily take the lead in setting up health maintenance organizations.

In 1977, some 7 years after the original InterStudy position paper and 4 years after the passage of Health Maintenance Organization Assistance Act, HEW Secretary Joseph Califano reaffirmed the new Democratic Carter Administration's commitment to the "fundamental" reform goal of assuring all Americans access to HMO care.[78] Efforts to attain this goal had, however, entered into a slower, more cautious, more "incrementalist" phase, in which more attention was being given to assuring sufficient commitment to a professional service ethic on the part of HMO providers as well as a reasonably egalitarian balance of social and political power between HMO providers and consumers.

Chapter 4

A POLITICAL–INCREMENTAL APPROACH

The New York State Moreland Act Commission on Nursing Homes and Related Facilities

INTRODUCTION

The New York State Moreland Act Commission on Nursing Homes and Related Facilities exemplifies that type of policy research which is most widely visible and familiar: the temporary investigatory commission established in the wake of some crisis or scandal-ridden situation which through media publicity has become a focus of public concern. As in the tradition of such commissions, the Moreland Act Commission research emphasized exposé, in this instance, of the laxity, ineptitude, and corruption of state nursing home regulation.

The commission's reform strategy sought to arouse and canalize the moral authority of public opinion via a series of public hearings in which the nature and degree of culpability of various high elected officials was assessed. Recommendations for structural change centered around the law—for example, redefining the legal rights of consumers vis-a-vis providers of long-term care as well as broadening or clarifying the legal authority of state government to regulate the nursing home industry.

Basic to the theory of social change underlying this focus on law was the belief that, through law, exploitation and injustice resulting from fundamental imbalances in power—among societal groups and between government and society—could be redressed. The intellectual assumptions underlying the Moreland Commission's approach to the problems of nursing home regulation, rather than being traceable to or compatible with a body of theory associated with an academic discipline (such as administrative science, organizational sociology, and economics in the preceding cases), are best characterized as belonging to the world view or professional mind set of two occupational groups: lawyers and journalists.

ORIGINS OF THE MORELAND COMMISSION

In the fall of 1974, allegations surfaced—soon followed by full-fledged scandals—concerning Medicaid fraud and abuse, poor quality care, and mistreatment of patients in New York State nursing homes. As one element of his official response, the governor appointed a special Moreland Act Commission to look into causes and correctives. At the time the Moreland Commission was created, the initial work of exposing the basic facts about nursing home abuses had already been accomplished by an earlier legislative commission (The Temporary State Commission on Living Costs and the Economy, chaired by State Assemblyman Andrew Stein and popularly known as the Stein Commission) and by the media. The governor had also appointed a new commissioner of health charged with carrying out a regulatory crackdown, as well as a special prosecutor to instigate legal action against individual wrongdoers. Accordingly, the Moreland Act Commission's mandate was to focus on longer-run, structural reforms that, by going to the root causes of nursing home abuses, would constitute preventive medicine.

The Moreland Commission had five members, including an elderly physician, the wife of a nationally known civil rights leader, and a socially prominent woman from upstate who was active in Republican party politics. However, only Peter A. A. Berle, a lawyer and former state legislator, and the commission's chairman, Morris B. Abram, also a lawyer and former president of Brandeis University, played active leadership roles.

The commission's staff was divided into two components, the legal and research staffs, which were to become almost two separate, unequal, and not well interrelated Moreland Commissions. The research staff, headed by Jonathan Weiner, carried out detailed studies of the mechanics of state regulation, with special emphasis on measuring quality of care and patient level of care need, the processes of certifying the need for and planning new nursing homes and related facilities, and the calculation and documentation of nursing home payment rates. The legal staff was headed by Chief Counsel S. Andrew Shaeffer who, together with Morris B. Abram, provided the day-to-day leadership of the commission. The commission lawyers focused on (a) holding public hearings concerning the responsibility of high public officials for the nursing home scandals, and (b) writing draft legislation intended to strengthen state regulation of nursing home patients as well as give nursing home patients more legal rights.

PLACING THE MORELAND COMMISSION
ON THE ANALYTIC GRID

Public Hearings and Legal Reforms: A Political Approach

Analytically the emphasis of the Moreland Commission reform strategy was on the political variables, power and consensus. The commission's public hearings mobilized consensus around moral values as well as political power in the related normative sense of the "power of public opinion." The package of legislative reforms the commission proposed was intended to strengthen somewhat the economic and coercive power available to state regulatory agencies or to private persons via the courts to deter or punish wrongdoing.

Thus a main purpose of the hearings was to canalize the public's sense of moral outrage over the instances of maltreatment, fraud, and abuse in nursing homes, and the political corruption in nursing home regulation. The commission leadership apparently believed that with the spotlight of public attention and expectation focused on nursing home reform, the sheer force of public opinion would cause the state legislature to pass the commission's reform bills. On another level the purpose of the hearings was quasi-judicial, to "bring before the bar of public opinion" various high public officials to determine their degree of responsibility for the scandalous conditions. Although some fact finding was involved, in the main it was a matter of piecing together, interpreting, and evaluating already available evidence to reach a verdict concerning a particular politician's active participation in corruption or passive shirking of responsibility.

The underlying implication was that those politicians found guilty of unethical conduct or shirking of responsibility would suffer a tarnished reputation and might even be punished at the polls; this, in turn, would serve as a warning to other politicians that the citizenry would demand a higher level of political ethics and public accountability from public officials in future.

Deviance on the part of some members from the norms of expected ethical or moral conduct provides society, as Emile Durkheim long ago observed, with an occasion for reassessing its moral values and the rules that express them and then to modify or reaffirm them. The Moreland Commission hearings on the conduct of various officials were thus apparently also intended to clarify to both politicians and public the ethical standards politicians should be expected to observe, most especially by delineating the boundaries between legitimate and illegitimate political influence, between responsiveness to constituents and serving special interests. According to the commission's final report,

> Nursing home owners and sponsors inevitably will seek political influence to obtain a public franchise or to maximize reimbursement from public funds. . . . The Commission believes that for the most part it is impossible to legislate away this fact of life. "Favors," as a high State Health Department official put it, were "the coin of the realm." They will remain so unless public attention and anger is continually focused and unless politicians are held accountable to the highest standards of conduct. Politicians must draw a line between the role of "ombudsman"—insuring, for example, through inquiry that bureaucrats are properly performing their assigned tasks—and abusing the public trust by exerting excessive and undue influence on regulatory processes.[1]

Finally, the hearings sought to point to certain widespread public attitudes and basic societal values that were held to be an underlying source of both the venality of so many nursing home operators and the failure of politicians to take effective action to protect patients. The commission's summary report cited the stigma attached to old age, dependency, and lack of economic productivity:

> Why did bad care and high profits fail to become political issues for so long? The fundamental answer, the Commission believes, is that the condition of elderly people cared for in homes and the plight of the elderly in general are matters which politicians—and the rest of us—would prefer to keep in obscurity. We are a society which celebrates youth and denigrates age. Old people no longer have a place in the economy and many, if not most of them, no longer have a place in the family. Increasingly they live long enough to suffer the full measure of ailments and infirmities of extreme old age. At this point they become a burden and an embarassment and, all too frequently, somebody else's problem.[2]

Although the primary focus of the Moreland Commission's public hearings was thus on various forms of consensus building, the main emphasis of the commission's legal reforms was on realignment of power relations. The legislative package developed by the commission's legal staff (in conjunction with state legislators and New York State Health Department officials) sought to bring about, via changes in the law, a new balance of power in relations between the state's private nursing home operators, and the patients. In terms of strengthening the regulatory powers of the State Health Department, the commission's legal staff made the following proposals:

1. Grant somewhat broader authority to suspend temporarily nursing home operating certificates or licenses in those cases in which the home's failure to meet regulatory standards is deemed a menace to the health and safety of patients.
2. Mandate the consideration of past performance of nursing home operators in certifying their "character and competence" to operate additional homes.
3. Authorize the state to sue for treble damages in connection with monies obtained via fraud, misrepresentation, or concealment of facts or false statements in documentation provided to regulatory agencies.
4. Require certification of all nursing home financial statements or information by independent certified public accountants who have no financial interest in the nursing home, along with felony liability for any CPA who knowingly certifies false information.
5. Authorize financial penalties of up to $1,000 dollars a day to be levied against nursing homes and residential facilities for failure to comply with regulations after a 30-day warning, and provision for docking the penalties from reimbursement fees.

6. Require two nursing home inspections yearly, at least one of which is to be unannounced.

7. Require annual full disclosure to the health department of persons having a financial interest in or receiving significant financial benefits from a nursing home.

8. Authorize the liability of "controlling persons" (i.e., all such persons who by virtue of direct or indirect ownership interests have the ability, directly or indirectly, to direct or cause the direction of the management or policies of a nursing home or related facilities) for any civil fines, penalties, assessments, or damages that may be levied against any residential health care facilities.[3]

To make the regulatory agencies less vulnerable to political corruption and to illegitimate or questionable political influence, the Moreland Commission's legal staff further proposed a legislative ethics bill that would prohibit on the grounds of conflict of interest state agency employees, state legislators, or members of their staffs from representing private law clients in the administrative law proceedings of state agencies.[4] In addition, the legal staff proposed a set of legislative reforms intended to strengthen the power of patients, their relatives, and the public at large in dealings with nursing home operators and the state. These included (a) the right to undertake law suits—in particular, class action suits—on behalf of patients of residential health care facilities, where such a facility deprives a patient of a right or benefit and the patient undergoes injury as a result; (b) public disclosure of inspection findings (via posting in a prominent place in the nursing home and making available to individual applicants for residency and their families copies of the latest state inspection report); and (c) the accompaniment of each New York State Health Department nursing home inspection by an evaluation of the facility by nursing home residents, family, and friends, with a system of public ratings for nursing home care to be based on both.[5]

Finally, the Moreland Commission proposed the creation of an administrative "advocate for the aging"—in effect, what is more usually referred to as an "ombudsman's office." The advocate for the aging would have investigatory authority, sub-poena powers (both upon complaint and on its own initiative), and right of on-site inspection of the premises and files of nursing homes. The advocate for the aging would also promote community contact and involvement with the patients, residents, and clients of facilities through the use of volunteers and volunteer programs. It would also advise and assist the health department in the development of methods for obtaining the participation and assistance of patients, their relatives, and friends in the evaluation of nursing home quality.[6]

Thus far our characterization of the Moreland Commission's approach as stressing the "political" variables, consensus and power, as the main levers for deliberate social change would seem to have ignored the work of the commission's research staff, which spent over a year studying the rational mechanics of bureaucratic regulation. In so doing, they devoted considerable attention to such "knowledge" issues as the measurement of quality and reasonable cost in nursing home care and such questions of organization as how proprietary and voluntary run nursing homes compare on various cost and quality measures. Their findings take up the bulk of the Moreland Commission's seven published reports.

The expected end product of policy research, however, is policy recommendations, of which the work of the research staff produced few. Rather, the six staff reports covering various aspects of nursing home regulation read as though the regulatory agencies were on trial and the Moreland Commission's research efforts were intended to assemble a record of evidence that would prove them guilty of incompetence, dereliction of duties, and corruption.

Where the research staff did suggest to health department officials specific improvements in regulatory procedures, these seldom involved changes on the policy level but rather focused

on relatively minor, highly technical improvements in existing
procedures and their methods of application.[7]

Where the research staff did produce findings of possible
use in formulating policy-level reforms, these were so far removed from the commission's main priority—enactment of the
draft legislation drawn up quite separately by the legal staff—
that they received little attention, and follow-up efforts suffered
accordingly. Finally, where research findings tended to contra-
dict a policy position that the commission leadership had
adopted a priori on the basis of a set of political values, the
findings were downplayed to the point of being almost totally
ignored. We will document the resulting neglect of major
knowledge and organizational issues below.

The Legislative Package: Legal Incrementalism

Throughout the 2-year period during which the nursing
home scandals were continually in the news, a number of relatively "fundamental" reform proposals were widely discussed.
Assemblyman Andrew Stein, for example, mounted a campaign to reorganize the provision of nursing home care from a
system of predominantly private, for-profit businesses to one
composed mainly of nonprofit organizations under religious,
civic, or senior citizen group sponsorship.[8] Congressman Ed
Koch proposed legislation whose aim was to encourage greater
reliance on home health services and less on institutional care
in nursing homes and related facilities.[9] A Center for Policy
Research position paper coauthored by Amitai Etzioni, the
Center's director and Professor of Sociology at Columbia University, and by Alfred Kahn and Sheila Kamerman, of the
Columbia University School of Social Work, supported such a
reorientation toward greater reliance on home health care.
Their position paper also recommended a fundamental change
in legal philosophy which would shift the burden of proof from
the state having to demonstrate to the courts a nursing home's

gross unfitness before being allowed to withdraw public funding to the nursing home having to demonstrate to the state its continued fitness before public funding could be renewed. In brief

> The basic principle underlying the relationship between the state and the providers would be fundamentally transformed to state the following categorically: No provider has a right or title to public funding. The right rests entirely with the state to confer or cancel eligibility for public funds according to judgments it makes on the basis of criteria it sets concerning acceptable or unacceptable services. The provider further agrees to waive all *a priori* right to litigation on this matter. A book publisher's right to decide which manuscripts submitted to it are worthy of publication can serve as the legal model.[10]

In contrast to these fundamental reform proposals, the Moreland Commission's legislative package was relatively incrementalist in character. The commission's ethics bill was the sole exception. It might be said to qualify as a proposal for fundamental reform, because this effort to disallow politicians from practicing law before state regulatory agencies, had it succeeded, would have removed a major means whereby politicians could intervene in the ostensibly objective, apolitical proceedings of regulatory bureaucracies on behalf of powerful vested interests, take money for it, and yet maintain an appearance of propriety.

Thus although several of the commission's bills sought to strengthen the regulatory powers of the New York State Health Department, they did so only in small measure. A case in point is the commission's amendment to Section 2806 of the Public Health Law which sought to define more precisely the conditions under which a nursing home's operating certificate (i.e., its license) could be temporarily suspended or limited pending a hearing on possible permanent suspension or revocation. According to the Moreland Commission's summary report,

Prior to the amendment, a temporary limitation or suspension was permitted for a period of up to 30 days in connection with a finding "that the public health or safety is in imminent danger." The amendment further empowered the commissioner to take such action upon a finding that "there exists any condition or practice or a continuing pattern of conditions or practices which poses imminent danger to the health or safety of any patient." The amendment thus made available a standard for temporary suspension or limitation specifically based upon the health or safety of patients rather than the more general standard of "public" health or safety.[11]

We characterize this reform as highly incremental, not simply because it involved only minor changes in wording but, more important, because these changes in wording broadened the state's regulatory authority by little more than a hair's breadth.

At issue in the rewriting of this statute was how the commission would decide to resolve, via the law, a basic value conflict between property rights and patient rights. That is, this amendment constituted the commission's response to the following philosophical question: Should society's first concern be for the nursing home investors who, if the home's certificate is suspended or revoked, will suffer financial loss and may indeed be forced "out of business"; or should first priority be given to the health, safety, comfort, and general well-being of nursing home patients who are almost entirely dependent on the regulatory authority of the state for protection? If we grant that each party has a legitimate interest to be safeguarded, the issue becomes one of balancing two risks. That is, which is society to view as the greater of two theoretically possible evils: that in taking away a home's operating certificate the state may abuse its regulatory powers and unfairly cause the owners and operators of the nursing home financial loss, *or* that by making it too difficult and time consuming for the state to withdraw certification, nursing home owners and operators will feel free to abuse or neglect the dependent persons entrusted to their care?

The Moreland Commission was well aware, or should have been on the basis of its own research, that state law concerning suspension or revocation of nursing home operating certificates, or at least the interpretation of such law by the courts, had for years frustrated the efforts of state health department officials to terminate the Medicaid funding of homes seriously in violation of federal fire safety regulations.[12] Indeed, for the state to invoke any kind of sanctions or penalties against noncompliant nursing homes had been extremely difficult. As Dr. Robert P. Whalen, Commissioner of Health, stated the problem in testimony before the Stein Commission:

> There must be the authority to impose penalties.
> In addition to that, it seems a little bit ridiculous to me that in our occupational health programs, OSHA, the new federal program, that inspectors can go into a factory where we have able-bodied working men and if there is a violation of the OSHA Act, fine them on the spot and have the hearing later. And let the owner justify the fact that he shouldn't have been fined.
> If we can give this protection to our working population, I don't see how we can give our elderly any less. . . .
> But the question always seems to get in another area. The question is: Was proper procedure followed? Property rights versus patient rights.
> And seldom do we get to the point: Are the older people getting good care?[13]

In effect, the law and its judicial interpretation had in the past served to force state health and welfare officials to leave Medicaid patients in firetraps because, without Medicaid funds, these homes could not remain in business; and for the state to take an action that would have the result of putting nursing homes out of business had been seen by the courts as tantamount to depriving their owners of property without due process. By making only minor changes of wording in the statute pertaining to the state's authority to suspend a nursing home's operating certificate without a prior hearing and full judicial appeal, the Moreland Commission agreed only to an incremental strengthening of the state's regulatory power and refused to make a fundamental reordering in the legal priority given to property over patient rights.

CONSENSUS AND POWER AS THE KEY LEVERS FOR NURSING HOME REFORM

Societal Consensus: The Limits of Public Opinion as a Force for Lasting Institutional Change

Of all the Moreland Commission's activities, its televised hearings were both the most publicly visible in terms of media attention and yet ultimately the most disappointing in terms of long-run impact. By the time the Moreland Commission began to hold its hearings, the Temporary State Commission on Living Costs and the Economy had already held extensively publicized hearings questioning the ethics and legality of the help and favors accorded Bernard Bergman, Eugene Hollander, and various other nursing home entrepreneurs by certain elected officials and their staffs, as well as officials in the state and city health departments. As a result of the revelations of inaction and ethically questionable conduct by bureaucrats, most of the implicated health department personnel had been ousted and a reorganization of and regulatory crackdown by the state health department was well underway. In brief, those "guilty parties" who were susceptible to immediate removal from office in response to public outrage had been removed. Those who were elected officials not up for reelection in the near future could— provided their skins were thick enough—"tough out" the public shaming, reasonably secure in the knowledge that the general public's memory span with regard to their state and local representatives barely extends to their names, let alone their records in office. Continuity in office would again depend heavily on gaining the support of powerful interest groups and individuals, nursing home owners and operators among them.

If going after individual miscreants had thus reached the point of rapidly diminishing returns, other functions could still be served by the hearings. One was to clarify for both the public and politicians the line between the latter's legitimate role as "ombudsman" for constituents (e.g., helping cut "red tape" in the processing of a nursing home application) and illegitimate influence (putting pressure on bureaucrats to change a decision properly arrived at in accordance with state law or administrative regulations in return for a payoff of some sort, whether an obvious bribe or something more subtle such as legal fees, insurance business, or political support). As Assemblyman Alan G. Hevesi, a member of the Temporary State Commission on Living Costs and the Economy, put it, "We've had testimony that there was a considerable amount of interest by public officials in certain nursing homes. The problem is defining what's improper and what's not."[14]

In addition, there was a need to propose structural reforms in the political and regulatory processes to lessen the temptations and opportunities for conflict of interest and illegitimate influence. In this connection the Moreland Commission hearings were ostensibly intended to mobilize public support behind passage of the commission's legislative ethics bill which sought to prohibit the conflict of interest inherent in legislators and members of their staffs practicing law before state agencies on behalf of clients seeking favorable administrative rulings. As noted earlier, the legislative ethics bill was a key element in fighting political corruption because, without it, politicians could continue to earn income legally from exerting what regulatory officials experienced as powerful political influence on behalf of vested interest groups.

In the midst of the Moreland Commission hearings, however, the legislative ethics bill went down to defeat. In part, this occurred because the commission hearings, although intended to sustain a climate of public concern supportive of the commission's legislative reforms, did not actually serve to focus the media's and the public's attention on the legislature's consideration of the ethics and other reform bills. Thus on June 2, 1975, Morris Abram opened the Moreland Commission's hearing by remarking that though his legislative package appeared likely to pass the state assembly, its three key elements—class action damage suits, stiff penalties for nursing home abuses, and the ban on legislators representing clients before state agencies— were in some jeopardy in the state senate. Most of that day's hearings, however, centered on the New York State Health Department's decision in 1971 to grant Bernard Bergman a license for a new nursing home despite the atrocious conditions inspectors had found in his other homes.[15] Shortly thereafter, when journalists objected that much of the testimony being presented at the Moreland Commission hearings involved allegations of misconduct already fully aired in the earlier Stein Commission hearings, an effort was made to provide the sort of "dramatic new developments" that would recapture media interest. Again these had nothing to do with either the ethics bill or the broader issue of conflict of interest. Rather, the Moreland Commission sought to expose the "shirking of responsibility" by such major figures as former Mayor John Lindsay and former Governor, then Vice President, Nelson Rockefeller. Thus during the period surrounding defeat of the ethics bill in the state senate, the newspapers were full of the suspense as to whether the Moreland Commission would decide to subpoena Vice President Rockefeller or simply "request" his appearance, as well as whether Rockefeller would or would not come in person, and so on.[16] Ironically, then, the Moreland Commission may actually have deflected public attention from what the commission leadership itself considered their single most important legislative proposal.

More deeply, however, the fact that the ethics bill went down to defeat during a high point of public concern about the nursing home scandals suggests a fundamental flaw in the commission's theory that public attention aroused and canalized by media reportage would be powerful enough to bring about structural reforms. Although there is no disputing that public

opinion can be, under cetain circumstances, extremely powerful, it represents a disorganized, hence a highly transitory, form
of power. Thus from the state legislature's perspective, it was
again a question of riding out a short-lived, if tempestuous and
troublesome, storm of public indignation. In order to put the
best possible face on the defeat of the ethics bill, however, the
legislature resorted to a tried and true technique known as the
"one-house" bill.[17] Since most of those tarred by conflict of
interest charges in connection with nursing homes were members of the assembly—including first and foremost Speaker
Stanley Steingut—the assembly enthusiastically passed the
bills, relying on the senate, which luckily had only a few members implicated as minor figures in the scandals, to defeat the
bills. Following the ethics bill's defeat, the Moreland Commission vowed to reintroduce it in the next session.[18] The bill was
indeed later reintroduced, but it made even less progress toward
passage the second time. By then, the Moreland Commission
was in the process of disbanding. The spotlight of media attention had moved on to new scandals—for example, fraud in the
federally funded school lunch program, real estate manipulations involving city-financed day care centers, and the like. The
forces of resistance had succeeded in waiting out the forces of
reform.

The Power of Law: Real versus Symbolic

Although the ethics bill was defeated, the other 10 bills the
commission proposed during its first year passed with relative
ease. Critics countered, however, that the bills passed so easily
because they represented, in fact, only minor unthreatening
changes; that is, to use our analytic terminology, they were too
"incrementalist." In June, 1975, State Senator Linda Winikow,
a member of the Temporary Commission on Living Costs and
the Economy, was quoted as saying, "The Moreland Commission bills don't go far enough. They take one step, but they don't
go far enough."[19] Alphonso Narvaez of the *New York Times*

characterized the legislative proposal put forth by the former members of the Stein Commission and their allies as going "much further than the Moreland proposals in attempting to end abuses."[20] Investigative reporter John Hess, in a postmortem of the Moreland Commission almost a year later, argued that taking the reform bills passed in the 1975 session as a whole, these were "in the main the work of legislators and health officials." Hess also criticized the Moreland Commission for being too willing to weaken the reforms by compromise. When the reform bills "ran into a roadblock in the senate, the Moreland Commission was prepared to settle for less, but the two sponsoring assemblymen made an all-or-nothing stand, and the senate gave way."[21]

Indeed, much more than others involved in the reform effort, the Moreland Commission seemed inclined to believe and be responsive to the claims of the nursing home lobby that particular reforms would infringe on their rights as owners of property, cause proprietary nursing homes to go out of business leaving residents "in the streets," or add burdensomely to their operating costs and, by extension, the already overloaded state budget.

In June of 1975, when the ethics bill had not yet been killed and the class action bill that later did pass was in trouble, Morris Abram told the press, "The effectiveness of this legislation can only be measured by the vociferousness of the industry's opposition to it. It has withstood the vetting of veteran legislators, and I stand ready to make any reasonable adjustment."[22] What Abram, however, regarded as "vociferous industry opposition" and "reasonable adjustment" could also be interpreted as merely a standard display of crocodile tears which the Moreland Commission was perhaps rather naive in accepting at face value. Thus, earlier, in May 1975, nursing home lobbyists had testified against the class action bill, characterizing it as the "most horrendous" of the commission's proposals because, they said, Medicaid would wind up paying huge liability insurance rates. "This package of bills is a nursing home lawyer's pension plan," argued Mr. Aronowitz, a nursing home lawyer, "because there is going to be an awful lot of litigation." In response the Moreland Commission amended its bill to require that plaintiffs prove actual damage rather than simply a failure to provide guaranteed care. This met the objection that courts usually insisted on proof of actual damage in a suit, but it also made the task of the plaintiff more difficult.[23] Indeed, despite all the publicity given to the new law, 1 year after its passage not even one such lawsuit had been undertaken.[24]

The reasons went far deeper than the concessions the Moreland Commission made to the nursing home lobby. They could be traced to fundamental flaws in the theory of social change that lay behind the commission's belief that once armed with the legal right to sue, as individuals or as a class, nursing home residents would have greatly increased power to protect themselves. By no means subtle, these flaws were readily detected by others well in advance of the legislation's passage. Thus Terrence Moan, legislative counsel to Assemblyman Stein, analyzed the proposed legislation and found "at least seven major defects which render it either ineffective as a deterrent against mistreatment in a nursing facility, or unconstitutional, or both."[25] Moan pointed out that the advanced age, ill health, poverty, and dependency of nursing home residents made them quite different from those consumer groups that had benefited from class action suits in recent years.

Thus class action suits take time, and time is a luxury 75- and 80-year-old persons in poor health do not possess. Statistics show that, on average, nursing home residents live only 2 or 3 years after placement, whereas law suits can easily take that long to settle. (At the Stein Commission hearings, one elderly nursing home patient who had suffered poor care, insults, and neglect from home personnel testified to a common attitude among elderly nursing home residents. He said he thought,

"Well, leave well enough alone. You're an old man, maybe you'll live a couple of more years, and then I'm going 6 feet under.")[26]

Moreover, persons who have suffered "actual damage" from poor care, mistreatment, or neglect may well not be healthy enough to fight back by seeking legal redress. Those nursing home patients most likely to be subjected to mistreatment—for example, the mentally confused, and those without relatives or friends who visit and keep tabs on their condition —are those least able to contact a lawyer or to obtain any outside help in contacting one. Consider also the position of those nursing home residents undertaking a lengthy suit to prove damage as a result of neglect or mistreatment against persons on whom they are, in the meantime, completely dependent for food, medical care, pocket money, perhaps even help in getting bathed and dressed, and so on. The Moreland Commission bill made no provision for immediate transfer of a patient from the first instant of lodging a complaint. (In such matters the attitude of regulatory officials has often resembled the old attitude of police toward rape victims. That is, there has been a tendency first to question the alleged victim's veracity and motives, since old people are seen as congenitally petulant and complaining, just "trying to get attention," and so forth.) Other factors could be cited, but they would all go to reinforce the same point: A practical powerlessness to act on legal rights renders all but meaningless their theoretical availability.

Despite these arguments, the fact that the Moreland Commission legislation did not inspire the expected wave of litigation on behalf of mistreated nursing home residents may still appear strange. After all, class action suits have provided the public interest law movement of the 1960s and 1970s with a main tool for safeguarding the rights of other politically powerless, dependent, and socially stigmatized groups, from mental patients, to imprisoned criminals, to retarded children. The case of *Wyatt* v. *Stickney* in which the federal court judge Frank Johnson ruled that Alabama state mental hospitals must meet quality of care standards developed by experts under the aegis of the court or else be required to release all patients involuntarily committed is a well-known example.[27]

It is important to note, howeve, that *Wyatt* v. *Stickney* and other such cases were primarily intended to effect policy-level reforms—for example, their success occurred in the large context of the "deinstitutionalization" movement or as a means of making incarceration and deprivation of the civil rights of non-criminals such as the mentally ill and retarded much more difficult. As instruments for obtaining justice and redress for individual complainants or as a judicial substitute for ongoing administrative enforcement of regulatory standards (which would appear to be the primary intent of the Moreland Commission legislation) they would have to be judged as cumbersome, costly, time consuming and, ultimately, of quite limited effectiveness.

Most of the other Moreland Commission reform bills sought to increase the regulatory power of the state by broadening or strengthening via clarification its legal authority. Ironically, during the course of its public hearings and in the background reports prepared by its research staff, the Moreland Commission had repeatedly taken the position that state officials already possessed the basic legal tools needed to regulate effectively the nursing home industry. The real problem was that officials had lacked the political will to do so.[28] The commission reports noted instance after instance in which state officials resorted to convoluted and far-fetched interpretations of state statutes so as to be able to plead limitations on their authority which would excuse them from taking legally permissible—indeed in some cases legally required—action.[29] From the standpoint of classical interest group political theory, the reason was obvious: Regulatory officials found themselves in constant contact with, and under constant pressure from, the representatives of the nursing home industry while the patients and public had no comparable counter lobby.

Conceivably the Moreland Commission could have taken

as one of its main missions the indentification and mobilization of groups capable of forming a public interest counterlobby. Amitai Etzioni, who was briefly the Moreland Commission's first staff director, suggested three groups that might be forged into such an activist coalition.

1. Relatives of nursing home residents who, if organized into associations, might well play much the same role in pressing for improvements in long-term care of the elderly that associations of parents of retarded children have played in recent years in improving care for the retarded.
2. Associations of older Americans—such as the National Council of Senior Citizens and its local affiliates —which have become increasingly active politically in recent years concerning government policies and programs affecting the elderly, such as health insurance, social security, pension laws, and mandatory retirement.
3. Religious organizations—for example, the American Jewish Congress, the National Council of Churches, Catholic Charities, and their local affiliates—along with labor unions, ethnic associations, and civic groups which might spearhead greater community involvement in nursing homes through advocacy, visitation, and guardianship programs aimed at protecting nursing home patients' rights, as well as increased voluntary group sponsorship of nursing homes and of alternatives to nursing homes.

Etzioni argued that without such a politically active constituency for nursing home reform, the Moreland Commission would quite likely be frustrated in its efforts to get its most important new legislative proposal—that is, the ethics bill— through the state legislature. Moreover, once the Moreland Commission completed its work and disbanded and the focus of the media and general public moved on to fresh scandals, there would be no institutionalized force for reform to keep up the pressure and make sure that the laws, both old and new, were enforced.[30]

It was not, however, until the fall of 1975—after the commission had held its hearings and seen 10 of its reform bills pass the legislature but met defeat on the ethics bill—that the commission leadership began to consider ways of institutionalizing the reform effort. The strategy chosen did not, however, focus on mobilizing a political constituency for ongoing nursing home reform, but centered instead around the creation, via new legislation, of an office of state advocate for the aging to act as a nursing home patients' "ombudsman."

Ironically, the legislation that would have created the state advocate for the aging office failed to pass the legislature because it had no organized political constituency to lobby for it. By the time the bill was introduced by the Governor, the Moreland Commission itself had disbanded, and there was no one left to fight for it.*

RELATIVE NEGLECT OF MAJOR KNOWLEDGE AND ORGANIZATIONAL ISSUES

Knowledge: The Evidence Required for Regulatory Enforcement

One of the main findings of the original Stein Commission and media investigations into the nursing home scandals was that the state health department and other state and local agencies charged with regulating the quality and cost of nursing

*Although a patient advocate's office was later established within the state health department, it was given few resources and was not the independent entity the Moreland Commission envisioned.

home services seemed quite literally not to know what they were doing. That is, despite federally mandated "periodic medical review" of all Medicaid nursing home patients and annual on-site "facility surveys" necessary to certify the eligibility of nursing homes for federal funds and to satisfy state licensing requirements, the state still did not know in any systematic, usable sense which homes delivered an acceptable level of patient care and which did not. Nor did the state know what relationship existed—if indeed there was a relationship—between higher and lower nursing home reimbursemnt rates and the quality of the patient care delivered. Indeed, it soon became apparent that the state possessed very little of the organizational intelligence it needed to regulate properly the nursing home industry.

As earlier noted, the Moreland Commission's research staff devoted considerable time and attention to studying various aspects of bureaucratic regulation of nursing homes, producing a total of roughly 1,000 pages of reports on issues ranging from measurement of quality of care to determination of level of care needs to establishment of reimbursement rates, and the like. It is difficult, however, to point to major policy impacts or even policy recommendations traceable to these efforts. We have already suggested as one reason the fact that the reports were more oriented toward providing a detailed, descriptive exposé of the failures of state nursing home regulation than they were toward formulating recommendations for reform. Typical of such an exposé-oriented approach are two of the findings, which were listed and underlined for emphasis in the Moreland Commission's first published report, issued 10 months after the commission's appointment:

> The State Health Department has failed dramatically to use its powers to enforce standards of acceptable patient care in nursing homes and in health-related facilities. Responsibility for firm action and leadership in enforcing standards of care was massively evaded in classic instances of bureaucratic buckpassing.[31]

Similarly, the commission's summary report listed the following as one of its major findings in the area of regulation:

> Despite early knowledge of poor care and patient abuse on an extensive scale in homes both in New York City and in upstate areas, knowledge which has been documented in inspection reports of the Health Department, use of regulatory tools to enforce minimum care standards was negligible up until the beginning of 1975.[32]

From a policymaking perspective it is difficult to know what to do with findings of this sort; that is, what implications for choices among alternative policies can they be said to suggest? They are not recommendations but condemnations. To the degree that such findings do imply action conclusions, these would seem to be little more that exhortations to the health department that in future they should try harder.

In other words, for purposes of reforming regulation, it was not enough for the Moreland Commission researchers to point to instances or areas where the regulatory agencies failed to perform as desired, expected, or required by law. They needed to define and propose solutions to particular structural problems that underlay and in large part served to explain poor regulatory performance.

One such structural problem is implicit in the Moreland researchers' statement quoted above that officials did, in fact, have "early knowledge" of the poor conditions in nursing homes yet failed to act on that knowledge. A closer look at the nature of that knowledge reveals, however, an enormous gap between what state officials and, in particular, nursing home inspectors "knew" informally, as individuals, about conditions in nursing homes and what the New York State Department of Health "knew" officially as an organizational unit of government. This gap was crucial because only the official knowledge of the organization could be used as the basis for regulatory action. Moreover, even official knowledge was usable only if it could meet the standards of proof required to survive a court challenge.

Given the training and experience of the Moreland Commission leadership as lawyers and the fact that the commission's main reform recommendations focused on the law, the Moreland Commission might have done an important service by dealing in depth with the issue of how the state health department could better conduct nursing home inspections, as well as process, organize, and present the information collected so as to provide the state with an adequate base of evidence on which to invoke legal penalties against substandard nursing homes. So long as nursing homes are looked upon by the courts as legally entitled to Medicare and Medicaid unless the state can show them grossly unfit to provide care and so long as nursing homes are granted virtually unlimited right to judicial appeal as a due process safeguard against arbitrary or abusive infringement by government on this "property right," the invoking of sanctions against nursing homes not in compliance with regulatory standards will continue to be severely hampered by the stringent burden of proof placed on government agencies and by the possibility of repeated court challenge. Evidence strong enough to meet standards and withstand such challenge must be collected via methods that are procedurally impeccable and that are objective and reliable enough to prevail against arguments that a finding of noncompliance was arbitrary or resulted from unfair abuse of administrative discretion.

Had they focused on this issue, the Moreland researchers might have noted that individual nursing home inspectors formulated their personal unofficial judgments on quality of care by collapsing all their observations into a summary assessment —for example, excellent, good, average, poor, and so on. If asked to give reasons for their judgments they would then cite particular criteria to which they gave special weight—for example, clean or dirty conditions, rude or helpful staff, frequent or infrequent cases of bedsores or infected catheters, and the like. In contrast, the official survey forms the inspectors filled out collected vast amounts of data on compliance or noncompliance with standards but provided no procedure for weighting and indexing the dozens of discrete items. As such, the state inspection reports represented, not evaluations of quality of care, but merely masses of undigested fact pertaining to assessment of quality of care.

Again, had the Moreland Commission researchers focused on this issue, they might at this point have recommneded that the health department develop a system for grading nursing homes based on indexing state and federal standards. In other words, inspectors' findings with respect to compliance or noncompliance with myriad individual regulations would be weighted and synthesized into an overall composite score.

Such scores could then be keyed to reimbursement rates in such a way as to create financial incentives for homes to meet or exceed code standards.[33] The composite scores might also have served as the basis for defining "serious operating deficiencies" with sufficient objectivity and reliability to meet legal standards of proof required to preclude arbitrary use and abuse of power by regulatory agencies. Thus homes scoring below a preestablished cutoff point defined as "serious operating deficiencies" might be denied Medicaid funds or have their operating certificates suspended.

Knowledge: Measuring the Quality of Nursing Home Care

Perhaps the major criticism the commission had of state and Medicaid nursing home regulations was that standards had little to do with the "quality of care" as either a medical professional or, alternatively, a lay person considering entering a nursing home or placing a relative in one would generally define as "quality."[34] Such medically relevant standards as existed focused mainly on mandating inputs—for example, professional staff qualifications, and the like—rather than evaluating the processes and outcomes of providing medical services.[35] In an effort to explore possible new methodologies for assessing the medical aspects of quality of care in nursing homes, the Moreland Commission staff contracted with the Fund for the City of New York to research whether the Fund's earlier work on developing disease—specific protocol evaluations of outpatient care—could be expanded to nursing home care.[36] This research effort produced some suggestive results. It was low on the commission's priorities, however, and never received the follow-up effort required to generate policy conclusions and recommendations.

The Fund researchers focused on developing medical treatment protocols for four disease entities thought to include at least 75% of the nursing home population: diabetes, hypertension, arterioschlerotic heart disease, and cerebrovascular insufficiency.[37] The protocols were designed to incorporate the generally accepted professional consensus regarding such "processes" as (a) the components of an adequate annual physical review both for persons known to have the disease or who are deemed at risk of developing it; (b) elements and schedule of appropriate laboratory evaluations and therapeutic regimens; (c) proper treatment response for particular clinical signs and symptoms; (d) proper preventative measures or remedial responses to common associated complications; and (e) criteria for admission to an acute-care hospital.[38] The protocols were then used to measure quality of care, based on data in patients' records, in two proprietary and one voluntary nursing homes in New York City.

As an example of the medical treatment "processes" measured: Diabetic nursing home patients are highly likely to develop ulcers and other skin conditions (generally known as "bedsores") as a complication of their disease. These conditions can usually be arrested and reversed if detected early. If not detected early, however, they become extremely painful to the patient as well as difficult and time consuming to treat. Accordingly, it is accepted as good medical practice that diabetics receive a monthly skin examination. The findings for the three nursing homes were as follows: In the 90-bed proprietary nursing home, 5.3% of diabetics received skin examinations on an approximately monthly basis; in the 400-bed voluntary home, the percentage was 39.1%; and in the 400-bed proprietary home, it was 14.3%.[39] The Table 4.1 lists the comparative performance of the three nursing homes with respect to several other measures of appropriate use of diagnostic tests. (This list is by no means exhaustive but meant merely to illustrate the kinds of medical processes about which the Fund was able to gather meaningful and potentially useful data.)

One of the suggestive findings of the study was that in many instances patients at risk for a given condition or complication were not tested with any greater frequency (and in a

Table 4.1

Appropriate use of diagnostic tests[40]	90-bed proprietary (percent)	400-bed voluntary (percent)	400-bed proprietary (percent)
Percentage of diabetics given regular blood glucose determinations (to measure level of control of the disease)	84.2	95.7	68.2
Blood-urea-nitrogen (BUN) assessments for diabetics (to detect possible renal complications)	15.8	60.9	38.5
BUN assessments for hypertensives (to detect possible renal complications)	16.7	29.6	58.1
Chest x-rays for heart disease patients (to track possibly worsening cardiomegaly)	12.5	21.9	21.6
Blood pressure readings for hypertensives	18.3	77.8	87.1
Cardiac exams for heart disease patients	65	74	82.4

number of cases were actually tested with less frequency) than those not at risk.[41]

The Fund researchers did encounter a variety of obstacles and disappointments in the course of their research. Among them the following:

1. Nursing homes tend to keep poor patient records.
2. Good or acceptable nursing care did not appear to be as susceptible to codification and measurement as good or acceptable physician care.
3. The cardiovascular insufficiency protocol did not generate enough usable or important indicators of physician performance to constitute a useful measure.[42]

Nevertheless, the Fund for the City of New York study dramatically demonstrated that a number of medically significant elements of nursing home care *can* be usefully measured. Indeed, several of the diagnostic procedures whose appropriate use was measured by the Fund researchers have potentially life and death significance (e.g., if a diabetic's rising level of blood sugar goes undetected, he or she may lapse into a dangerous diabetic coma without the staff being able to take preventative measures.)

The findings of the Fund for the City of New York study were of considerable potential policy significance because they challenged the prevailing view that the poorly developed "state of the art" of quality assessment as well as the nature of the chronic conditions afflicting nursing home residents effectively precluded all but the crudest and most indirect measures of quality of care in nursing homes. At the same time, however, the Fund for the City of New York research was precisely that —research. Its methodology could not simply be taken and immediately incorporated into regulation. Much consideration needed to be given to determining which aspects of the Fund methodology might be appropriately or feasibly assimilated and via what means. (For example, it might well be argued that the heavy dependence of the Fund for the City of New York indicators of quality of care on cooperative record keeping by nursing homes, along with other attributes, makes this methodology much better suited to an educational effort aimed at improving medical care rather than a punitive process of setting minimum acceptable standards, monitoring compliance, and invoking sanctions against substandard performance.)

In order to disseminate the Fund's research, assess its meaning, and begin to explore how this methodology might be implemented as part of ongoing processes of regulation, two small meetings of physicians and other health professionals were convened (December 5 and 14, 1975) under the auspices of the New York Academy of Medicine.[43] At the first meeting the quality of the study was highly praised. Nonetheless considerable skepticism was expressed with respect to the use of disease-specific protocols; and many who attended the meeting stressed the conventional wisdom in the field, which held that a preferable method, in principle, would be one that evaluated the functional status of patients on a longitudinal basis. (The difficulty with this stance is, however, that many uncontrollable factors besides medical care affect such functional outcomes, and efforts to date to factor out the effects attributable to medical care alone are not well developed. Hence, to say that functional status measures of health outcomes are preferable to disease-specific protocols measuring medical care processes is on the one hand to reiterate an abstract principle everyone agrees with, but as a practical matter tacitly to advocate doing nothing.) At the second meeting, somewhat greater progress was made in suggesting how some of the methods developed by the Fund researchers could begin to be incorporated into regulatory processes.

At this point, though, when the follow-up work on disseminating, evaluating, and drawing policy recommendations from the findings of the Fund for the City of New York research had only just begun, the Moreland Commission was phased out. Like most such special investigating commissions, it had been designed to have a longevity of 1 to 1½ years, and although that term might have been extended, the commission leadership apparently felt they had achieved most of what they wanted or might expect to achieve. The Moreland Commission was thus structurally unable to provide the kind of long, slow, continuous follow-up effort that was needed to transform the innovative research of the Fund for the City of New York into innovative regulation. To some extent the lack of continuity of the Moreland Commission was made up for by the ongoing involvement of the Fund for the City of New York, whose staff met with health department officials on several occasions after the commission disbanded. Health department officials expressed what Fund staffers believed to be sincere interest in incorporating the research findings into the regulatory process; however, as of 3 years after the phaseout of the Moreland Commission, no implementation had as yet taken place.

Organization: The Controversy over For-Profit Facilities

From the onset of the nursing home exposés (in which proprietary homes had been implicated virtually exclusively), the question was repeatedly raised whether for-profit homes were inherently more prone to financial fraud and abuse and poor quality care than voluntary homes and, if so, what policy conclusions should be drawn. John Hess, investigative reporter for the *New York Times,* brought up the issue early[44] in his continuing series and returned to it again and again during the year and a half he covered the nursing home scandals.

On February 26, 1975, Assemblyman Andrew Stein, head of the Temporary State Commission on Living Costs and the Economy, which had been active in first bringing nursing home abuses to light, announced plans to recommend to the legislature that profit-making nursing homes be gradually phased out of New York's government-financed, long-term care system. "Our elderly deserve institutions which seek to provide quality care, not which provide only profit for unscrupulous investors," he stated. He further said that months of investigation had convinced him that private interests were capable of breaking any reimbursement formula written by the state. Stein's plan called for a moratorium on the construction of new proprietary homes and vigilant supervision of existing proprietary institutions "to prevent future patient abuse and instances of Medicaid fraud." Homes not providing quality care would gradually be phased out. As a long-run strategy he proposed that the state enter upon a conscious policy in favor of encouraging qualified charities, community hospitals, and nonprofit facilities to care for the elderly.[45]

On April 11, 1975, the Health Committee of the New York State Assembly heard a majority of witnesses testify in favor of greatly expanding the voluntary sector's role in long-term care. That same day, 800 delegates of the Golden Ring Council of Senior Citizens' Clubs unanimously approved a "white paper" denouncing reported abuses in nursing homes and calling for nonprofit alternatives.[46]

In May, 1975, when the Moreland Commission's initial package of legislative proposals came before the assembly, Assemblyman Stein criticized the package for its failure to address "the root of corruption," the profit motive. He again urged a moratorium on the licensing of new proprietary facilities and added that "since the existing voluntary organizations will not fill the vacuum," the state should encourage existing old people's centers to build nursing homes.[47] David Weisen, testifying at the same hearing for the Community Council of Greater New York, stated "after a great deal of soul searching we feel we have to raise with your committee the very serious question as to whether there isn't something basically inconsistent about the presence of the profit motive in the field of institutional care of old and disabled people."[48]

By June, 1975, Assemblyman Stein had obtained 100,000 signatures on a petition for a nonprofit system.[49] He had also obtained a ruling from HEW that New York State could legally halt the issuance of new licenses to for-profit facilities without, as critics of Stein's plan had alleged, violating federal regulations with respect to patients' "freedom of choice."[50]

During this entire period, Morris Abram, Chairman of the Moreland Commission, consistently refused to consider the possibility either of deemphasizing of phasing out for-profit facilities. According to Abram, such a policy was not worth serious consideration because, he claimed, "people would be thrown out into the streets." Furthermore, Abrams argued, the representatives of Catholic, Jewish, and Protestant charities were on record as saying that the voluntary sector could not, at any forseeable time, take the place of the proprietary sector."[51]

More generally, Abram also denied the superiority of voluntary homes. Abram stated that he had seen at first hand several for-profit nursing homes that provided high quality care at apparently reasonable cost. In effect, what this statement did was to deny that any general conclusions about the comparative performance of voluntary and proprietary homes could be based on evidence of statistical differences among groups of profit and not-for-profit facilities. That is, Abram appeared to be taking the position that as long as even one "good" for-profit facility—or, alternatively, one "bad" voluntary—could be found, then no inference that one form of organization was preferable to the other could legitimately be made.

The main point worth noting here is that by making these and other arguments against Stein's proposal as strongly as he did, and when he did, Abram committed the Moreland Commission to a position defending the for-profit nursing homes before the commission could possibly have had time to research the question. In brief, Abram could at that point have legitimately disagreed with Stein and Hess about the proper interpretation of their investigations, but he had no new findings of his own on which to base his position. Indeed, a look at Abram's arguments quickly reveals that they were not induced from the investigative evidence so far uncovered, but rather deduced from a priori philosophical assumptions. Overall, Abram's arguments had the effect of identifying the defense of New York

State's for-profit nursing homes with the defense of American capitalism in general. In contrast, many of those who supported Stein's proposed shift toward greater reliance on voluntary nursing homes believed simply that for-profit nursing homes had shown themselves peculiarly attractive to fast-buck operators, the New York State Department of Health had shown itself incapable of keeping such fast-buck operators out of the industry, ergo the best solution was to ban future for-profits in favor of voluntary homes sponsored by legitimate religious, senior citizen, or other "civic" organizations.

By committing the commission to a position so strongly defensive of for-profit facilities so early in the commission's work, Abram all but precluded the possibility of the commission making an objective research-based assessment of the issue. Future research could only tend to justify or to undercut the preestablished position.

The results of a subsequent staff study comparing state survey inspection findings in a sample of proprietary and voluntary homes appeared in the commission's first published report, issued in October, 1975, roughly 9 months after Abram had publicly committed the commission to a defense of proprietary homes. The findings—whatever one's judgment of their significance or validity—could scarcely be interpreted as supportive.

Quality of care in voluntary and proprietary homes was assessed by performing a statistical analysis comparing the scores of a sample of 54 proprietary, voluntary, and public[52] nursing homes in New York City on the Medicare–Medicaid facility survey and the periodic medical review (the two Medicaid-required quality of care measurement instruments). Actually, the Moreland researchers' methodology was somewhat peculiar in that homes closed by a state regulatory crackdown in the wake of the nursing home scandals (all of which were proprietary homes) were treated as a separate category entirely, thereby weakening a priori any association that could be found between proprietary sponsorship and a lower quality of care. Even so, an association remained as Tables, 4.2 and 4.3 show. (Note: Higher scores both on the survey and periodic medical

Table 4.2   Periodic Medical Review (PMR) Index[*]

Ownership	0–.49	.5–.99	1.0–1.99	2.0–2.99	3.0 and up
Voluntary	6	3	3	0	1
Proprietary	1	7	5	7	3
Closed	2	2	3	4	2

Source: Moreland Commission Report No. 1, p. 106.
[*]This index was derived by totalling all PMR items marked deficient (with the exception of two items thought to assess the patient's condition independent of quality of care) and dividing by the number of patients to get an index of *unsatisfactory items per patient.*

Table 4.3   Survey Index[*]

Ownership	0–15	16–30	31–60	61–80	81 and up
Voluntary	1	8	2	0	0
Proprietary	9	6	3	4	0
Closed	0	1	2	3	6

Source: Moreland Commission Report No. 1, p. 107.
[*]This index represents the total number of conditions, standards, elements, and fire safety items for each home marked "not met" on the survey form.

review (PMR) indicate lower quality of care since these figures represent numbers of deficiencies noted.)

When the closed facilities are added to the category of proprietaries, and the tables recomputed, the association becomes even more striking (Tables 4.4 and 4.5). The figures in parentheses represent cumulative percentages. Thus it can be observed, to cite one example, that over two-thirds of the voluntary facilities fell in the lowest two categories on the index of periodic medical review deficiencies, whereas only one-third of the proprietaries had as few periodic medical review deficiencies.

The tables comparing the performance of voluntary and proprietary homes in respect to Medicaid standards were relegated to an appendix. In the body of the report the findings received only the briefest of mentions, that is, "As a general

Table 4.4   Periodic Medical Review (PMR) Index

Ownership	0–.49	.5–.99	1.0–1.99	2.0–2.99	3.0 and up
Voluntary N = 13	6 (46%)	3 (69%)	3 (92%)	0	1 (100%)
Proprietary N = 36	3 (8%)	9 (33%)	8 (56%)	11 (86%)	5 (100%)

Table 4.5   Survey Index

Ownership	0–15	16–30	31–60	61–80	31 and up
Voluntary N = 11	1 (9%)	8 (72%)	2 (100%)	0	0
Proprietary N = 34	9 (26%)	7 (47%)	5 (62%)	7 (82%)	6 (100%)

rule, voluntary homes were found to have better survey and PMR ratings than proprietary homes, but several proprietary facilities ranked with the best voluntary institutions on both reports."[53]

In brief, the authors of the report presented the findings but sought to deemphasize their importance. A main reason the Moreland researchers downplayed the comparatively poorer performance of proprietary versus voluntary homes on the survey and periodic medical review indices was no doubt their belief that these instruments were themselves poor measures of quality of care in nursing homes. Whether or not the Medicare–Medicaid facility survey and the periodic medical review can be considered good or adequate measures of quality of care (or something else equally useful and relevant such as fire safety) and whether or not the criteria and methods the Moreland Commission employed in assessing the value of the survey and periodic medical review were sound are complicated issues we cannot deal with here. Suffice it to say, however, that federal law does *require* (although the requirement has not been enforced) skilled nursing homes to meet the standards set forth in the facility survey in order to receive Medicare and Medicaid payments.

Thus had these findings concerning the comparative performance of voluntary and proprietary nursing homes on the federally mandated quality measures been picked up by the media, they probably would have proved rather embarrassing to the commission's arguments against a policy of shifting away from reliance on for-profit facilities. By this time, however, the political momentum behind Assemblyman Stein's proposal to prohibit future proprietary construction and shift toward greater reliance on voluntary institutions had long since peaked. The Stein proposal had been defeated; the Moreland Commission's official stance had won out. In sum, the time when such evidence might have made a difference was past, the political verdict was already in, the point was now moot.

CONCLUSION

We have seen that the reform strategy developed by the Moreland Commission in response to the problems of poor quality care and financial fraud and abuse in nursing homes was one that focused on the political variables, power and consensus, as the main levers for effecting deliberate social change. The Moreland Commission sought to mobilize societal consensus, in the form of outraged public opinion, via a series of public hearings exposing corruption and shirking of responsibility on the part of highly placed and well-known elected officials. Public indignation was also expected to provide sufficient moral force to cause the state legislature to enact the commission's legislative proposals, the majority of which sought to strengthen either the legal rights of nursing home residents and their families so that they might better protect themselves from mistreatment or the authority of the state to impose regulatory requirements on nursing homes.

With, however, the sole exception of the legislative ethics bill (which, had it not been defeated, would have closed a major avenue of legal corruption of public officials by powerful vested interest groups), the Moreland Commission's legal reforms were highly "incrementalist." As such, they failed to redress the prevailing bias in favor of property rights over patients' rights. In addition, the Moreland Commission evaded or downplayed the issue of the comparative quality of voluntary and proprietary nursing homes, refused to consider fundamental reorganization of nursing home care from for-profit to not-for-profit sponsorship, and failed to provide much in the way of alternative recommendations for ridding the nursing home industry of fast-buck operators. Finally, although the commission repeatedly stated that the main weakness of state regulation of nursing homes was not the inadequacy of existing laws but the inadequacy of law enforcement, the commission did not properly address the "knowledge" deficiencies that were largely responsible for the health department's poor enforcement record. Chief among these was the fact that findings of compliance or noncompliance with regulatory standards obtained via periodic nursing home inspections were not systematically collected, analyzed, interpreted, and evaluated in such a way as to enable the state to sustain the burden of proof required to invoke sanctions against substandard homes and withstand repeated court challenge.

The disbanding of the Moreland Commission in May, 1976, left many observers with the feeling that despite the new laws on the books, the seven published reports, and the ritual shaming of key political figures during the Moreland Commission's televised hearings, the Moreland Commission had left the roots of the nursing home scandals largely undisturbed. Investigative reporter John Hess of the *New York Times* wrote, in an article entitled "Literally, It Is Business As Usual in the Nursing Homes," that "Nothing basic has changed."[54] Indeed, Morris Abram predicted in his final letter of transmittal to Governor Carey that "another investigation will most certainly be required in 5 to 10 years." Abram, of course, did not mean by this that he perceived the commission's reforms to be ineffective. The fundamental problem, as he saw it, lay in the deeply entrenched values of a "society which celebrates youth and denigrates age."[55]

All said and done, the highly publicized drama of its public hearings accomplished little more than a repeat performance of previous exposes. Most of the package of reform legislation proposed by the commission was passed, but, of the two most important proposals, the legislative ethics bill failed to be enacted, and the class action suit legislation did not generate the expected results. In sum, the Moreland Commission appears to be a virtual textbook case of "symbolic politics," defined by Murray Edelman as political activity that serves simultaneously to provide tangible benefits to elites and symbolic benefits to mass publics, by quieting potential unrest, deflecting political demands, and blurring the true allocation of rewards.[56]

Similarly, it could be said of the Moreland Commission what Robert Alford concluded when he applied Edelman's concept of symbolic politics to an analysis of a series of New York City health care investigating commissions 1950–1971. Namely, "None of the reforms has touched the basic power of the private sector and its institutions. Instead, state power has reinforced private power."[57]

Our analysis also suggests, however, that if in the end an investigatory commission fails to generate more than symbolic reforms, this not simply because those social groups having a "structural interest" in reform are politically weak while those social groups with a corresponding "structural interest" in the *status quo* are politically powerful.

The Moreland Commission case study shows that even persons sincerely desirous of reform and who do not stand to benefit directly and personally from the defeat of a reform effort may be unwilling to subject to fundamental criticism cherished values that in effect preclude meaningful reform. In the case of nursing home regulation, these unexamined values pertain to particular definitions of legal rights, particularly the right to due process, which so long as they remain above challenge will virtually ensure that the property interests of nursing home owners will for the most part be given precedence over the personal well-being of nursing home patients.

In addition, the case study of the Moreland Commission illustrates that reform interests are not politically powerless. At the height of a reform effort, the collective power of an aroused public is at least as great, and probably much greater, than that of the vested interest groups who resist structural change. This power dissipates rapidly, however, due to lack of organization. Thus the true power of vested interest groups is staying power. And the Achilles heel of reform movements lies in their transient character. A *temporary* investigating commission is appointed. It holds a series of hearings that *temporarily* focus media, hence public attention on the need for reform. Laws put on the books during such a period represent the crystallized remains of aroused public opinion. Public attention and indignation cannot, however, be sustained at a high pitch for long. Like Weber's notion of "charisma," the reform spirit must be routinized, rationalized, and given some form of ongoing, organizational expression. Otherwise, once the spotlight of public opinion aroused by the media has dimmed—or, perhaps more commonly, moved on to a new focus of concern—the law loses its animating force.

There are thus two possible responses to this volatility. One is to accept the transient character of reform movements as a "given" and work within its limitations. This suggests that, like the Moreland Commission when it disbanded, one should call for the periodic repetition of reform theatrics. An alternative response is to look for ways to harness some portion of the quicksilver reform spirit and institutionalize it. In the next chapter we shall explore in the "consumer participation" theory, one such effort.

Chapter 5

A FUNDAMENTAL–POLITICAL APPROACH

Heal Yourself. The Report of the Citizens' Board of Inquiry into Health Services for Americans

INTRODUCTION

Our fourth and last example of an attempt to bridge thought and action, policy research and policymaking, concerns the reform strategy of consumer participation. *Heal Yourself,* the Report of the Citizens' Board of Inquiry into Health Services for Americans, urged the involvement of consumers of health care in the decision making of health services institutions, agencies, and programs. The Citizens' Board report exemplified the thinking of a much broader consumer participation movement. Grounded intellectually in concepts of alienation which have been a part of social criticism of industrial society since the mid-19th century, a basic premise of the consumer participation ideology was that social service institutions and programs were largely unresponsive to the needs and preferences of the consumers of services. This was because decision making was the virtual monopoly of service professionals and, in the case of government programs, of government bureaucrats. The consumer participation ideal stressed local community participation and participation by social groups that had historically been politically passive, powerless, and were thought to feel especially alienated—that is, the poor as well as disadvantaged racial and ethnic minorities.

Clearly, the "consumer participation" thrust of the 1960s and 1970s was and is related to other efforts both ongoing and historical to open up the processes of social, economic, and political participation in American life to previously excluded groups (e.g., the civil rights and labor movements).

Moreover, although consumer participation theory owes much to the traditions of the European intellectual left, it also has many elements that are characteristically American. In particular, there is a strong strain of the kind of populism that at earlier points in American history gave rise to such "direct democracy" reforms as primary balloting, initiatives, referenda, and recall, all of which aimed at bringing the reality of American politics more in line with the civic textbook model of individual citizen participation.

Although American populism shares with European socialism a radical egalitarian thrust and a tendency to view politics as a struggle of the people versus the powerful, it differs markedly from European socialism in emphasizing solutions that are high in individualism, pluralism, localism, and self-help. Thus the traditional approach of the European left to remedying inequality, by which the national government assumes ownership and operation of an industry or service on behalf of the citizenry as a whole but gives individual citizens no role in shaping the policies of that industry or service is incompatible with populist values.

The consumer participation ideology of the 1960s and 1970s differed, however, in at least one major respect from the core assumption underlying most American political reform movements during the past century. Typically, such efforts to expand democratic participation focused on traditional mechanisms; that is, political parties, procedures for nominating and electing public officials, access to the courts, and so on. In contrast, the consumer participation movement has focused on democratizing institutions and processes which for many years were thought of as inappropriate to direct democratic political participation, being instead the province of neutral expertise. Thus, following the victory of civil service reform over the spoils system, the accepted ideal (if not quite the actual practice) was that government bureaucracy should be insulated from political pressures and political biases. Similarly, in the so-called private governments of business corporations, universities, hospitals, and other voluntary service institutions, the dominance of managerial and professional elites, whose authority was justified by claims to expertise, has been largely taken for granted. Thus in calling for both public and private bureaucracies to open participation in decision making to outside constituencies, the consumer participation movement strongly challenged the prevailing arguments that these institutions can and should be above or at least outside politics, that expert authority ought to be granted precedence over democratic political authority, and that expertise is apolitical, that is, objective, and value neutral.

ORIGINS OF THE PROPOSAL:
THE CONSUMER PARTICIPATION MOVEMENT

Regulation and policymaking are generally conceived of as governmental activities. This does not mean, however, that only government is active while society is either passive or merely reactive. Indeed, as Alexis de Toqueville observed as early as 1835 and Almond and Verba's *The Civic Culture* reconfirmed in 1965, a high level of citizen activism (compared to other nations) is a characteristic feature of American politics.[1] Moreover, American government (as compared to the governments of other countries) is highly open and responsive to citizen activism. Thus in many instances the impetus behind a new social policy, a new regulatory effort undertaken by or through government, comes from outside the government, from an active, "public spirited" citizenry.

A case in point is the growth during the 1960s and 1970s of consumer participation as an ideological and social movement which ultimately affected nearly every variety of social service institution and government social program. The heterogeneity of the movement's participants can be seen in the wide range of slogans, each with its own particular ideological connotations. Thus the "New Left" theorized on the theme of "participatory democracy" and called for "power to the people." Urban minority groups demanded "community control" of schools and other social services, while mayors and city administrators sought to placate them with various proposals for "community participation" and "neighborhood government."[2] The front-line units of the War on Poverty were the community action programs (CAPs), whose legislation mandated "maximum feasible participation" of the poor, although government programs, community action programs, grew out of a private foundation's innovative community organizing efforts, the Ford Foundation's Mobilization for Youth project.[3]

Because equality, community, and participation are all old American themes, in a deep sense the community participation movement of the 1960s and 1970s was part of an ongoing American tradition of periodic political revivalism. As earlier noted, it did, however, have some distinctive features: (a) the focus on consumer participation in decision making by *bureaucracies,* both public and private; and (b) the challenge to the primacy of "expertise," both professional and bureaucratic, in particular to the claims that by virtue of knowledge the expert is rendered completely disinterested and objective and that the proper relationship between expert and nonexpert is for the lay person to defer almost totally to the expert or professional's "better judgment."

Another distinctive feature of the "consumer-community-citizen" participation thrust of the 1960s and 1970s has been the self-consciousness afforded by the extensive role of social research in both shaping and evaluating the results of participatory efforts. The best known work is, of course, Daniel P. Moynihan's *Maximum Feasible Misunderstanding,* an intellectual postmortem of the community action programs. Moynihan in turn traces the origins of the "CAPs" (and of the earlier Ford Foundation Mobilization for Youth program) to the opportunity theory of delinquency set forth by social scientists Richard Cloward and Lloyd Ohlin and, more indirectly, to the writings on community of two social essayists, one radical (Paul Goodman, *Growing Up Absurd*) and one conservative (Robert Nisbet, *The Quest for Community*). Moynihan's book presents the disappointments of community action as a cautionary tale regarding the influence of social science on social policy. Liberals who desire to effect social change "constantly underestimate difficulties, overpromise results, and avoid any evidence of incompatibility and conflict, thus repeatedly creating the conditions of failure out of the desperate desire for success." Moreover, "This danger has been compounded by the increasing introduction into politics and government of ideas originating in the social sciences which promise to bring about social change through the manipulation of what might be termed the hidden processes of society."[4]

The participatory mechanisms instituted in government programs also became a fertile field for evaluation research. The Department of Health, Education, and Welfare contracted with management consulting firms and research institutes from, Booz, Allen Public Administration, to Rand, to the Urban Institute to study, evaluate, and make recommendations for improving various mechanisms for citizen participation in agency programs.[5]

In the area of health services specifically, however, consumer participation efforts have been most influenced not by the research efforts of the professional intelligentsia (i.e., academic social scientists, social essayists–philosophers, or evaluation researchers) but by the growing trend of advocacy research by citizen activists and public interest groups. Advocacy research is characterized by its rejection of the traditional scientific stance of value neutrality. Advocacy researchers are frank (and indeed often passionate) about their commitment to a set of political values. Although advocacy research exists across the political spectrum (the American Enterprise Institute is an example of a conservatively oriented advocacy research institute), most of the advocacy research done in the health services field has been by researchers with perspectives ranging from left liberal to avowedly Marxist. For example the New Left theory of participation was applied to health services by Health-PAC (the Health Policy Advisory Center), a radical research, education, and action group.[6] They defined their missions as "providing information and analysis of immediate usefulness to people who are active or might become active in health issues" and serving the larger movement for radical social change in America, by making health a "case study in the need for democratic restructuring of American institutions."[7] Ralph Nader and his "Raiders," who popularized the ideas of consumer advocacy and consumer evaluation, established an organization specifically devoted to health issues, the Public Citizens' Health Research Group.[8]

Despite the greater visibility of these two organizations, it can be argued, however, that the manifesto of the consumer participation movement in health was written by the Citizens' Board of Inquiry into Health Services for Americans. A kind of self-constituted equivalent to a Presidential commission, the Citizens' Board of Inquiry was conceived and organized by C. Arden Miller, M.D., then Vice Chancellor of Health Services at the University of North Carolina. Its membership was composed mainly of liberal elements of what was typically referred to during the 1960s as "the Establishment"—that is, representatives of government, major universities, corporations, and labor unions. (Examples include Hon. David Bazelon, Chief Judge, U.S. Court of Appeals, Washington, D.C.; Rashi Fein, Ph.D., Professor of the Economics of Medicine, Harvard University; Peter McColough, President, Xerox Corporation; Nathan Stark, Vice President, Hallmark Cards; Jerry Wurf, President, American Federation of State, County, and Municipal Workers.) Other members included well-known social activists and representatives of minority groups who had chosen to work for change "within the system" and who, in some instances, also occupied "Establishment" positions. (Examples include George Wiley, Ph.D., Director, National Welfare Rights Organization; Bayard Rustin, Executive Director, A. Philip Randolph Institute, New York, New York; and Marian Wright Edelman, attorney, then with the Washington Research Project.) Finally, there was also a sprinkling of representatives of the poor who were discovered by and then recruited to serve on the Citizens' Board of Inquiry during the course of the board's public hearings. (Victoria De Lee, Ridgeville, South Carolina; Bertha Johnson, Detroit, Michigan; Dorothy DiMascio, Anchorage, Alaska.)

The most active members of the Citizens' Board of Inquiry were those who served on its executive committee. In addition to C. Arden Miller, they were as follows: Lester Breslow, M.D., Chairman, Department of Preventive and Social Medicine, UCLA Medical School; the Hon. Julian Bond, Georgia State House of Representatives, Atlanta, Georgia; Harry Huge, attorney, Arnold and Porter, Washington, D.C.; and Lisbeth Bamberger Schorr.[9] The Citizens' Board also had a staff, headed by Leda Rothman. The staff organized the public hearings held across the country and carried out the site visits from which most of the illustrative examples and anecdotal evidence found in *Heal Yourself* were drawn.

In contrast to our three other case studies of policy research, the Citizens' Board of Inquiry had neither a specific policymaking client in the government nor specific bureaucratic, legislative, or national policy aims it sought to accomplish. The audience for, as well as the objectives of, *Heal Yourself,* were much broader and more ill defined. According to C. Arden Miller, the first printing of *Heal Yourself,* about 10,000 copies:

> Was distributed largely on request to persons who had learned of the report in a variety of ways. Many requests were made by health agencies with lay advisory boards or with consumer training programs. Universities used the report in classes on public policy and health planning and medical, dental, and nursing schools requested it for uses as a textbook. In addition, there were many requests from "interested citizens."[10]

A second edition was published and distributed under the auspices of the American Public Health Association, whose executive director, James R. Kimmey, M.D., wrote in the preface,

> The key to an effective national health care program is citizen understanding of the factors operating in society to abridge his right to health care. *Heal Yourself* represents an important step toward achieving that understanding. If those who read this report are moved to act to correct the inequities it highlights, then the work of the Citizens' Board of Inquiry shall have been effective indeed.[11]

It might be said that the dissemination of *Heal Yourself* reflected the underlying philosophy of the Citizens' Board of Inquiry that in a democracy the ultimate policymakers should be the citizens themselves.

LOCATING *HEAL YOURSELF* ON THE ANALYTIC GRID

A Political Diagnosis: Socioeconomic Inequalities in Access to Health Services and Professional Dominance in Decision Making

In our three previous case studies, the policy researchers,

for most part, focused on finding and proposing solutions to a given situation (e.g., inefficient management of a government program, or an old-fashioned, overly fragmented health care delivery system, or lax enforcement of law and regulations due to illegitimate political influence) that they took for granted was widely accepted as the basic problem. In constrast, much of *Heal Yourself* was devoted to defining social injustice as the common root of multiple problems in the health system and making a convincing case to the reader to accept this definition of the situation as valid.

The central thesis of *Heal Yourself* is that America, the wealthiest nation on earth—a nation with ample health care resources in terms of the proportion of physicians, dentists, and hospital beds per population as well as the nation that spends the highest percentage of its gross national product on health care—nevertheless fails to meet the health needs of most of its people.[12] Thus

> For millions of Americans—the poor and near poor who live in the rural backwaters of this nation or populate its inner cities—the medical care system is not merely inadequate. It is almost nonexistent. In addition, it is often an added source of injustice and oppression. For Americans who are not poor but earn less than $20,000 a year, adequate medical care is becoming evermore elusive and evermore expensive.
>
> But good care does exist. Wealthy or privileged Americans have access to the finest medical care in the world, even though it is fragmented. An influential elite can rest assured that financial considerations will not be a barrier to superlative medical care.[13]

In other words, health care in America is inadequate principally because access to it is grossly unequal. According to the Citizens' Board of Inquiry, adequate health care, like a basic education, should be the right of every citizen, not a privilege accorded on the basis of income or membership in a social or occupational elite.

Why is quality health care distributed according to class

and status criteria, rather than on the basis of medical need? According to the Citizens' Board of Inquiry,

> The answer, though seemingly complex, can be simply put: Health care providers often act from the narrow bases of institutional or professional interests, unrestrained by consumer influence, by rules of the marketplace or by government regulation. The interests of the providers differ from the interests of health care consumers. Consumers are left powerless to deal with obvious inadequacies and injustices, while conscientious and well-meaning professionals get caught up in a system that does justice neither to their skill nor to their intent.[14]

That is, access to health care is not democratically distributed, because health system decision making is procedurally undemocratic. Decision making is unjustly dominated by the interests and values of health professionals.

The traditional solo-practice, fee-for-service system of delivering ambulatory care is one major expression of the dominance of professional interests. The skewed geographical distribution of physicians and their choice of specialties are others.

Physicians favor the *solo* practice fee for service ambulatory care because it maximizes each individual practitioner's income and decision-making autonomy. As for consumers:

> The nation lives with a faded tintype image of a family physician. He is a kindly old gentleman riding behind a team of horses, off on a late night trip to be at a patient's side. But this image is far from the needs of today, if indeed it ever was accurate. Yet in many ways we cling to the paternalism it represented as the comforting operating principle of our medical care system. Dependence on this paternalistic vision has permitted health providers to shape health policy almost by themselves.[15]

Consumer dissatisfaction with health care often reflects the failure of real physicians to meet the unrealistic expectations embodied in this image.

> The doctor is like other human beings: His own well-being and that of his family are concerns that understandably influence the conduct of his professional life. He is not superhuman, but lacking an organized health system, we too often attempt to solve our medical care problems as if he were. The doctor's inability to sacrifice all his time—to be always available—has led to consumer frustration with the traditional fee-for-service office visit.[16]

Still more important, however, the inability of most physicians to conform to the ideal and the frustration this breeds have diverted attention from the defects of the ideal itself. Thus

> Even if everybody could afford private office calls, and if the doctor were always there, such visits would still remain crisis care, often inefficient and uncoordinated, and not, broadly speaking, health care at all.[17]

If solo practice is inherently inefficient, uncoordinated, crisis-oriented "candy store medicine," as one critic is quoted as characterizing it,[18] the fee-for-service method of reimbursement insures that access to the medical candy store will reflect the social class structure to a high degree. High-quality medical care is treated like any other luxury product of a profit-oriented, business society. That is, in the words of one local medical society president, "Each is entitled to what he can get. The public is entitled to expect that good medical care will be available, but it should be available on the marketplace like a Cadillac or anything else."[19]

According to the Citizens' Board of Inquiry, access to medical services reflects ability to pay more than need for and potential to benefit from such services mainly because

> Health professionals function as businessmen who earn their living from fees paid by sick people. As a result, they may turn away patients who cannot pay, or reject Medicaid patients if the level of reimbursement mechanism seems cumbersome. The tautness in physician supply leaves them free to determine their

own fees according to their own needs rather than their patients'.[20]

A similar class bias and nonresponsiveness to consumer need characterize hospital care. Professional dominance in decision making concerning what types of services a hospital will provide, who will be admitted as patients, and who will be told to go elsewhere, as well as how resources will be allocated among such priorities as research, teaching, and service to the surrounding community is justified on the grounds that hospitals are "private institutions." The Citizens' Board of Inquiry observes, however, that

> Only a very few of America's hospitals can truly be considered "private" establishments. Except for a small percentage, American hospitals are nonprofit, tax-exempt institutions ... These privileges have been extended without attendant responsibilites. Hospitals have not been subject to effective government regulation to ensure that they act in the public interest.[21]

The dominance of professional and institutional interests over the public interest in hospital decision making is reflected in the insistence on providing prestigious services such as open-heart surgery even though other hospitals in the community can more than meet the need and even provide higher-quality services. The result is a costly and wasteful duplication of equipment and facilities. In the meantime, serious community health needs may go unmet as private practitioners leave the inner cities, while those remaining often refuse to treat Medicaid patients, and the urban poor must increasingly rely on hospital emergency rooms and outpatient clinics rather than private doctors as their main source of primary care. Instead of considering how they might adapt their services to meet this need, voluntary hospitals have complained about "misuse" of hospital services and have often set up financial or other barriers to entry.[22] Hospitals also tend not to be responsive to those community health needs that have a strong social component and require outreach, such as screening for lead poisoning and anemia among the children of the urban poor.

Access to hospital care reflects ability to pay as much as does access to office-based physicians' services. Even economically well-off consumers, however, can exercise little freedom of choice because they must generally go to the hospitals where their family physicians have staff privileges. This system in turn contributes to the two-class system of hospital care, because voluntary hospitals allocate the bulk of their inpatient beds to doctors with staff privileges. The result is discrimination against patients without a private doctor, including many Medicare and Medicaid patients, as well as poor persons with no third-party insurance coverage who are thus directed to overcrowded and understaffed public hospitals.

Health insurance is seen by the authors of *Heal Yourself* as having had considerable impact on the practices of doctors and hospitals as well as on the health system as a whole, but not via insurers exercising the bargaining power of their policy-holders in the consumer interest. Rather,

> The health insurance industry has been free to shape its involvement in the health system to suit its own interests, though often these conflict with consumers' needs. As a result, health insurance coverage is limited, despite resultant hardships to consumers; insurance programs have tended to distort priorities in the delivery of health care and health insurance has served as a stimulant to the inflation of health care costs.[23]

Health insurance organizations, according to the Citizens' Board of Inquiry, are "completely ill suited" to represent the consumer interest within the health system because, from their inception, the nonprofit insurance companies have been closely allied with hospital and physician interests, and private profit-making insurance companies are trapped by constraints inherent in the insurance busines.[24]

Governmental financing of health facilities (e.g., via Hill-Burton and later the Comprehensive Health Planning Agencies), of education and manpower (e.g., via the National Health Services Corps), and of medical services (e.g., Medicare and Medicaid) is similarly critiqued for shoring up the status quo rather than encouraging change. As with private insurance, certain forms of government subsidy, Medicare and Medicaid in particular, are seen as fueling medical inflation, thereby raising the cost of medical care to the already hard-pressed consumer, including, not infrequently, these programs' own beneficiaries. Thus

> Despite the fact that the health care delivery system is settled into patterns of provider dominance and orientation, often at great social expense, federal government programs have done little to break the patterns, to redress the imbalance, or to encourage major innovation in delivery. The programs have, in fact, reinforced the dominance of physicians and hospitals, delegating to them, directly or indirectly, the power to make decisions of broad social importance with little or no public accountability.[25]

A Political Prescription: Consumer Participation in Shaping Health Policy

The corrective, as seen by the Citizens' Board of Inquiry was to restructure the health care delivery system so that it would reflect the needs, interests, and preferences of consumers. This would be accomplished by according consumer representatives "the dominant role at all levels in the decision-making process of the health care system."[26] The various levels include "facility, service system or program, and neighborhood, city, state, region, or nation."[27] Through such control or influence over institutional and programmatic decision making,

> Consumers must be able to establish goals, objectives, and priorities of the newly structured delivery systems and make them effective in the organization and delivery of health services.[28]

Power is seen as *the* lever for change, power that "should include, but not be limited to, making policy, controlling assets (including capital expenditures), facilities, equipment, and services."[29]

Provider dominance must be replaced by consumer dominance because, with respect to consensus, the Citizens' Board of Inquiry espoused a form of social conflict theory whose intellectual assumptions precluded much possibility for provider–consumer agreement on basic values. That is, although consensus within the consumer and provider constituencies was taken for granted, consensus between the consumer and provider camps was considered to be all but impossible due to each group's fundamentally opposing interests. Thus much like the relationship of capital and labor in Marxist theory, an adversary relationship was seen as structurally built-in by virtue of the differential relationship of consumers and providers to the "means of production" of health care.

A Fundamental Redistribution of Resources and Reordering of Values

If providers and consumers have diametrically opposing interests and value preferences, it follows that the Citizens' Board of Inquiry expected replacing provider dominance with consumer dominance to produce a fundamental restructuring of the health delivery system. Such a restructured system would be virtually the mirror opposite of the present system. Thus the Citizens' Board envisioned a health system shaped by consumers to reflect their needs, preferences, and values as having the following characteristics:

1. It would give much higher priority than the present system to routine and preventive care as opposed to crisis care for acute illness.
2. It would eliminate barriers to equal access from race, ethnicity, language, transportation to eligibility procedures, location, and hours of services, as well as economic barriers.

3. In contrast to the current impersonality of health care and the deference physicians in particular require from patients, the restructured system would ensure prompt access to services and an atmosphere of friendliness, dignity, and personal identification between health personnel and patients.
4. An individual's and family's care would be continuous and coordinated, by means of information technology and the development of alternatives to solo-practice, fee-for-service ambulatory care. Such alternatives would be locally organized and could be of a variety of types including, for example, prepaid group practice, neighborhood health centers, and medical school-sponsored foundations; they need not have defined physical settings, but would require a coherent organizational and administrative framework that reflects consumer wishes.[30]

CONSUMER PARTICIPATION THEORY

The Citizens' Board Approach to Implementing Consumer Power: Neglect of Organizational and Knowledge Factors

We have seen that *Heal Yourself* issued a strong call for redistribution of power over health system decision making from provider to consumer dominance. The Citizens' Board of Inquiry recommendations were rather vague, however, concerning the means through which such a redistribution of power could be brought about.

In principle, one means of establishing consumer control over the health system might be for consumers to band together to hire their own doctors, set up their own facilities—in brief, to create an entire "countersystem" designed to be responsive to consumer needs and preferences and in which consumers would claim for themselves the dominant policymaking role.

Indeed, *Heal Yourself* devoted one long, sympathetic chapter to health co-ops and free clinics. In it, however, the Citizens' Board noted that such groups had been most active in the 1920s and 1930s. Although many of them had succeeded in providing services within limited geographical areas, or, in the case of labor union sponsored co-ops, to their own organizational membership, none "was directed at or was able to make fundamental changes in the delivery system."[31] The need, therefore, according to the Citizens' Commission, was for consumers to work through government to gain control of the existing health delivery system.

Thus all those favoring a dominant role for consumers in health care policymaking were urged to "work for enactment of legislation at all levels of government to shift to consumers the power to make health care policy."[32] Advocates of consumer power were also urged to "initiate and support legal action to provide stronger consumer representation on provider-dominated health care bodies. . . ."[33] Beyond this, the Citizens' Board appealed to health care institutions to voluntarily redistribute power to consumers:

> Agencies or institutions that render medical services and that spend public funds or enjoy tax advantages should examine whether having providers of their services in positions of authority over the governance of the same agency or institution is in the best interest of that agency or institution or the services that are provided.[34]

Although the Citizens' Board clearly intended for consumers to exercise power in the decision-making processes at every level of both public and private health bureaucracies, their recommendations did not spell out specific organizational structures, processes, and mechanisms that would translate the rhetoric of consumer power into day-to-day reality. We shall see in a later section that majority representation of consumers on the governing boards or other decision-making bodies of health services institutions, agencies, and programs has provided the principal organizational means utilized in practice to operationalize consumer participation in health policymaking. The Citizens' Board reviewed the performance of a number of these boards and committees and, although not rejecting this approach outright, appeared to take the position that they were inherently weak and tokenistic. At the same time, however, the Citizens' Board failed to suggest any other organizational mechanism as a replacement.

Thus the theory of consumer participation as outlined by the Citizens' Board of Inquiry gave insufficient attention to the organizational attributes that differentiate real or symbolic, effective versus ineffective consumer power. In addition, the Citizens' Board also gave little attention to the issue of which organizational structures and processes would serve to link consumer representatives to their consumer constituencies.

Similarly, the Citizens' Board greatly downplayed the importance of knowledge or expertise as a tool that consumers might need to help them make wise or effective use of decision-making power. The Citizens' Board indeed made a highly persuasive case against the traditional argument that the gap between professionals and consumers in the possession of medical knowledge necessitates professional dominance of health care decision making. They did so by carefully differentiating individual treatment decisions—where it is conceded that medical expertise should be the determinant—from decision making concerning the health system or health policy. Thus according to the Citizens' Board,

> Health professionals should make individual decisions affecting the health of their patients while the public should become the ultimate determinant of the health care system and how health care services are delivered, paid for, and organized.[35]

Concerning any knowledge members of the public might require to make decisions about health systems and about how health care services are delivered, paid for, and organized, the

Citizens' Board exhorted them to "become well-informed about the financing, operations, and mechanisms of the health care delivery system and their particular part of it."[36] The report went on to note that, "In some cases, consumer representatives will need a professional staff or consultants whose prime responsibility is to consumers and not to the provider mechanism."[37] Despite one or two such minor concessions, however, the basic position of *Heal Yourself* is one that implicitly denies the necessity for consumers to obtain specialized knowledge to participate in health system decision making. If not precisely anti-intellectual, the perspective of *Heal Yourself* is certainly "anti-expert." According to the Citizens' Board of Inquiry the experience and common sense—in effect, the "folk wisdom"— of the common man would suffice to guide consumer participation in health policymaking. Behind this definition of democracy, however, there would seem to lie a spirit of radical egalitarian populism which rejects any major concession to the need for specialized knowledge in health decision making as opening the door to an elitism based on expertise. Hence the quote from John Dewey which serves as the heading for the chapter of *Heal Yourself* entitled "Conclusions and Recommendations":

> No matter how ignorant any person is, here is one thing he knows better than anyone else, and that is where the shoes pinch his own feet, and that is because it is the individual that knows his own troubles, even if he is not literate or sophisticated in other respects. The idea of democracy as opposed to any conception of aristocracy is that every individual must be consulted in such a way, actively not passively, that he himself becomes a part of the process of authority, of the process of social control; that his needs and wants have a chance to be registered where they count in determining social policy.[38]

In sum, the Citizens' Board of Inquiry advocated consumer participation in decision making based almost entirely on criteria of personal need and preference—that is, individual value judgments—with little or no attention being given to the function knowledge performs in "reality testing" decisions that might otherwise prove utopian or invalid due to excessive personalism and subjectivity or ideological distortion. Moreover, each consumer is portrayed by the Citizens' Board as possessing a clear and well-developed consciousness of his or her own interest and by implication the consumer class interest. The assumption that membership in a group automatically confers awareness of the group interest is one that suggests little need for consumer organization, most especially little need for establishment of organized means of expressing, communicating, and debating alternative views of the "consumer interest" as well as little need for organized mechanisms and procedures to arrive at intragroup consensus regarding the consumer interest. Here again, the view that common sense and personal experience are sufficient basis for each consumer participant to determine "the consumer interest" is radically egalitarian and antielitist in that it denies the need for a consumer leadership whose task is to inform and educate the mass base.

We now turn to examine the validity of the board's theory of consumer participation in the light of actual efforts to implement consumer participation in practice. First, it must be noted that the diffuse dissemination of the Citizens' Board report makes it difficult to trace direct impacts on specific attempts to implement consumer participation as a result of exposure to the report. Indeed, in some instances consumer participation efforts preceded the Citizens' Board report. As such, the Citizens' Board report is probably best characterized as a distilled expression of the thinking that animated the movement for consumer participation in health as a whole. Thus regardless of whether the report itself actually influenced efforts to establish consumer participation mechanisms in health facilities and programs, we believe it can be shown that efforts to implement consumer participation in practice were grounded in much the same intellectual assumptions contained in the report of the Citizens' Board of Inquiry.

CONSUMER PARTICIPATION IN PRACTICE

Evaluating Consumer Participation: Process and Outcome Indicators

Consumer participation of some degree and type was incorporated into nearly every federal health program of the 1960s and 1970s: for example, in Medicaid, Office of Economic Opportunity neighborhood health centers, community mental health centers, experimental health services delivery projects, comprehensive health planning agencies, and the health systems agencies that replaced them.

Occasionally consumer representation was also required under the auspices of state and local government health programs: for example, in New York State's Article 28 planning and review process for new hospital and nursing home construction, in New York City's municipal hospitals, and in those voluntary hospitals that received funds for ambulatory care from the New York City Health Department's Ghetto Medicine Program. Many of these consumer participation mechanisms were already in place at the time the Citizens' Board of Inquiry was conducting its research and were evaluated by the board. In a number of instances these evaluations included site visits and interviews with consumer representatives. In all but one or two cases, the assessments were highly critical. For example, the Hill-Burton and Comprehensive Health Planning Agency mechanisms were characterized as "ineffective."[39] The Boston Department of Health and Hospitals experiment with consumers was declared "a sham," which served to illustrate "one of the common fallacies about consumer involvement: Having some people on a board who are labeled 'consumers' is sufficient whether or not the board has any powers, how frequently it meets, and whether or not it is listened to."[40]

Since the publication of *Heal Yourself,* some of the consumer participation mechanisms studied by the Citizens' Board have been phased out, or all but phased out, along with the

Great Society programs of which they were a part. Others, however—most notably those having to do with planning—have continued to evolve and, apparently, grow stronger. In the remainder of this chapter, we will draw on the rather large body of evaluation research that has grown up around consumer participation to suggest some analytic distinctions between those efforts to implement consumer participation that have been more, versus less, effective. Although some of these analytic distinctions can be thought of as explaining why consumer participation implementation fell short of the consumer participation ideal, others suggest that the ideal itself, as exemplified in Citizens' Board recommendations, was flawed.

In assessing the effectiveness of consumer participation in practice, two broad sets of criteria will be used. They can be thought of as "input" and "process" versus "output" measures of participation or, alternatively, as indicators of procedural democracy on the one hand versus substantive social change on the other.

Among the first group of indicators we include the following: How much legal authority has been granted to the consumer participation mechanism? That is, has it been granted authority to control or simply to advise decision making? Are its control or advisory functions vague or ambiguous, or are they clearly spelled out and delimited? Over what specific functions does the participatory structure have jurisdiction: Budgetary decision making? Final approval of all major policy decisions? Amenities of patient services?

Do the laws and regulations call for participation exclusively of consumers or do consumers participate together with government officials or health care providers, or both? If participation is shared, are consumers legally required to constitute a majority or only "some" of the participants? Finally, are there de facto barriers to consumer participation that preclude or seriously inhibit consumer's ability to exercise their "de jure" authority?

With respect to substantive social change, the central questions are whether consumer participation makes a difference in the character of the policy decisions made: if so, what kind, and how great a difference. More specifically, does consumer participation appear to have the kind of transforming impact expected by the Citizens' Board of Inquiry?

Power: How Much, How Real?

We have seen that the Citizens' Board of Inquiry into Health Services for Americans defined "consumer power" as "consumer dominance" or "consumer control." Government programs have tended to operationalize consumer control as majority; that is, at least 51% consumer representation on whatever boards, committees, or councils are created as mechanisms of consumer participation. The findings of a 1973 Rand study of consumer participation in HEW programs suggest, however, that a more important prior issue is whether the consumer participation mechanism—that is, the board or committee the consumer majority controls—itself has control over anything.[41] In other words, to what extent do the consumer participation mechanisms make decisions or merely give advice?

Based on a review of 51 examples of consumer participation in HEW programs (including both health and other social programs), the Rand researchers concluded that 69% of governing boards (i.e., citizen participation mechanisms with policy-setting functions and ultimate budgetary authority) versus 52% of the committees (having only limited authority or of a strictly advisory character) were judged as having implemented citizens' ideas to a significant degree.[42] The Rand researchers further suggested that the statistical differences would be greater if it were taken into account that some legally constituted governing boards are in fact weak and quiescent whereas some ostensibly advisory committees have managed to gain and exercise de facto governing powers.[43] Thus the Rand study found that whether the consumer participation mechanism was legally a board or a committee, the most significant correlate with program impact was whether or not the board or committee actually exercised substantial influence over the facility or program budget. Seventy-nine percent of those that did were able to achieve significantly high implementation of citizen views as compared to only 38% of those that did not.[44]

In view of the Rand findings, it is noteworthy that consumer participation mechanisms in health services institutions and programs have typically been constituted both in law and actuality as advisory rather than governing boards. For example, the voluntary hospital boards set up in connection with the New York City Health Department's Ghetto Medicine Program were required to have majority consumer representation, but as their titles—ambulatory services advisory committees—indicate, they were granted advisory authority only. Similarly, the consumer participation mechanisms set up within the New York City municipal hospital system by the 1970 New York City Health and Hospitals Corporation Act were also advisory bodies, although they were ostensibly to participate in setting priorities, allocating funds, judging the acceptability of services to patients, and areawide planning. The only specific authority they were given was concurrence in the selection of an executive director for the hospital.[45]

In the neighborhood health center program of the Office of Economic Opportunity, consumer participation was permitted in law to be either via governing or advisory boards. One study of 27 such neighborhood health centers (40 were eventually set up) carried out between 1967 and 1970, found that only 3 of the 27 neighborhood health center's participatory mechanisms were actually constituted as governing boards, and one of these was quiescent—although five advisory committees were found to have achieved de facto governing board status. Using a variety of indicators, scored on the basis of site visits to neighborhood health centers that involved discussions with consumer and provider representatives and project staff, as well as observations of board meetings, the authors rated the degree of consumer involvement of the neighborhood health center consumer boards and committees. Involvement was defined as actual participation of the consumer group in the major and minor policies, practices, and operational decisions of the project. Seven centers were rated high in consumer involvement, nine moderate, and ten low.[46]

The 314(e) projects of the Public Health Service Act were set up to provide health services to local target populations, especially low-income groups, via such facilities as family health centers, neighborhood health centers, and—it was hoped eventually—health maintenance organizations. Each project involved a relatively large grant: $500,000 or more. A 1972 HEW-sponsored study of the 314(e) projects found that all had some sort of consumer representation, and that one-half had governing boards with consumer representation. However, citizen representatives formed a majority in only one-fifth of all projects.[47]

Thus far we have reviewed only programs that involved consumer participation at the local level, within particular service delivery institutions—for example, hospitals, ambulatory clinics, neighborhood health centers, and the like. Medicaid, the second largest government health financing program, also had consumer participation incorporated into its law and regulations at both the state and national levels. However, such participation, which was only advisory to begin with, proved to be embarrassingly pro forma. According to the *Washington Report on Medicine and Health* (March 10, 1969), the 21-member Federal Medical Assistance Advisory Council established under the Social Security Amendments of 1967, rapidly gained the reputation of being "one of the least used panels in HEW's large stable of advisory councils." Although the federal Medical Assistance Advisory Council was legally required to have a majority of consumer representatives, a 1970 Senate Finance Committee staff report noted that, of the 21 Medical Assistance Advisory Council members, only 4 might possibly be characterized as "representatives of health services."[48] Congress abolished the federal Medical Assistance Advisory Council in the Social Security Act Amendments of 1972.

At the state level the 1973 Rand study concluded with respect to Medicaid that "the committees have played a largely perfunctory role, and have not influenced policymaking."[49] Moreover, the report noted that "providers of medical services have overwhelmingly dominated the work of the advisory committees and the administration of the Medicaid program."[50] Provider dominance was clearly reflected in the membership of the state medical advisory committees. A HEW survey of the state medical assistance advisory councils, carried out in late 1970, found that representatives of medical services accounted for about 70% of all members; only 15% of the members represented citizens. Although the federal guidelines stressed participation of Medicaid recipients, actual Medicaid beneficiaries constituted only 4% of the total membership. Thirty-two states did not have a single Medicaid recipient on their committees and several states had no citizen membership of any kind.[51] According to Medicaid historians Robert and Rosemary Stevens, the consumer participation "ideology" apparently achieved its peak influence on Medicaid during 1971, when the Social Rehabilitation Service, Medicaid's parent agency within HEW, determined that consumer participation would be a "program priority" in fiscal 1973 and established a Study Group on Consumer Involvement to write a handbook.[52] According to the handbook,

> The major goal of SRS [Social Rehabilitation Service] is to aid the individual to return or regain his ability for self-care and self-determination. . . . From the point of view of the consumer client, therefore, the most decisive and immediately apparent form of significant involvement in the agency's program is his own active participation in the determination of what services he needs and may receive through the community program from which he is seeking help.[53]

As Stevens and Stevens point out, however, the idea that committees of welfare recipients would be permitted to supersede Congress and state legislatures in determining what kinds of services Medicaid would finance was quite unrealistic.

Overall—although it falls far short of what the Citizens' Board of Inquiry had in mind by "consumer control"—the most successful implementation of consumer participation to date has been in health planning. At first glance this might well appear surprising, since both our popular conceptions and political and sociological theory look on planning as among the most bureaucratic of activities. So foreign is the notion of democratic political participation to our usual connotations of planning that the very word tends to conjure up in many people's minds visions of Russian-style "five year plans" imposed dictatorially by remote, highly centralized government agencies, whose functionaries are out of touch with, and uninterested in, local conditions, preferences, and needs.

In truth, however, the United States has a long tradition of voluntary health planning at the local level. Historically such efforts were dominated by the local health facilities, indeed, were carried out via interorganizational mechanisms that the facilities themselves had developed.[54] At the same time, these processes did involve considerable consumer or citizen participation, although the consumers and citizens in question were typically members of the same business, professional, and managerial elite as those who ran the Community Chest, and other voluntary charitable and civic associations and who served on the boards of trustees of the local health facilities.

Shortly after World War II, however, efforts were made to strengthen and coordinate these voluntary, local efforts under federal government auspices, beginning with the Hill-Burton Hospital Survey and Construction Act of 1946 and later the Comprehensive Health Planning and Regional Medical Programs of the mid-1960s. The comprehensive health planning (CHP) program, in particular, sought to incorporate requirements for consumer participation that would transfer power over local and regional health planning from the local hospital and other provider elites to groups more representative of the public as a whole. We have already noted that the Citizens' Board of Inquiry considered the comprehensive health planning agencies ineffective. This was largely because the 1966 Comprehensive Health Planning Act gave these agencies only advisory authority and also included, at the insistence of the medical lobby, an assurance that there would be no "interference with existing patterns of private professional practice."[55]

Nevertheless, as a 1974 GAO report noted, 21 states had enacted "certificate of need" laws by 1973 that gave comprehensive health planning agencies varying degrees of control over construction of health care facilities.[56] The General Accounting Office report also cited statistics and examples of unnecessary construction or other capital expenditures that had been prevented; proposed new construction or services that had been modified; new health services to meet community needs that were implemented; and existing services that were made more efficient, economical, or accessible.[57]

On a more negative note, however, the General Accounting Office report was critical of consumer participation in the comprehensive health planning agencies reviewed (three statewide and six areawide councils) pointing out that consumer attendance at council meetings for most agencies was generally less than 50% and that only two agencies had consumer majorities attending half their meetings. In addition, these agencies were not always geographically and socioeconomically representative. Two agencies did not even have the legally required consumer majority.[58]

In order to strengthen both health planning and consumer participation in health planning, Congress enacted the Health Planning and Resources Development Act of 1974 which merged and superseded the Hill-Burton, Comprehensive Health Planning and Regional Medical Programs. This legislation, PL 93-641, mandated the creation of approximately 200 regional "health systems agencies" as well as state health planning and development agencies, statewide coordinating councils, and a national council on health planning and development. Although the national council is a purely advisory body to HEW, the state and regional health planning agencies exercise considerable decision-making authority. Their teeth is in the form of administration of state certificate of need programs, capital expenditures review (under Section 1122 of the Social Security Act), and the responsibility for review and approval of federal health grant and contract funds (of which the new law authorized $390 million over the first 3 years for health facilities construction and modernization). What this means in practice is that before hospitals, nursing homes, and other health care institutions can build new facilities, expand or modernize old ones, or make capital expenditures of almost any sort involving construction of facilities or purchase of major equipment, they must first obtain the approval of the appropriate regional and state health planning agencies.

The 200 regional health systems agencies are required by PL 93-641 to have 51% to 60% consumer representation on their governing bodies. The statewide coordinating councils are required to have at least 16 members appointed by the governor. Of the council's total membership, 60% must be representatives of health systems agencies, and at least half of these must be consumer representatives.

In June 1977 the Orkand Corporation completed a study for HEW of the composition of the health systems agencies' board and executive committee membership. Data were collected in 1976 on 134 health systems agencies' governing boards (66 of which had executive committees). Consumers were forced to constitute an average 52.8% of the governing board membership and 53.1% of the membership of the executive committees. There were 12 health systems agencies that had fewer consumers than prescribed by law on their governing boards; two health systems agencies had more consumers than the law allowed. Eight health systems agencies had less than 50% consumer members on their executive committees, whereas five agencies had more than 60%. Although women were underrepresented, and health systems agencies consumer board and executive committee membership is strongly biased toward the upper middle class (65% of consumer board members have professional or managerial occupations), main racial and ethnic minority groups were actually overrepresented on the health systems agencies' boards and executive committees in comparison to the percentage of these groups in the geographic area served by each health systems agency.[59]

Thus unlike most previous efforts to implement consumer participation in health decision making either at the level of local institutions or government financing programs, the health systems planning agencies have both actual consumer majorities and a legal mandate to exercise real decision-making power. Although the authority of the health systems agencies over individual health services institutions is confined almost entirely to the area of capital expenditures, it extends to virtually all such institutions within the agency's geographical jurisdiction, and it is clearly a "governing" authority, since final decision making rests with the hierarchy of planning bodies, not the health services institutions.

We shall explore in the next several sections, however, a number of factors not adequately foreseen by the Citizens' Board or other consumer participation theorists that hinder the effective exercise of consumer power, even where, as in the health systems agencies, not only substantial formal authority but considerable real power is available to consumer representatives. Since the health systems agencies are as yet so new, there has been little opportunity to study their decision-making behavior. We therefore will need to rely for data illustrative of these factors mostly on studies of consumer participation, in which the consumer role has been an advisory rather than a governing one. We hope to be able to make a persuasive case, however, that structurally the problems posed by consensus, knowledge, and organizational factors are much the same whether consumer representatives act in a purely advisory capacity or wield actual governing power.

Conflict versus Consensus: How Well Does Conflict Theory Predict the Attitudes and Behavior of Health Care Consumers and Providers?

As was noted earlier, the theory of consumer participation set forth in *Heal Yourself* implies a conflict model of health care provider and consumer relations. In particular, consumer participation is expected to lead to fundamental transformation of the American health system because health care providers and consumers are seen as having opposing interests that arise out of their different positions in the social structure. For example, it is said to be in the consumer interest to promote equal access to health care regardless of financial considerations, although it is in the provider interest to have a class-based system that maximizes their own individual or institutional income. Similarly, consumers are viewed as having a structural interest in comprehensive health care delivery systems which, in turn, creates a consumer interest in moving toward more organized modes of delivering health care such as group practice, ambulatory care clinics, and prepaid care provided by health maintenance organizations. Providers, on the other hand, are expected to manifest a diehard attachment to traditional fee-for-service solo practice because it maximizes both their autonomy and earnings. Finally, given the choice of how to spend available funds, providers are portrayed as nearly always ready to invest more in teaching, in medical research, or in high technology to diagnose and treat exotic diseases, whereas consumers would favor more community outreach programs to deal with socially relevant health problems (e.g., lead poisoning among ghetto children), improvements in routine medical care (including more ambulatory care clinics with longer hours), and more emphasis on preventive medicine.

These and other structural interests of consumers and providers are presented by the authors of *Heal Yourself* as so diametrically opposed that persuasion, compromise, negotiation, and other such consensus-generating techniques rate no mention in their participatory model. Rather, the solution is seen as one of replacing provider dominance with consumer dominance.

In effect, then—although it may seem rather unexpected for such a theory to come from such a group of "Establishment" figures as the members of the Citizens' Board of Inquiry —the relations between health care providers and consumers depicted in *Heal Yourself* are essentially those of a Marxist-style class struggle, with health care providers cast in the role traditionally reserved for the capitalist bourgeoisie, while the health care consumers become the medical proletariat. Among the assumptions underlying this model are (a) political values are dictated by self-interest, mainly economic self-interest; (b) self-interest is a function of position in the socioeconomic structure; and (c) in the case of health care politics, the relevant structural positions are only two, provider and consumer.

There is, however, considerable empirical evidence that these assumptions do not hold up well when compared to the reality of consumer and provider value preferences and decision-making behavior. First, the theory that consumers and providers are locked in a kind of class struggle due to their fundamentally opposed structural interests has difficulty dealing with the discrepancies that are actually found between what the theory claims are the objective structural interests of consumers and providers and what empirical evidence indicated are the values, beliefs, and preferences actually held by members of these two groups. Classical Marxist theory, of course, has long recognized this "problem of consciousness," as it relates to the differences between what Marxists see as the objective interests of the working class versus individual workers' consciousness of their interests. Marxism early on developed a sophisticated theoretical response, whose lynch pin is the doctrine of false consciousness. It explains the lack of awareness among the working class of the proletarian class interest as due to their indoctrination with the ideology of the ruling class.

Some academic sociologists who employ conflict theory to analyze the health system rely on a variant of the false consciousness thesis to explain why the majority of health care consumers appear to hold less radical beliefs and values than they should on the basis of their structural interests. They stress, for example, the promotion of traditional beliefs and values associated with the provider interest by the public schools, the communications media, and other agents of mass socialization and opinion formation. According to sociologist Robert Alford,

> People come to accept as inevitable that which exists and even to believe that it is right. . . .
> Thus, the formation of consensus around the provision of health services by a professional monopoly of physicians is not an independent causal force in its own right. Rather the reinforcing and reproducing power of the institutions which guarantee the monopoly generates legitimating symbols and beliefs.[60]

The essential point we wish to make here, however, is that many consumer participation advocates—the Citizens' Board of Inquiry being a case in point—have largely failed to perceive that there is a discrepancy between the fundamental change they believe is in the "consumer interest" and the rather traditionalist beliefs and value preferences many consumers actually hold. The "problem of consciousness" is of crucial importance because when real flesh and blood consumers begin to participate in decision making, they will do so, obviously, on the basis of their own values and perceived interests. Moreover, in terms of the effect on consumer participation, it does not matter whether this consciousness is true or false. If there is a discrepancy between the subjective value preferences actually held by consumer participants and the objective interests ascribed to the consumer class by consumer participation theorists, then, clearly, consumer participation is unlikely to have the kind of impact on policy its theorists envision.

There are additional problems with the conflict model of provider and consumer relations. Although for certain purposes it may be useful to reduce the complexity of real people to simplified analytic categories—for example, provider or consumer—the fact remains that the real world is synthetic; thus the behavior of real people can seldom be predicted on the basis of one dimension of social structural status. Real people are multidimensional; in the language of structural-functional sociology they are subject to "cross-cutting status sets." For example, health care consumers differ among themselves according to age, income, occupation, ethnicity, and so on. Providers, in particular, can be differentiated according to whether they are physicians, hospital administrators, academics, health insurers, and the like. There is much empirical evidence to suggest that differences of opinion associated with these contrasting statuses can be as great or greater among consumers and providers as between them. More deeply, the empirical evidence also suggests that the beliefs and value preferences that individuals hold as well as those that correlate with particular social statuses (such as income or occupation) are not necessarily the ones that accord with economic self-interest. That is, the actual beliefs and value preferences held by individuals and social groups often manifest a far higher degree of altruism than a conflict theory based on assumptions of opposing structural interests can allow.

To document these points we will look first at the findings of an attitude survey which compared the opinions and policy preferences of hospital administrators, consumer representatives, and a scientifically random sample of community residents in one New York City health services catchment area.[61] The area in question included three hospitals—one municipal, two voluntaries—and two ambulatory care clinics—one hospital affiliated, the other independent. At least 2 years prior to the start of the study, each facility had instituted consumer participation in the form of an advisory board. In terms of social class, the community was approximately 41% lower class, 22% middle class, and 37% upper class.[62] Ethnically, residents were 24% black, 24% Hispanic, 41 white, and 11% "other."[63] Compared to the community as a whole, the membership of the consumer advisory boards was biased toward greater representation of low-income and ethnic-minority groups.[64]

Hospital administrators, consumer representatives, and a scientifically random sample of community residents were surveyed concerning their assessments of local health problems and services and their policy preferences with respect to changes that ought to be made. Although the study did find greater similarity of views between the community and consumer representatives than between the hospital administrators and either the community or the consumer representatives, the most striking finding was the overall lack of strong differences in views among the three groups.[65] Thus out of a set of 34 questions relating to the assessment of local health services and policy preferences, there was consensus (i.e., no statistically significant differences) between the views of the community and those of local health administrators on all but eight items. What is especially worth noting here is that majorities of the community and the administrators were in actual disagreement on only one item. This question involved which facilities hospitals should expand. Community residents favored expanding emergency room facilities; administrators preferred to expand outpatient clinics.[66] In the other seven instances, majorities among both the community and administrators were in agreement; the statistical differences were in the size of the majority or the intensity of agreement.[67] In other words, most of the differences of opinion concerned matters of emphasis or priority. As examples, although majorities of both community residents and administrators favored more preventive care, the administrator majority was significantly larger. Similarly, although both community residents and administrators agreed that each hospital should have its own ambulance, that waiting times in emergency rooms should be reduced, and that patients should receive more individualized treatment, the community majorities favoring these changes were significantly greater. Finally, as an example of differences in intensity, the majority of community residents considered allowing interns to examine patients as part of their training "extremely important," whereas most administrators considered this "indispensable."[68]

It is particularly interesting to compare the attitudes of community residents, consumer representatives, and hospital administrators with respect to the importance of medical research in hospitals, since it is one of the central tenets of consumer participation theory that the importance of medical research is a professional priority, whereas consumer interest is in more expenditures for medical services, especially routine and preventative services. The study found, however, that the attitudes of administrators, consumer representatives, and community residents were in accord in attaching great importance to medical research.[69] Interestingly, it was the lowest-income, least-educated community residents who attached the greatest importance to medical research—greater importance, in fact, than the hospital administrators did.[70] Although this and several other traditional attitudes that were most common among the most disadvantaged groups in the community might seem readily explainable in terms of "false consciousness," a number of other class differences in attitudes are much less so.

In particular, there were strong differences among ethnic groups and among lower-, middle-, and upper-class community residents in their degree of satisfaction or dissatisfaction with locally available medical care. Whereas majorities of blacks (58.5%) and Hispanics (61%) indicated little or moderate dissatisfaction, most non-Jewish whites (50%) and Jews (69%) indicated that they were either very or extremely dissatisfied with the medical care available.[71] Similarly, 60% of the lower-class persons were only a little or moderately dissatisfied, whereas 53% of the middle-class and 54% of the upper-class respondents were very or extremely dissatisfied.[72] Moreover, a closer examination revealed that the dissatisfaction of the middle- and upper-class residents was not with the care they themselves were receiving, but with the care they thought was available to others.[73] Thus middle- and upper-class community members were much more likely than either Medicaid recipients or the poor in general to say that Medicaid patients received worse care than those who could pay by other modes.[74] Among consumer representatives, parallel differences existed among persons from different social classes and ethnic groups.[75] In particular, the most "radical" members of the consumer boards were housewives from families with annual incomes over $15,000.[76] By "radical," we mean that they were more likely to favor community control (including hire–fire authority over doctors) and to believe that the proper role of consumer representatives was to effect changes in the types of medical services available, as opposed to providing merely a channel of expression for community views.[77]

One of the more curious findings of the study was that although the actual views of the majority of consumer representatives and the majority of community residents were closely matched, the consumer representatives were not aware of this and, in fact, projected attitudes on the community that the community did not hold. It is intriguing to note that most of the attitudes the consumer representatives mistakenly imputed to the community were in line with the so-called consumer interest as defined by the Citizens' Board of Inquiry. For example, when the consumer representatives were asked what the average community resident would pick as the most important health problem in that community, over half the representatives thought it would be routine care.[78] In fact, majorities of the community, the consumer representatives, and local hospital administrators all agreed that socially relevant health problems were the most important.[79] (It is interesting to note, in this context, that all three groups manifested confusion and uncertainty, as indicated by a lack of clear majority consensus both

within and among themselves, as to what kinds of health programs hospitals and other local health institutions should undertake to deal with socially relevant health problems.[80]) This
may well be because a major cause of such problems was said
to be "living conditions."[81] Asked what programs the community wanted but that had not been instituted, those most frequently mentioned both by administrators and residents were
alcohol and drug programs.[82] (Again, both residents and administrators were in agreement in perceiving the main obstacle
to these programs as lack of funding.)[83] Consumer representatives were even more mistaken in their evaluations of how the
community felt about the importance of teaching medical students and doing medical research in hospitals and of providing
care for "outsiders" as well as local community residents. Although most consumer representatives themselves rated these
activities as very or extremely important, they believed that the
majority of community residents would rate them as not at all
important or as only somewhat important. In fact, 86% of the
community agreed that teaching was a very or extremely important hospital function, 78% felt the same way about medical
research, and 68% about the responsibility of the hospital to
provide care to "outsiders."[84] Finally, consumer board representatives tended to underestimate the community's preference
for private physicians over clinic care. Although 44% of consumer representatives thought the community preferred private
care, 60% of the community selected private physicians as their
first choice. A third of the representatives thought the community would prefer free-standing clinics (on the model of neighborhood health centers). In fact, the 28% of community
residents who preferred clinics, preferred the traditional hospital outpatient clinics.[85] It appeared to the researchers that community residents, when asked to name their preferences, picked
the modes of care they themselves used or at least were familiar
with, whereas the consumer representatives projected on the
community their own, comparatively greater, tendency to favor

new organizational forms. The principal champions of clinic care, however—both in hospital outpatient departments and in free-standing clinics—were the hospital administrators.

In sum, then, this study suggests that—at least in terms of the subjective perceptions of hospital administrators, consumer representatives, and community residents—the "structural interests" of providers versus consumers may not be as clearly divergent and opposed as consumer participation theory would lead us to expect. Ironically, the one issue on which consumer representatives appeared to be truly at loggerheads with the hospital administrators was the issue of participation itself, or, more precisely, the issue of "community control." In this respect, however, the consumer representatives were also clearly more militant than their communities.[86] Although 71% of the consumer representatives endorsed the idea that organizations designed to serve the community—like public schools and hospitals—should be controlled by members of the community, only 46% of community residents agreed;[87] and whereas a third (34%) of consumer representatives thought that community people should have control over hiring and firing of doctors, less than a fourth (23%) of community residents agreed.[88]

The question must, of course, be raised as to how typical of health care providers and consumers generally are the attitudes of hospital administrators, consumer representatives, and community residents in one New York City health services area. The data needed to answer this question scientifically are simply not available. There is evidence, however, to *suggest* that these attitudes probably are fairly characteristic of American provider and consumer attitudes generally.

Some such evidence comes from a national survey comparing the attitudes of statistically representative samples of American health care consumers and American physicians toward U.S. health care and toward government health policy. Many of the findings of the study, which was carried out in 1971 (i.e., during the same period as both the New York City study and the Citizens' Board report), strongly echo those cited above.[89] For example, Steven Strickland, author of the published findings, observed that the "strongest sentiment for change seems to lie in the middle class."[90] Among Americans generally, those groups most convinced of the need for basic changes in the health care system were professional and businessmen (67%), white collar workers (67%), and the college educated (68%). Those groups least likely to perceive a need for basic changes were the nonwhites (49%), the grade school educated (51%), persons over 60 (53%), and persons not in the labor force (55%).[91]

Although persons from all backgrounds who had little or no confidence in their own ability to obtain good medical care were the strongest advocates for change (89%), it is worth noting that the businessmen, professionals, and college educated—that is, those among the different social groups who were most convinced of the need for basic changes— were also those who had the greatest confidence in their own ability to obtain good medical care.[92] As the study's author, Steven Strickland, observed,

> Altogether the pattern of responses makes clear that there is no "class struggle" over the merits of the present health system or the need for changes in it. Those for whom our system of health care personally works well are also concerned that the system should work better for all citizens.[93]

Like the New York City study, the national study also found that the American public generally preferred the traditional system of obtaining primary care from fee-for-service private practitioners as opposed to a more organized or comprehensive delivery system.[94] One question, for example, described the concept of the health maintenance organization and then asked whether the respondent thought it was a good idea or whether sticking to one doctor was preferable. (as part of the description of health maintenance organizations, respondents were told that "some people feel this kind of a program provides fuller medical care than they are able to get from their own family doctor. Other people feel that changing to this kind of a program is too much of a risk because they are not sure they will be able to see the same doctor all the time.")[95] Of those surveyed 58% said it was preferable to stay with one doctor.[96] Although the author considered it impressive that even one-third of the respondents considered health maintenance organizations a "good idea,"[97] given their lack of personal experience with them, he nonetheless was forced to conclude

> The public does not identify the reorganization of existing health care facilities, or the alteration of traditional medical practice, as among the most important steps to improve American health care. . . . Even the potential advantages of better preventive care, probable lower cost, and more comprehensive treatment—heralded by the proponents of health maintenance organizations— are viewed skeptically by most of the people, who fear they may be forced to sacrifice the still more central value of personal attention by one doctor whom they know and trust.[98]

The national study also confirmed the enthusiasm of the general public for research. When asked to rank 11 proposals for government action to meet U.S. health needs, the respondents ranked sponsorship of health research second only to removal of cost barriers.[99] In contrast, the physicians' sample ranked research last, among seven options for government action presented to them. Even physicians themselves engaged in teaching and research ranked research no higher than fourth.[100]

Perhaps the most interesting feature of this study is the opportunity to compare the public's versus the doctors' assessments of the health system and their preferences for government action. Once again, the findings indicate a much higher level of consensus between consumers and providers than consumer participation theory would lead one to expect. According to the author, "Overall, physicians' assessments of needed actions were not markedly different from those of the public."[101] Indeed, on the questionnaire as a whole, differences among categories of physicians often appeared much greater than differences between physicians in general and the public. The principal line of cleavage was between office-based, solo-practicing general practitioners and all other physicians (i.e., specialists, hospital-based physicians, and those engaged in teaching and research). It appears that the traditionalist or conservative views typically ascribed to doctors are, in actuality, mainly the views of general practitioners. Other categories of physicians tend to be more liberal, some extremely so. For example, hospital-based physicians and physicians in teaching and research ranked national health insurance as their first priority for government action.[102] Similarly, if reorganization of health care delivery is ultimately in the consumer interest, these two groups of physicians are far ahead of the general public in championing that interest.[103]

Between "consumers" and "physicians," the greatest split to be found was again over the issue of participation itself. According to the study's author,

> The public singles out no special villains to blame for present problems. Indeed, approval and support is expressed in various ways for all the established health institutions, professions, and organizations. But while recognizing the importance of professionalism, citizens also believe there should be a role for themselves as "consumers" in the administration of the health care system, particularly on the local level.[104]

In contrast to the public's willingness to include and to place a high level of trust in the essential fairness of virtually all interested parties, physicians tended to be exclusionary. Steven Strickland drew the following conclusion concerning physicians' attitudes toward the participation of other groups in health policy:

> Highly professionalized, most U.S. physicians would prefer to keep the health care system under their complete control if possible, sharing direction only with private insurance compa-

nies and excluding, with evenhanded firmness, both lay citizens and other health professionals such as hospital administrators.[105]

Once again, however, there were considerable differences among different categories of physicians on this score. One of the ironies this produced was that the general public manifested greater confidence in the AMA to produce fair and workable policies than did the doctors.[106] The apparent reason for this was that general practitioners gave the AMA a considerably higher vote of confidence than did other categories of physicians. It is worth noting, however, that with the sole exception of hospital-based physicians, no category of physicians gave consumer groups a positive confidence rating.[107] Curiously, physicians engaged in teaching and research, a group that generally has quite liberal or progressive views on substantive issues, expressed the *least* confidence of all physicians that consumer groups would propose fair and workable health care policies.[108]

Let us now consider what all these attitude survey findings add up to—what they mean. First, because our main concern is with the character and quality of the knowledge that underlies proposals for policy reform, it is worth noting that the majority of academic social scientists would see few if any of the findings from the two attitude surveys discussed above as surprising. Moreover, most mainstream sociologists and political scientists would likely consider the theoretical points we have made in this section so well known as to scarcely bear repeating. The truly interesting question is, thus, if the theoretical insights are so obvious to mainstream social scientists and the empirical findings presented so readily predictable, why did consumer participation theory not take them into account? Or, put another way, why have consumer participation advocates taken as theoretical guides assumptions—about the nature of intergroup conflict, the "mirror-image" of political ideology, and individual or group economic self-interest, and the like that several generations of social scientists have tested and found wanting?

The answer would seem to be that the theoretical assumptions underlying consumer participation theory are derived not from social science but from the social activist tradition. In its origins, of course, the "social conflict" paradigm that animates the social activist tradition did develop out of social science— 19th century social science. Over the past 100 years, however, the conflict paradigm—at least in its nonacademic popularized forms—has lost its character as a scientific theory, open to intellectual challenge and subject to the need for empirical verification. Rather, it has rigidified into a set of assumptions its adherents accept as an article of faith. In part, this is because the world view it represents is part of the heritage that one generation of social activists passes on to the next. In this sense, espousal of the conflict perspective (whether in the form of a Marxist or non-Marxist theory) "goes with" becoming an activist in much the same way that a bohemian lifestyle goes with a life in the arts. It is equally important to point out, however, that although academic social science has discredited empirically many of the expectations conflict theory fosters, it has not (partly due to its preoccupation with value neutrality, partly due to its concern for predicting and explaining as opposed to influencing social change) provided those concerned with achieving a greater measure of social justice with an alternative theoretical guide.

Contemporary social activists pay a high price for their continued allegiance to certain assumptions of conflict theory. This is especially true for reform activists such as advocates of consumer participation. In particular, certain of the intellectual assumptions of conflict theory are fundamentally at odds with the democratic ideals of the consumer participation advocates.

The democratic ideal does not assume consensus, but it does assume a capacity for consensus building. That is, democracy does not require all citizens of a polity to share the same interests and values. Neither does it require that their disagreements be merely minor ones and weak in intensity. Democracy does require, however, that the individuals and groups who make up a society possess sufficient ambivalence, uncertainty, empathy, altruism, and the like, to enable them to change their minds, see the other side of an issue, and tolerate disagreement. Finally, democracy assumes that through the use of certain procedures—for example, persuasion, compromise, voting, and majority rule—it is possible to arrive at collective decisions even though the individuals or groups or both, who participated in the process continue to disagree.

Conflict theory with its description of society as divided into warring camps of class or status groups or both, with implacably opposing structural interests denies the possibility of democratic consensus. Politics, according to the conflict model, is not a process whereby individuals and groups overcome dissension to reach collective decisions all participants can accept as legitimate, but is an all-or-nothing struggle in which the social group identified as the virtuous carrier of social change must wrest dominance from the group identified with stasis and resistance.

Quite apart from the incompatibility of the conflict model with democratic values, it causes consumer participation advocates to make serious tactical and strategic errors in promoting the substantive changes they wish to effect in the health system. In particular, it causes them to reject or alienate individuals and groups among the "providers" who might otherwise be allies.

This problem was amply apparent in the work of the Citizens' Board of Inquiry itself, one of whose two practicing physician members felt impelled to write a minority, dissenting opinion, in which he stated,

> There is an inherent bias in the rhetoric of the majority report, which serves no constructive purpose, and, in being accusatory rather than informative, does a disservice to a dedicated profession. Such rhetoric serves to undermine the cooperative effort between consumer, provider, and government that is necessary if we are to correct the obvious and poignant inequities in the

provision of health care. . . .To denigrate the responsible role the provider must share in guaranteeing the appropriateness, relevance, and success of solutions is a disservice to our democratic processes and our pluralistic heritage.[109]

Concerning the question of provider versus consumer dominance, Dr. Besson wrote,

> This minority report agrees that consumer representation must not be a sham nor should providers be responsible for contributions to policy decision if there is any conflict of interest. The essential ingredients for an effective, responsive institution are clearly articulated needs, shared control and responsiveness of provider to policy making bodies that function as community trustees. The majority report seems to be a clarion call only for the assumption of power and not a search for equity.[110]

He concluded by urging the readers of *Heal Yourself* to consider "that dialogue between provider and consumer acting as community trustees rather than power struggles of vested interests will best serve consumer needs."[111]

Another serious strategic problem results from the emphasis conflict theory causes consumer advocates to place on the class, ethnic, and other status affiliations of consumer representatives. As earlier noted, the consumer participation movement has tended to define "representativeness" largely in terms of demographics. That is, if 15% of the community is black, then 15% of the consumer representatives should be black, and so on. Although this stress on mirroring the racial, class, and ethnic distribution of the local population is intended to ensure the participation of those who have been excluded in the past, and it is difficult to come up with another mechanism that would as readily assure the presence of persons from low-income minority backgrounds on consumer boards, it is nonetheless counterproductive in some other respects to the aims of consumer participation. The main problem is that it is difficult to reconcile the requirements for demographic representation with the kinds of procedures that would allow consumers or consumer organizations to elect the persons they wish to represent them, thereby establishing lines of communication and accountability between the representatives and their constituencies. That is, there is no way to ensure that free elections by consumers or consumer organizations would result in demographic parity between the representatives chosen and the community. Indeed, it is highly likely that such parity would not result. In part, this is because, although people may show a certain preference for representatives who share their own background characteristics, they often give equal or greater weight to what they perceive as the superior personal qualities (e.g., leadership ability, knowledgeability, integrity) of particular individuals. In a truly egalitarian society, we would expect the imbalances in selection of representatives from diverse backgrounds to cancel each other out. The emphasis of the consumer participation movement, however, has been on parity in each and every case. Moveover, one must realistically recognize that the historic political apathy and low level of organization among the poor and certain racial and ethnic minorities, as well as latent prejudices against them, would likely skew the processes of organized representation against them.

Yet if ensuring the proper proportional representation of the poor and minorities thus virtually requires that representatives be appointed by some one omniscient person or committee charged with obtaining the right "mix," then it is also clear that whoever makes these appointments has the power to "stack the deck." Indeed, in practice it is usually the established power group (i.e., the representatives of local health institutions) who are charged with recruiting the Indians, welfare mothers, and other representatives of disadvantaged groups. Obviously the potential that consumer representation of disadvantaged groups will degenerate to mere tokenism under such circumstances is quite high. Indeed, in some instances uncovered by the Citizens' Board, the "tokens" were appointed without even being asked, as part of an apparent exercise in paper compliance —a matter of providing names with the right ethnic and class tags attached to satisfy legal requirements.[112] Even where such representatives do participate in decision making, however, the way in which they were chosen and their consequent lack of links to a constituency tend seriously to undermine their effectiveness.

Finally, as we have seen, certain of the intellectual assumptions of conflict theory cause consumer participation theorists to impute to consumers, especially poor and minority consumers, an interest in fundamental transformation of the health system that empirically is not now present in their subjective values and beliefs. By simply assuming consumers to be more change oriented than they actually are, consumer advocates have neglected the need for consumer education and what the feminist movement calls "consciousness raising." They have also set up unrealistic expectations for consumer participation as a means of rapidly effecting fundamental reform of health care.

The conflict theory on which the analysis and recommendations of *Heal Yourself* is based portrays the consumer interest as a single, well-defined entity that can be readily perceived and understood by individual consumers provided they just take the time to reflect on their own personal experience. Because the consumer interest is seen as grounded in the logic of social stratification, however, conflict theory also accords it a kind of objective existence independent of individual consumers' perceptions of it.

In contrast, our analysis of attitude surveys suggests that if one's aim is to maximize the potential of consumer participation to social change in the health care system, it is probably more fruitful to define the consumer interest, rather differently, as the product of a process of consensus building among individual consumers and consumer groups. Viewed from this perspective, the consumer interest becomes a variable rather than a constant. That is, whether or not a consumer interest can be said to have an existence that is anything other than purely theoretical depends on the existence or nonexistence of channels of upward consensus building whereby actual consumers can formulate positions on various issues, based on a common understanding they have reached concerning the consumer interest. It is important to note here that, unlike traditional conflict theory, in which becoming conscious of a group interest is viewed largely as a process of discovery or "seeing the light" (hence rather similar, in fact, to religious conversion), the "consumer interest" that arises out of a process of consensus building is quite clearly something created by the participants. As such the character of the process itself has a highly important shaping influence. Altering elements of the process might be expected to result in quite different definitions of the consumer interest. Clearly, this perspective makes issues of organization and knowledge (including such factors as leadership, communication, training, and education) crucial to the evolution of the consumer interest. As we shall see in the next two sections, however, it was precisely these organizational and knowledge factors that were given little attention in the Citizens' Board of Inquiry theory of consumer participation.

Knowledge: The Need for Consumer Expertise

Concerning the knowledge gap between health professionals and consumers, we have seen that the basic stance taken by the authors of *Heal Yourself* was to downplay its importance. According to the Citizens' Board of Inquiry, health policymaking as opposed to medical treatment decision making does not require specialized expertise. One's personal experience, that is, knowing "where the shoe pinches," in John Dewey's phrase, is sufficient.

A review of the literature on consumer participation suggests, however, that although common sense and personal experience may be sufficient for dealing with problems pertaining to the sensitivity and humaneness of patient care (e.g., rude staff, over-long waiting times, drab and uncomfortable surroundings, etc.), lack of greater knowledgeability also tends to limit consumer representatives to these concerns. Moreover, according to a New York City Health Department study of consumer participation on voluntary hospital advisory boards under the Ghetto Medicine Program:

> Throughout many hours of committee discussion ran the thread of individual experiences of committee members, e.g., particular complaints such as "I had to wait for 2 hours before I was seen in an emergency room" or "last week my mother-in-law fractured her hip and she had to wait over one hour to have an x-ray taken." The personal experience syndrome has wastefully drained off energy as committee members have concentrated excessively on putting out fires without dealing with the source of ignition. It has been hard for some committees to abstract from personal experiences and move on to effective action.[113]

To make their influence felt in areas of policy other than patient amenities, consumer representatives need various types of knowledge and information. For example, when it comes to resource allocation within an individual hospital, clinic, or other health facility, consumers can make certain of the basic decisions concerning priorities on values alone. Translating value preferences into action, however, also requires a certain amount of reality testing and adaptation. Thus consumer representatives need to become knowledgeable about the specific institution's financial situation: How much money or other resources the institution has available, what are its financial commitments or debts, where is the slack in the budget, what additional sources of financing for new programs are there (e.g., is there federal money available for alcoholism programs, but not for geriatrics; for manpower training, but not construction, etc.). Consumer boards often experience great difficulty gaining access to such information. According to Laurelyn Veatch, who studied consumer participation in New York City municipal and voluntary hospitals,

Acquiring information is a common problem for laypersons. The lay members of community boards are essentially volunteers (they receive a small compensation) who have other jobs and commitments. They are up against health professionals who have training in, daily contact with, and control over information which would be useful to community board members. The Health and Hospitals Corporation *Interim Guidelines* give community boards "the right to consult with responsible officials and outside authorities"; but "consulting with" does not assure full disclosure. Most of the community boards are dependent primarily on the executive director of the hospital for information, and secondarily (in New York City municipal hospitals) on the director of community affairs, who is usually hired by and responsible to the executive director.[114]

One consumer board at a voluntary hospital that could not obtain copies of the architectural plans or sufficient financial information about a proposed new facility filed a lawsuit; but although their public interest lawyer won a preliminary legal battle with the large Wall Street firm representing the hospital, the board members, who were all volunteers, subsequently decided they could not afford the time to pursue the lawsuit and to fight for reelection. They then resigned en masse and released their reasons to the press.[115] Although the legal rights of consumers to information are being expanded, they remain ambiguous or at least contestable in many cases; and as this instance illustrates, they can be difficult and time consuming to enforce.

A survey of consumers involved in health planning in four cities (Birmingham, Alabama; Chicago; Los Angeles; and New York), carried out under contract to HEW by the Consumer Commission on the Accreditation of Health Services, elicited numerous complaints concerning providers' easier access to and control over information and expertise as a means of intimidating consumers:

On HSA [health systems agencies] and SHCC [State Health Coordinating Council] boards and committees, consumers feel the provider presence and know of provider expertise. They are required to respond to provider proprosals and, lacking knowledge and staff, feel pressured to endorse programs without understanding their content or intent.[116]

Consumers serving on health planning bodies also complained about the sheer volume of technical material they must review prior to meetings, frequently on short notice and with insufficient explanation.

At least as serious a barrier to consumer effectiveness is lack of legal or bureaucratic expertise. The health planning law is extremely complicated and many consumers do not fully understand it. Among those consumer representatives surveyed by the Consumer Commission on the Accreditation of Health Services, roughly one-third (37%) were health systems agencies' board members. Of this, in effect, leadership group, two-thirds indicated that they neither knew nor understood the role and function of the State Health Coordinating Council. One-third were unaware of the 10 national health priorities set down in PL 93-641. Three-fourths said they did not know or understand the role and function of the National Health Planning Council. One-fourth considered themselves neither well informed on health issues, nor did they have a working knowledge of PL 93-641, the legislation under which they exercise their authority as consumer representatives. Some indicated that they did not understand the concepts of review and comment, certificate of need, and the definition and purpose of the Health Systems Plan and the Annual Implementation Plan.[117]

The authors of *Heal Yourself* did recommend that consumer boards be given their own staff. According to the Rand study of 51 cases of consumer participation cited earlier, 75% of those consumer boards and committees that had their own staff were able to achieve significant or high implementation of citizen views, as compared to 42% of those without staff.[118] The researchers concluded that staff made possible a continuity and expertise not otherwise available to a board made up of part-time volunteers.[119]

The literature on consumer participation also suggests,

however, that the cases of consumer participation that are the most innovative and carry the greatest impact are those in which consumer representatives use their staff, not only to wrest information from hospital administrators or program bureaucrats who are reluctant to share it with consumers, but also to collect and process new types of information. These activities can serve as a means of redefining the whole scope and nature of the policy issues raised. This appears to be especially true in cases in which the aim is to move from considering particular health facilities and the various services they do or should provide in isolation from one another toward considering all the services provided by facilities in a given area in relation to one another and to the unmet health needs of the area's residents.

To date, consumer participation advocates have shown perhaps too great a tendency to view knowledge as an already existing power resource monopolized by provider and bureaucratic vested interests. However, as Harry Cain, Director of HEW's Bureau of Health Planning and Resources Development and Frances V. Dearman, information officer with the bureau, point out, the knowledge base needed for health planning is at present largely nonexistent. Thus, according to Cain and Dearman,

> The law calls upon us to provide the agencies with technical assistance in the form of planning approaches, methodologies, policies and standards for appropriate planning and development of health resources as if we had this information on hand. The problem is that we do not know, for example, how many of what kinds of health services a given population needs. Often we know what the hospitals and other providers want to provide, but how do we measure what they need? The lack of such information represents a fundamental gap in our technical assistance armamentarium.[120]

Although some of the needed knowledge can be gained by assuring the health systems agencies and their consumer representatives access to population health statistics collected by local and state health departments as well as data collection and analyses of health services utilization and quality of care carried out by the physician-dominated professional standards review organizations, considerable new research and development will also be required.

There is evidence, albeit anecdotal, that by taking an active role in such research and development, consumer representatives can greatly enhance their policy influence. Thus according to one study of consumer participation in the Moon Valley (Pennsylvania) Experimental Health Services Delivery System Project (EHSDS), "Systematically collected data became the key by which the total community could have input into planning decisions."[121] Because the federal grants for the Moon Valley experimental demonstration projects included generous funding to hire staff and conduct research, the community management board (called the "Moon Valley Health and Welfare Council") was able to obtain various types of information useful for area planning. For example, based on data collected by the Moon Valley Experimental Health Services staff concerning community health needs and population projections, the community management board was able to obtain several changes in plans for a proposed new hospital facility (such as its location and number of beds) and for utilization of two existing hospitals. As a result, the authors found that the hospital board had begun to rely more and more on the community board's research component. In 1972, a valleywide survey was conducted to obtain information from residents about their health problems and health care. Planned and conducted in cooperation with the National Center for Health Statistics, the Moon Valley survey used the same methodology used by the National Center in its national health surveys. One of the findings was that the average American had nearly 50% more contacts with physicians than the average Moon Valley resident, although the latter had over 50% more sick bed days.[122] In addition, the Emergency Medical Care Committee, organized in early 1974, employed data collected by Moon Valley Experimental Health Services staff to plan improvements in area ambulance service.

The authors of the study stressed the political as well as purely rational uses of these data, mobilization of the community being one such use. Thus

> As has been the case with consumer involvement in most of the current health care activities in the Moon Valley, the initial formal impetus was provided by council staff, but it is the public concern which maintains each activity's viability. The key factor in this process is the data pertaining to the problem at hand. Without relatively complete and accurate information, the staff could not arouse interest on the part of community leaders in working toward improvements in the system. In the typical situation, providers tend to monopolize and control the available data. This often leads to an intimidation of less adequately informed consumers.[123]

The authors also pointed out that rational persuasion based on new knowledge provides consumers with an alternative tactic to conflict and confrontation in their dealings with providers. Although there may be times when confrontational tactics are necessary, rational persuasion when it can be employed is less alienating and provides a better basis for long-term cooperative interaction, since it is a technique for building consensus as opposed to flexing power. Moreover the self-image of health care providers as experts who base their opinions not on self-interest but on knowledge of the facts makes it difficult for them to resist arguments backed up with compelling data. Of course, the persuasive power of new knowledge works both ways. Thus the authors report an instance in which the board's research served to build greater consensus between Moon Valley consumers and providers, by causing the consumers to change their views. In 1972 the community management boards research staff conducted a survey of local physicians' attitudes and opinions regarding major Moon Valley health problems and their solution. The survey was conducted at the request of a committee set up to study the feasibility of starting a health maintenance organization in the valley. The committee also hired a consultant to estimate the economic viability of a health maintenance organization. Based on the consultant's report, which was negative, as well as on the survey findings that most Moon Valley physicians were opposed to prepaid care and considered a shortage of physicians to be the valley's major problem, the Moon Valley Health and Welfare Council and the local labor unions which had provided the initial impetus in favor of a health maintenance organization were led to reconsider their position and ultimately to seek a different approach.[124] There is a danger, however, in consumers becoming overly dependent on federal financing. Unless the consumer participation movement develops—in addition to federal financial support and apart from the federally created health planning structure—an independent organizational and resource base, it risks the fate of the Great Society's community action agencies which sought to organize and facilitate the maximum feasible participation of the poor in the antipoverty war. Having no organizational existence apart from that established via federal legislation, and having been sustained throughout its history via federal funds, the movement for community participation in the inner cities was vulnerable to political pressure exerted by opposing interest groups and to a conservative shift among American voters to a degree that equally controversial but more independent movements (e.g., labor, civil rights) never were.

Organization: The Need to Create Upward Linkages Between Consumer Constituencies and Consumer Representatives

Among the most serious defects of consumer participation, both in theory and practice, is the relative inattention to organizational structures, processes, and mechanisms that would serve to link consumer representatives to their constituencies. Such linkages are essential to the performance of the following functions:

1. *Communication* from constituents to representatives, so that the representatives will be aware of their constituents' opinions and values regarding health issues: and *communication* from representatives to constituents, so that representatives can play an educational and leadership role vis-a-vis constituents.

2. *Accountability,* so that consumers will not only know who their representatives are and what positions and actions they have taken, but so that consumers can also participate in choosing them and have an opportunity periodically to decide whether particular persons should continue as representatives.

3. *Mobilization* of the constituency in support of representatives, so that whenever a conflict makes it necessary, the group as a whole can express consensus or display its power.

4. *Legitimation* of the representatives, so they can act as authentic spokesmen and bargaining agents for their constituencies.

Societal guidance theory refers to the organizational structures and processes that serve these functions as upward consensus-building channels, as contrasted with downward controlling ones—epitomized by bureaucracy—whose functions are primarily managerial. In political science, structural functional systems theory refers to channels of "interest articulation and aggregation."

Consumer participation advocates have tended to stress the importance of establishing organizational mechanisms for consumer representation within private and governmental health bureaucracies, but have neglected the organizational structures and processes that would link the representatives "inside" to their constituencies "outside." Thus the Citizens' Board of Inquiry report suggests only the following rather vague recommendations for ensuring the authentic "representativeness" of consumer representatives:

1. The process for selecting consumer representatives must be well known and clear to the community or to the consumer group to which services are being provided.
2. Individual consumers and consumer groups must be able to affect the process of selection.
3. Consumer representatives must be accountable and responsible to the group that they represent.[125]

The Citizens' Board of Inquiry did not, however, suggest what particular organizational mechanisms could serve to implement these requirements.

Lack of such organizational mechanisms produces anticipatable dysfunctions analogous to the functions earlier listed, that is, nonexistent or poor communication between consumers and their representative, lack of accountability of representatives to consumers, low capacity for constituency mobilization, and reluctance or refusal on the part of others, especially provider representatives, to accord legitimacy to consumer representatives. One consequence that can result from inadequate communication between consumers and their representatives is a state of pluralistic ignorance. An example of such pluralistic ignorance is provided by a finding (which was cited earlier in a different context) from a study comparing the assessments and policy preferences regarding local health services of hospital advisory board consumer representatives and a scientifically chosen sample of community residents in one New York City service area. The finding was that although majorities of the representatives and their constituents actually held almost identical views, the representatives were unaware of this identity of views.[126] Indeed, when asked to predict community attitudes, the representatives ascribed to their constituents much narrower, more self-interested views than those the representatives and the community in fact shared.

Lack of accountability of representatives to constituents can easily result in representatives exploiting their positions for their own or associates' personal gain. This is illustrated by an instance of corruption uncovered during the course of 1975–1976 New York State nursing home investigations.

A wealthy Republican businessman named Samuel Hausman had for some years played an influential role in New York State politics acting as what testimony before the Moreland Act Investigating Commission termed Governor Nelson Rockefeller's "eyes and ears to the Jewish community."[127] Although Hausman was active in fund raising for many Jewish charities and served on the board of directors of several prominent Jewish institutions, his political role as a spokesman for the Jewish community was unofficial and self-appointed. It was, however, because of this role that Hausman obtained an appointment to the State Hospital Review and Planning Council, a health planning body established under New York State's Article 28 program. Among the responsibilities of the Hospital Review and Planning Council was participation in administering New York State's "certificate of need" legislation, which required would-be nursing home operators to submit new construction applications to a process of review by a hierarchy of health planning bodies. Approval had to be granted before any nursing home construction could begin. At the time they recommended Hausman's appointment to the Hospital Review and Planning Council, state health officials already knew that Hausman desired the position, not to further the public interest as a representative of the Jewish community but to promote the business interests of nursing home entrepreneur Bernard Bergman. Bergman, who was later convicted and jailed for Medicaid fraud, had several times been refused a certificate of need for new construction because of repeated violations of state law and regulations. Most pointedly, he had demonstrated poor "character and competence" in the operation of his existing nursing homes. Once on the New York State Hospital Review and Planning Council, Hausman indeed sought to intervene on Bergman's behalf, most notably by seeking to influence the recommendations of the local community planning board and the areawide planning agency.[128] Although Hausman apparently did not have a personal financial interest in any of Bergman's nursing home operations, he was able to establish lucrative business dealings with Bergman for one of his relatives.[129]

The relative lack of organization of health consumer constituencies as well as the poorly developed linkages between consumer board representatives and consumer constituencies undercuts the credibility of the views the representatives express. In comparison, providers are highly organized, and there are well-developed linkages between provider organizations and provider representatives serving on various boards and committees. The Consumer Commission on the Accreditation of Health Services study of consumer participation in health systems agencies noted

> Provider representatives on HSA [health systems agencies] boards have organized constituencies and they are politically credible and accountable. When, for example, an American Hospital Association representative speaks at an HSA board meeting, that person is speaking for, and with the weight of, many of the country's inpatient acute care health facilities.[130]

In contrast,

> Whether HSA [health systems agencies] and SHCC [State Health Coordinating Council] consumer board members represent the interests of, or are responsive or accountable to, an identifiable constituency is often questioned by providers and by other consumers. Although HSA consumer representatives are legally required to be broadly representative of the demographic characteristics of the population (i.e., the social, economic, linguistic, and racial groups and the geographic areas of each health

service area), there is often no other relationship between HSA consumer board members and the community they represent.[131]

The lack of organizational linkages between consumer representatives and their constituencies can be best understood by looking at how consumer representatives are selected. There are four basic modes available: (a) appointment, (b) self-selection, (c) election, and (d) organizational representation. Although each method has its advantages and disadvantages, it is worth noting, for our purposes, that appointment and self-selection are alike in that they tend not to create linkages between consumer representatives and their constituencies, whereas elections and organizational representation do.

ALTERNATIVE PROCEDURES FOR SELECTING CONSUMER REPRESENTATIVES

Appointment and Self-Selection. Although, analytically, appointment and self-selection are two distinct methods, in practice they tend to be found together. "Appointment" means that consumer representatives are chosen by some person or group of persons in authority. These may include elected officials (e.g., the governor), health agency bureaucrats (who rarely have the official authority to appoint representatives but often make or shape the choice of elected officials or others), hospital and clinic administrators (especially in the case of institutional level boards and committees), and, finally, consumer representatives already in office. (Critics refer to health systems agencies in which board members typically choose their own successors as self-perpetuating boards.) "Self-selection" means that would-be consumer representatives volunteer for the positions. Appointment and self-selection generally go together because, although some appointees are actively recruited (especially to satisfy minority and low-income quotas), most appointees are chosen from among those who put themselves forward as candidates.

A main drawback of appointment of consumer representatives by public officials is that it tends to assimilate these positions into the traditional system of political patronage. In the case of Samuel Hausman (discussed above), who used his appointment to a New York State Article 28 health planning and review body to lobby on behalf of an associate's business interests, there is little question that Hausman's personal campaign contributions and his fund-raising activities in the Jewish community on behalf of Governor Rockefeller were a major factor in his appointment (as a "representative of the Jewish community") to the Hospital Review and Planning Council. Where institutional consumer board representatives are appointed by administrators, staff, or trustees of the health facilities, there is, of course, the danger that consumer representatives will be chosen for their compliance or may be participants in name only. (*Heal Yourself* reported a number of instances in which institutions appointed consumer representatives who were not even aware of having been chosen.) In several cases the New York City Health Department initially rejected ambulatory service advisory committees under the Instudy Ghetto Medicine program as insufficiently representative of the community and suspiciously tokenistic.[132]

Elections.   A quite different mode of selecting consumer representatives is by holding at-large elections in which all adult citizens residing in a defined geographic area (e.g., a health planning region or a health services catchment area) may participate. In contrast to appointment and self-selection, the election process is designed, in principle, to create links between consumer representatives and their constituencies by providing a mechanism for the constituents to choose those who will participate on their behalf.

Electoral politics has, of course, traditionally been the legitimate mode of organizing citizen participation in the United States. In an electoral system, citizens participate directly as individuals. Each person expresses his values and exercises his modicum of power via the vote. An obvious advantage of elections is their ability to involve large aggregate masses of citizens in a decision-making process on a relatively egalitarian basis. Electoral politics, however, has its disadvantages. A main one is that, between elections, there are almost no regularly institutionalized mechanisms of communication between constituents and their elected representatives. What this means in practice is that electoral politics relies heavily on the media—television, radio, newspapers—to keep the citizenry informed about what actions their representatives are taking on their behalf. Where media coverage of politics is poor or highly routine, which not infrequently is the case on the state and local level, representatives become less and less accountable to the citizenry. Beyond this, electoral politics leaves it largely up to individual representatives and citizens to keep the lines of communication open. American political ideology exhorts citizens to write letters to their representatives and to the editors of the local newspaper and attend public meetings (when and if these are held) but offers few other mechanisms of participation for citizens, as individuals, between elections.

Prior to the 1960s there were few attempts to apply the electoral model outside its traditional province of national, state, and municipal representation to the particular social service areas. The major exception to this rule was in education where, typically, local school districts were governed separately by their own elected school boards. School boards can serve as a prototype of consumer dominance, since on matters of overall policy and allocation of funds lay school board members have the final say, over and above the professionals, that is, the school administrators and teachers.

Because of the wide acceptability and apparent high effectiveness of local school boards, many of the consumer participation efforts of the 1960s consciously or unconsciously imitated them. Applied to other service areas, however, the electoral model has been less successful.

The principal problem is the low rate of participation in elections for consumer board members. As one study by the Rand Corporation of a wide variety of consumer participation efforts noted, the turnout is often so low as to raise questions about the legitimacy of the consumer representatives.[133] Those seeking to design consumer participation mechanisms find these low participation rates especially frustrating because, on other criteria, elections are superior to either appointment or self-selection for choosing representatives. The Rand study, for example, found that less than half the appointed consumer boards versus 60% of elected and self-selected boards were successful in influencing the program in line with their views; only 30% of appointed and self-selected boards versus 81% of elected boards had a unifying impact on the community.[134]

Data from a Center for Policy Research study of consumer board elections in one New York City health catchment area underscore the problems that plague the electoral model when it is applied to local health care institutions. Although all of the relevant consumer advisory boards had been in existence for at least 2 years at the time of interviewing and had been advertised widely, only 21% of a statistically representative example of area residents knew of their existence. This was in an area 2 miles long and less than 1 mile wide.[135] Of the 616 respondents, 51 and 40, respectively, knew which hospitals and clinics in the area had boards or knew if there were people from the community on them. Twenty-two people said they knew someone who was a member of such a board, yet only 4 of these could tell us what board the person was on. Because of this, only 54 respondents attempted to say one way or the other whether they felt the board members represented their views and feelings.[136]

Of the 616 recipients, only 9 had voted in a board election (many of which were ostensibly communitywide), and only 8 could say which board they voted about. Although 10 had signed a petition to help someone get on a board, only 2 could say which board. Of the 7 recipients who had attended a meeting called by a board, 6 could say which one. Although 15 maintained that they had discussed problems relating to health care with a board member, only 2 could say on which board the member served.[137]

Channels of regular communication from board members to constituents and vice versa were virtually nonexistent. Only

12 of the 616 residents said they had ever received any letters, announcements, or other information from such boards (2 could say which one). Only 11 of 616 community residents interviewed thought that the boards were effective in representing community views.[138]

It is interesting to speculate on why the electoral model has been more successful at generating community involvement when applied to education than to health. (Although it is well to bear in mind that school board election turnouts, although higher, are still quite low compared to general elections.) Several hypotheses have been advanced. One stresses the differential salience of education and health to Americans generally. Traditionally, education has occupied a very special position in the American value system, being viewed as the ticket to equal opportunity and upward mobility for oneself or one's children. The Center for Policy Research study, cited above, asked a representative sample of residents of a New York City health services area to rank health in importance compared to three other issues. Health ranked last, after housing, education, and jobs.[139]

There are also a number of structural differences between education and health services and their governance that may affect salience and participation. It is worth noting in particular that education is frequently supported by an entirely separate financing system (e.g., the property tax) from other municipal services and that besides voting for school board representatives who control allocation of these monies, citizens often have an opportunity to vote directly or indirectly on the school tax itself or on school bond issues. Not only is the connection between level of taxes and the amount and quality of services so much more visible under these circumstances, but citizens have some direct power with respect to core issues of resource allocation since they may, for example, approve or disapprove school bond issues intended to make possible new school construction, higher teacher salaries, a new football stadium, and so on. Federal and state aid notwithstanding, most educational funds are still generated locally and most educational policy decisions are still made at the local level. The same is not true in the case of health care institutions.

Many of the dissatisfactions and problems consumers experience with their local health services are not local problems in the sense of being particular to their area, nor, more important, are they amenable to local solutions. The high cost of health care, specifically, the high cost of health insurance, which surveys suggest is among the most serious problems Americans perceive in the health system, is an example.[140] So is the problem of the shortage and maldistribution of physicians and other health personnel. Although local efforts—particularly in planning—may ameliorate *aspects* of these and other problems, the problems remain fundamentally systemic problems. Hence the principal point of leverage for dealing with them must be at the national level.

Organizational Representation. The fourth and final mode of consumer representation is via organizations. In the case of consumer representation on hospital boards, health planning bodies, and the like, organizational representation takes the form of allocating seats to consumer organizations, which in turn choose their individual delegates by election, self-selection, or appointment. It is important to note, however, that organizational representation, in contrast to the other forms of consumer representation discussed so far, transcends the specific mechanism of the consumer board. That is, in addition to representing consumers via these institutionalized bureaucratic channels, consumer organizations can serve many other mutual-benefit and political functions for their members and even, in many cases, for nonmember constituencies. For example, they may engage in consumer health education (e.g., by holding natural childbirth classes, organizing health fairs, or setting up consumer self-help hotlines or health information libraries). They may perform a watchdog role (for example, by visiting nursing homes, clinics, and hospital emergency rooms to check on conditions, hear grievances, and then bring these to the attention of responsible authorities). They may also engage in lobbying or other politicking on behalf of legislation in the consumer interest or more effective enforcement of existing proconsumer legislation. Finally, local consumer organizations can link together to form a network of state and national organizations to broaden the scope of activities just listed.

Organizational representation is geared to a definition or theory of democracy that stresses interest-group pluralism. Pluralist theory holds that there are in the political arena a large variety of groupings, in which citizens who have similar needs or vested interests or who support the same cause unite to press their demands on the government. Virtually any socially relevant shared attribute—for example, race, class, ethnicity, age, occupation—could constitute a basis for interest-group formation. In practice, however, interest groups vary greatly in their level of cohesion (i.e., consciousness of common interests) and mobilization (i.e., what percentage of the relevant category of persons they have succeeded in organizing), the amount of resources they have at their disposal (e.g., money to mount lobbying efforts), as well as the degree of persuasive power they have with their members (i.e. the ability to form a group consensus and exercise power via collective action).

It is for these reasons, obviously, that interest-group politics is highly inegalitarian: Some interests are well represented, others only poorly, still others not at all. Though such inequality is an extremely serious defect from the standpoint of democratic values, it is well to note that interest groups exhibit many positive attributes as well. For example, certain organized interests that may be seen as undemocratic from a societal perspective, because they so overpower those with opposing interests, may yet be highly democratic internally. The American Medical Association is an example. Although political organizations in general are often not internally democratic, both professional associations and public interest groups tend to be exceptions to Michel's iron law of oligarchy. This is especially true of the public interest groups, because participation itself, rather than economic advantages, is the main benefit they have to offer their members.

Moreover, unlike electoral participation, which is intermittent, organization allows interest groups to maintain continuity of effort and to gain access to resources that would normally be quite unavailable to individual participants (e.g., such as hiring medical, legal, financial, or other experts). Organized interest groups also provide for considerable freedom of choice and spontaneity in political participation. Interest groups are continually organizing, disbanding, growing or losing in strength, and redefining the issues they focus on according to those that are most salient to their membership and constituencies. The problem of apathy or low participation that plagues electoral politics is comparatively rare because organized interest groups draw political activists. Organizational participation also promotes a higher level of knowledgeability.

American political tradition, however, accords organized interest groups little ideological or institutional legitimacy. Although voluntary associations per se are an esteemed American tradition, politically active voluntary associations have typically been portrayed as subverting the civic textbook vision of democracy which stresses individual participation in electoral politics almost exclusively.

According to political scientist Grant McConnell,

> From time to time we have cherished the illusion that power need not exist, sometimes even that it is a myth. Parts of our political tradition seem to encourage these beliefs. They are dangerous, for they prevent understanding and contribute to the evils we would cure.[141]

The idea that organized political interests "ought not" to exist in a true democracy did not lead to their disappearance but rather to their power becoming, according to McConnell, the "open secret" of American politics. This, in turn, has led to our curious national pattern of recurrent exposé without meaningful reform.

In recent years, however, there has been a movement away from such institutionalized hypocrisy or naivete—however one chooses to see it. In other words, instead of denouncing the evil influence of lobbies and then allowing their activities to proceed unchecked, there has been a trend toward granting legitimate institutional expression to interest groups, while at the same time using these very processes of legitimation to distinguish between acceptable and unacceptable interest-group activities so as to channel them in what are considered socially desirable directions. Limitations on, and reporting of, campaign contributions is a case in point, as are "freedom of information" and "sunshine" laws which make it much more difficult for legislators and bureaucrats to leak information to favored interest groups while withholding it from others. This approach recognizes that where major interests are fairly equally represented, interest-group politics is highly democratic and, indeed, fills a participatory need not adequately met by electoral politics, in the sense that it provides for a high level of continuous, focused participation with respect to issues of special saliency to different parts of the citizenry.

The call for majority consumer representation on decision making and advisory boards within both public and private bureaucracies can be viewed as part of this trend. It is important to note here, as McConnell has pointed out, that "Boards and committees of 'representatives' of private groups, sometimes officially making policy and sometimes merely advising (another distinction often lost in practice) deal with matters at all levels of government. These practices are so widespread that the very idea of constitutionalism sometimes seems to be placed in question."[142] It is precisely the rising view, however, that it is not the existence per se of such boards and committees that is undemocratic, but the fact that their representation of interest groups has traditionally been so one-sided. According to this view, it is undesirable as well as unrealistic to try to abolish these and other channels for the expression of group values and flexing of group power vis-a-vis bureaucracy. Even if successful (which is doubtful), the only result would be to render bureau-cracy more insulated and less responsive, to reinforce the myth of a purely rational—that is apolitical—bureaucratic expertise, and, in general, to increase the power of government over and above the citizenry. Rather than seeking to eliminate interest-group power as evil, consumer participation theorists advocate an egalitarian redistribution of power, which, then, instead of being an open secret, will be officially recognized, institutional-ized, and controlled.

Hence the call for 51% to 60% consumer representation on health facility and health agency boards and committees. Although consumer participation theory has recognized the need for representation of consumers as an interest group, how-ever, it has tended to ignore the fact that group interests are typically represented in politics via organizations.

Some observers view this neglect of political organization as deliberate. According to William Morrow, contemporary politics is characterized by a "revolution seeking more direct participation by citizens in policy making." He states that,

> In contrast to the tendency for institutions to represent orga-nized interests, this resurgence of participatory democracy seeks direct citizen access to decision centers and involvement in deci-sion making regardless of any connections or affiliations that the participants might have with organized interests. In fact, the participation movement has stressed representation of unorgan-ized publics that have been given only casual concern in policy areas.[143]

Others stress the special difficulties involved in organizing health consumers (e.g., the intermittent rather than continuous contact most consumers have with the health system and conse-quent diffuseness of the consumer interest in health care) that tend to discourage organizational efforts.[144] Whatever the reasons, the consumer participation move-ment has, until recently, been markedly individualistic in its approach to consumer representation. That is, it has been considered enough that consumer representatives be individuals who are themselves consumers ("consumers" being defined as including all persons who have no financial stake in providing health services). Similarly, it has been thought that the special needs and concerns of black, women, low-income, and the like consumers would be best represented by including among consumer representatives appropriate numbers of individuals with these class and status attributes. Thus the legislation setting up the health systems agencies requires consumer representatives to be broadly representative of the consumer population. Although this legislative interest has not yet been translated into specific, enforceable regulations, most consumer activists believe it to mean that the racial, ethnic, gender, and class attributes of individuals serving as consumer representatives should reflect proportionately the demographic mix in the geographical area covered by the planning agency.

Sometimes consumer representatives are also affiliated with organizations such as labor unions, welfare rights organizations, local civic groups, and so on. (Official or semiofficial organizational representation appears to be more common in the case of planning boards.) More often, however, consumer representatives serve in an entirely individual capacity. In contrast, as the Consumer Commission on Accreditation of Health Services notes,

> Providers are organized in powerful associations, societies, affiliations, etc., on local, state, regional and national levels. As a political force and as a technical arm of providers, these associations concentrate the effectiveness of their representatives on boards and commissions which determine and implement health policies, standards, programs, and finances.[145]

Indeed, several years ago it was revealed by an informant in the AMA's Chicago headquarters that the organization had instituted rather elaborate procedures (e.g., hiring a management consulting firm to design a computer program) to ensure that only physicians with the "right" (i.e., AMA-sanctioned) attitudes would be appointed to the hundreds of bureaucratic decision-making and advisory panels nationwide.

As a memo from the consulting firm observed, the referral system was considered important because the advisory panels "not only influence the development of federal health policies and program regulations, but they also influence the distribution of health grants, funds which affect the investment in various health trends, programs, etc. It is, therefore, vital that the views of the AMA be represented in the executive branches' deliberations on health policy."[146]

Not all provider representatives serve as official or unofficial representatives of provider organizations. It is important to note, however, that almost all health professionals—physicians especially—belong to one or more professional associations. Because of this high degree of organizational mobilization and the well-developed channels of communication within the medical and other health professions, provider representatives will likely be acquainted with how their colleagues feel about particular issues as well as the official positions of the various organizations. Provider representatives also know that if they take maverick positions on issues, they will probably hear about it from their colleagues.

Consumer representatives, in contrast, operate in a vacuum. They seldom have any way of knowing in advance whether the positions they plan to take on issues are representative of consumer opinion generally, nor do they often receive much feedback on the positions they take from their consumer constituents. The end result is that most provider representatives are supported by the collective voice and collective power resources (expertise, funds, personnel, etc.) of one or more organized interest groups, ready to come to the aid of the representative, provided he does indeed "represent" the group position. Again, as the Consumer Commission on the Accreditation of Health Services study points out:

Provider representatives of well-organized institutional or professional associations have access to most source information; technical staff to accumulate and analyze data; and professional staff to shape policy and program proposals. There are existing mechanisms for them to poll and/or educate their constituencies on proposals under consideration; they have the financial resources to hire planners and any other experts required to further their interests. When a provider representative suggests a course of action, comments or votes on a proposal, it is in the language of the specialists and supported by quantified data; the probable outcomes have been considered, reconsidered, analyzed, dissected, and projected by multiple experts each working for the goals of providers.[147]

Behind most consumer representatives there is either no organizational backup or a much weaker one. As a result, consumer representatives must rely for influence much more heavily on sheer force of personality since they have no other power base; although, here again, provider representatives may be just as likely to have forceful personalities. It is little wonder, then, that providers so often dominate decision making and advisory boards even when the proportional mix gives consumers numerical superiority.

The Rand study, cited earlier, of 51 cases of consumer participation, found that, provided they had staff to supply continuity and cohesion, the most effective consumer boards were the so-called umbrella organizations whose members were delegates elected by a variety of constituent organizations. Effectiveness was measured both in terms of program impact and in terms of unifying various groups in the community.[148] In addition, a comparison study of community participation efforts in Chicago, Philadelphia, and New York by Paul Peterson suggested that given the low rate of community participation in general elections, the best way to establish that consumer representatives do in fact speak on behalf of some larger consumer base is to hold elections for representatives within constituent organizations or among delegates or organizations.[149]

A different approach, recommended by the Consumer Commission on the Accreditation of Health Services, calls for the establishment of an integrated national, state, and local consumer health network:

> Through a series of contracts, network affiliates corresponding to each local and state health planning agency would be established. Consumer groups meeting established criteria would be eligible to become fully affiliated with the network. Individuals, organizations, and institutions wishing to support the network could become members by making a contribution or by paying established member fees. Regional offices of the central corporate body would be developed to provide expert assistance to affiliates and to foster consumer awareness and organizing.[150]

Under this model, consumer representatives on health planning bodies would not be the official delegates of the consumer network affiliate organizations, but they could turn to the network for technical information and assistance, consumer education, and political mobilization.

CONCLUSION

Heal Yourself, the report of the Citizens' Board of Inquiry into Health Services for Americans, is an example of advocacy research growing out of a social movement. As such, the Citizens' Board report was a political manifesto, intended to express and argue passionately for a particular set of values and their policy implications and to arouse individual citizens to voluntary political activism in their behalf.

The report called for fundamental reform of the American health care system in the direction of greater equality of access to health care, with special emphasis on the elimination of socioeconomic barriers to care. It further urged a reordering of societal value priorities as these are reflected in the health system. Instead of a health system shaped primarily to serve the

economic self-interest, desire for autonomy, and other professional and institutional interests of health "providers" (including not only physicians but hospitals and health insurance
plans), the restructured health system envisioned by the Citizens' Board of Inquiry would be responsive to the needs and
preferences of health care consumers. These needs and preferences were assumed to include availability of high-quality comprehensive care at affordable costs; ready access to routine and
preventive services as well as crisis care; and dignified, personal-
ized, nonalienating interactions between patients and medical
personnel.

According to the Citizens' Board, the principal lever for
bringing about such a transformation was consumer power, in
the form of consumer participation in policy decision making
at every level of the health system—local, regional, and national. Special emphasis was accorded, however, to the exercise
of consumer power in bureaucratic settings, both within private
health bureaucracies, such as a local voluntary hospital and
government agencies administering various types of health programs. Indeed, the Citizens' Board of Inquiry report strongly
urged that provider dominance of health facility and program
decision making be replaced by consumer control.

Implicit in the Citizens' Board of Inquiry recommendation
for consumer control was a challenge to the hegemony of expert
authority and to the claim that authority based on expertise is
objective, disinterested, and value neutral. Indeed, advocacy of
consumer control is predicated on the notion that there is a kind
of underlying class conflict between the interests of health care
providers and consumers, which has been obscured by the providers' claim that their decision making is derived from knowledge, not self-interest. The centrality of certain intellectual
assumptions derived from conflict theory—in particular, the
assumption that when providers and consumers participate in
health care decision making, they will do so on the basis of
conflicting interests associated with their different positions in
the health social structure is somewhat ironic in view of the
liberal Establishment composition of the Citizens' Board itself,

especially the fact that roughly one-third of the Citizens' Board of Inquiry members were physicians (albeit mostly medical school professors).

More important, however, consumer participation in health system decision making cannot be expected to bring about the kind of transformation of the entire American health system anticipated by the Citizens' Board of Inquiry unless the theoretically posited opposing interests of health care providers and consumers are actually manifested in the opinions, attitudes, and beliefs of the real flesh and blood people who participate in decision making. This is true whether consumer representatives are merely advisory or exercise real governing power. If, for example, most American health care consumers do not perceive a need for government intervention designed to eliminate all socioeconomic inequalities in availability of and access to health services, then they can scarcely be expected to promote such a goal once accorded the opportunity to participate in health policymaking.

Indeed, analysis of available data on the attitudes of health care consumers and providers (including the attitudes of consumers who are in fact exercising some measure of decision-making power or influence on health facilities and programs through participation on consumer boards and committees) indicates that value conflicts among different categories or types of consumers and providers are often greater than those between consumers and providers, taken as a whole. Moreover, the opinions and preferences that consumers and particular subgroups of consumers (especially those with low incomes) express are often not in line with what, according to the Citizens' Board, is in the consumer interest.

This does not necessarily mean that the Citizens' Board was "wrong" in its definition of the consumer interest. To assume this would be to assume that the attitudes and opinions of the average health care consumer are knowledgeable and well thought out, based on exposure to arguments pro and con, followed by a reasoned choice. This is unlikely to be the case.

Rather, the lack of congruence between the consumer interest, as defined by the Citizens' Board of Inquiry and the findings of attitude surveys suggests that it is important for advocacy researchers to distinguish carefully between the concept of conflicting interests as a heuristic device and the theoretical assumption that such a concept accurately describes empirical reality. As a heuristic device, the idea that "consumers" in general share certain common attributes and experiences that logically or morally should give them reason to favor a health system restructured in a certain way whereas "providers" in general have reason to favor maintenance of the status quo is a useful tool for consumer advocates seeking to educate, inspire, and mobilize for purposes of political activism persons defined as belonging to the "target" constituency of health consumers. This is quite different from making the intellectual assumption that persons characterized, analytically, as occupying a particular position in the social structure will by virtue of their common attributes and experience naturally evolve a shared perspective on various issues and, if placed in a decision-making role, will automatically act on behalf of such group interests. Although common attitudes *may* tend to develop naturally among the members of a class or status group, such intragroup consensus is likely to be considerably weaker than that achieved via processes of deliberate consensus building. Thus the degree of congruence between the group interest as an inspirational ideal and the empirically measurable level of agreement among members of the group on both general principles and specific issues is a function of the ideal's intrinsic responsiveness to group concerns and also to the ability of advocates of the ideal to make a persuasive case.

The Citizens' Board defined the "consumer interest" in much the same way that sociological conflict theory has traditionally defined any group interest—as a set of perceived needs and preferences that persons occupying a given position in the social structure will more or less spontaneously come to identify and act upon as "theirs." We are suggesting, however, that, especially from the standpoint of those who seek to effect deliberate social change, it is both more accurate and more fruitful to look on the consumer interest as a "malleable variable." That is, the consumer interest, to the degree that it has an empirical existence, is the outcome of a process of successful political mobilization and indeed has been shaped in its content by that process.

This latter perspective requires, however, that considerable attention be given to the "rational" variables, knowledge and organization, in so far as these can provide mechanisms for generating consensus among health consumers at large and for ensuring that consumer representatives will be aware of and responsive to the needs and preferences of their constituencies when exercising decision-making power on their behalf.

We have seen, however, that in challenging the hegemony of professional expertise, the Citizens' Board of Inquiry quietly downplayed the need for consumer knowledgeability. Thus virtually no attention was given in their recommendations to the issues of consumer education in the broad sense or to ways of meeting the various knowledge needs of consumer representatives serving in decision-making roles. Similarly, the Citizens' Board report neglected to specify either the organizational processes and mechanisms that could most effectively serve to implement or operationalize consumer power in a bureaucratic setting or the forms of political organization that could build cohesion among consumers and create linkages of communication and accountability between consumer representatives and their constituencies.

The failure of the Citizens' Board of Inquiry report to give sufficient attention to knowledge and organizational factors gives the *Heal Yourself* recommendations an appearance of pure rhetoric. Failure to give sufficient attention to these factors in practice hinders existing consumer participation mechanisms from fulfilling their potential as instruments of substantive social change.

Chapter 6

A THEORETICAL BASE FOR SOCIAL POLICY RESEARCH AND POLICYMAKING

ALTERNATIVE CONCEPTS OF THE MAIN LEVERS FOR CHANGE

In the preceding chapters we have analyzed four health policy studies and their recommendations for bringing about deliberate social change in the health care system. A main theme of the analysis has been that alternative approaches to social regulation flow in large measure from alternative concepts or theoretical assumptions concerning the social factors that can most effectively serve as levers for deliberate social change.

Some approaches, for example, stress the need for more and better knowledge about the problem or problems regulation seeks to correct as well as feedback or evaluation about the effectiveness of corrective efforts. Among the four case studies analyzed in this book, the Medicaid Task Force report and recommendations exemplify such a strategy of relying on knowledge as the main lever for deliberate social change. The Task Force recommendations called for the development and

implementation of a nationwide integrated Medicaid management information system to collect, analyze, and evaluate data
on the program's performance with respect to such goals as cost
control and cost efficiency, necessary and appropriate utilization of medical services, and accessibility of services to those
who need them.

Other strategies for social regulation give primary attention to the importance of designing appropriate organizational
structures to implement change. Of our four cases, this is the
principal thrust of Interstudy's "health maintenance strategy,"
which proposed to reorganize the American health services
delivery system in such a way as to create self-regulating market
mechanisms (i.e. health maintenance organizations") that, besides promoting more competition in the health services industry would also introduce elements of modern corporate
bureaucratic rationality into a historically overfragmented and
underorganized field of endeavor.

Still other approaches to social regulation focus on the
significance of societal consensus, that is, agreement on values.
Two main tools available for expressing, institutionalizing, and
influencing consensus are the law and mass communications.
Because the law embodies prevailing value preferences and priorities and codifies these in terms of rules to guide behavior, the
shaping of law provides a major opportunity to employ consensus as a lever for deliberate change. Mobilization and channel-
ing of public opinion via the communications media is another.
The case study of the New York State Moreland Act Commission's strategy for nursing home reform exemplifies reliance on
both these methods of employing consensus as a lever for
change.

Finally, some approaches to social regulation focus on
power as the principal lever for deliberate social change, calling
for realignments in "vertical," that is, government vis a vis
society, or "horizontal," that is, intrasocietal group power relations, or both. Frequently such strategies portray conflict between classes or interest groups as the motor for social change;

hence deliberate social change is seen as entailing deliberate efforts to sharpen such conflict and bring it to a head. *Heal Yourself,* the report of the Citizens' Board of Inquiry into Health Services for Americans, is a case in point. The analysis stresses the opposing group interests of health care "providers" (e.g., doctors, hospitals, health insurers, etc.) and "consumers" (e.g., patients and the public at large). According to the Citizens' Board of Inquiry the American health care system as it presently exists reflects the power of health care providers to shape the system to serve their interests. Making the system more responsive to the needs and preferences of patients is seen as requiring a redistribution of decision-making power to give consumers the dominant role in policymaking at every level of the health system: facility, service system, city, state, region, and nation.

Alternative approaches to social regulation may also imply alternative concepts of decision-making strategy; specifically, whether deliberate social change is best effected via incremental modifications versus more fundamental criticism and reform of the status quo. Among our four case studies, the Medicaid Task Force and Moreland Act Commission recommendations illustrate an incremental approach to decision making because the changes proposed are remedial and differ only in a few respects, that is, "incrementally," from existing policy. In contrast, the Interstudy "health maintenance strategy" and the recommendations of the Citizens' Board of Inquiry into Health Services for Americans exemplify proposals for fundamental reform in that they challenge not just existing policy but its basic premises. In the case of the Interstudy health maintenance strategy, the principal challenge is to the professional's traditional autonomy where medical practice is organized according to a solo-practice, fee-for-service system. In the case of the Citizens' Board of Inquiry report the principal challenge is to health care providers' claims to a virtual monopoly on decision-making authority in the health system based on professional expertise as well as to their claim that professional expertise is wholly objective, disinterested, and value neutral.

The Societal Guidance Approach

In seeking via the four case studies to analyze and explicate the differing concepts of deliberate social change underlying alternative strategies for social regulation, our aim has been to illustrate a central thesis concerning the theoretical knowledge base required for effective regulation. Derived from Amitai Etzioni's theory of societal guidance, this thesis is that strategies for social regulation will tend to be more effective in achieving their goals (and result in fewer of what Robert Merton terms "unanticipated consequences of purposive social action") to the extent that they take into account the interdependence of five sets of social factors: knowledge, organization, power, consensus, and decision making. It is true that depending on the nature of the problem social regulation seeks to correct and the goals it seeks to accomplish, one or two of these factors or variables may appear to provide more leverage for change than the others and may hence play the primary role in shaping the basic character of the intervention. It is our contention, however, that the interrelationship of the five "societal guidance variables" is such that a regulatory strategy must take into account the need for compatible readings on the other variables if the main intervention is to work as intended and expected.

At this point it is essential to note that the requirement for compatible readings on the five main variables does not necessarily mean that there is one and only one right answer or right approach to social regulation in any given case. There may well be a number of workable combinations. Conversely, if the malleability of one or more of the five factors is highly limited (as is often the case), the range of combinations will also be limited and indeed there may be no fully satisfactory combination, only a lesser of evils solution. (A typical example might involve the nonmalleability of power. If a politically powerful minority is adamantly opposed to a regulatory policy, supporters of the policy must activate a constituency or coalition of constituencies with sufficient countervailing power, or else tailor their proposals to what the veto group will accept. A concrete case in point is gun control. Although favored by a majority of Americans, its supporters have as yet not been able to mobilize the kind of organized lobbying strength its opponents can easily mount.)

An analogy between regulatory and architectural design can perhaps further illustrate what we mean by the need to achieve appropriate readings on several variables without there being one and only one right approach. Just as a regulatory policy must be designed with both rational and political considerations in mind, so an architectural plan must meet two roughly analogous criteria: It must be structurally sound and it must satisfy the needs and preferences of the client–users. In principle, a number of building designs might meet both criteria. In any given instance, however, the architect needs to take into account and ensure proper interrelationship among several main factors, including engineering requirements, aesthetics, physical habitability (i.e., meeting the biological needs of human beings for heat, light, water, sanitation, etc.), and the social purposes for which the building will be used. Failure to take any of these factors sufficiently into account can have negative results ranging from the inconvenient to the disastrous. Obviously, a failure to take engineering principles adequately into account is likely to produce defects that will make the building unsafe. There is also a growing recognition of the unintended consequences that can result from failure to consider social factors. For example a public housing project may be functional and aesthetically pleasing when first built, but rapidly deteriorate because its design inhibits the development of the community and thus encourages crime and vandalism.

As important as taking each factor separately into account, however, is creating a design that appropriately relates the various factors to one another. Thus if a client insists for, say aesthetic reasons on a particular material that has serious structural limitations, the architect must somehow reconcile aesthetics and engineering, perhaps via an innovative design that overcomes the previous limitations or by persuading the client that another material would be safer and equally beautiful. Again, the architect's degrees of freedom may be restricted by the limited malleability of one or more factors; for example, if climate or cost and availability of materials pose particular engineering problems and constraints.

To return now to the design of regulatory strategies, it is worth noting that of the five social factors whose importance and interdependence we have said it is essential to take into account, none is new in the sense that its causal significance has not been known or appreciated. Historically, however, different analytic disciplines or professions have tended, for a variety of reasons, to focus on certain factors and give little or no attention to others. Concerning regulations of health care, for example, as we pointed out in the first chapter, the medical profession has traditionally stressed the importance of knowledge, specifically, the professional expertise possessed only by doctors. The idea that only practicing physicians had the knowledge required to design and carry out social regulation of health care was widely accepted both intellectually (e.g., among sociologists of medicine, such as Talcott Parsons) and in practice (virtually all regulation of health care prior to the mid-1960s was via peer review, either purely voluntary or under government auspices.)

Beyond this, however, the various disciplines and professions that nourish policy research make differing assumptions about which social factors are more effective levers for change and how one can gain a handle on them. Persons trained in business or public administration, law, economics, sociology, or political science, and so on, will tend to carry these assumptions with them when they move from the traditional concerns of their discipline or profession into policy research or policymaking. Thus administrative science tends to focus on those factors we have characterized as the "rational" variables—knowledge and, especially, organization. A policy researcher with a business or public administration background is likely to approach deliberate social change first and foremost from the perspective of the organizational structures and processes that will implement and manage the proposed changes. Similarly, persons with administrative training and experience will tend to make more "voluntaristic" assumptions concerning the degree to which change can be deliberately created and controlled, and thus will give more explicit attention and emphasis to decision making and to forms of decision making that stress planning.

Lawyers, quite naturally, tend to focus on the role of law in effecting deliberate social change and to be more attuned to political concerns—specifically, the societal attitudes and values as well as the relationships of power and authority that the law reflects and embodies. Because of the relationship of law to history and cultural tradition, lawyers may also be more likely to view decision making and change from a perspective that emphasizes gradual evolution which is partly deliberate and partly proceeds spontaneously according to its own inherent logic.

Economists, in turn, tend to approach deliberate social change as a problem of how to create and maintain the economic incentives and disincentives to motivate change, and they are likely to focus on organizational structures (e.g., markets) primarily as instruments that can serve to institutionalize such economic motivation.

In contrast, the sociologist's world view is one that pays greater attention to motivations other than economic (e.g., power, prestige, altruism) and that sees society more in terms of organic groups (e.g., communities, social classes, ethnic groups, etc.). In particular, sociologists who are deeply concerned with deliberate social change and identify themselves as social activists as well as scientists and intellectuals often tend to see conflict or struggles for power among social groups as the main levers for change. They are also likely to perceive or at least to look for possibilities for revolutionary as well as evolutionary change.

Each of these different disciplinary and professional perspectives has validity. Indeed it is precisely our contention that to establish an intellectual foundation sufficient to approach social regulation and social policy scientifically requires an interdisciplinary synthesis. This book's emphasis on the interdependence of knowledge, organization, power, consensus, and decision making as levers for deliberate social change represents an attempt to propose such a synthesis and argue its merits.

To show, however, that all five factors need to be taken into account in analyzing and recommending strategies for deliberate social change, it is necessary to demonstrate that if a particular factor is given little attention or if its role and interaction with the other factors are misunderstood, the results and the effectiveness of social action guided by the analysis and recommendations will not be as expected. This was the main theme of the case studies.

THE CONCEPTUAL ROOTS OF UNANTICIPATED CONSEQUENCES

Neglecting the Political Variables, Power and Value Consensus

Each of the four policy studies was chosen because, analytically, it illustrates an intellectual approach that identified a particular combination of guidance variables and readings on those variables as providing the leverage for deliberate social change, while neglecting or downplaying the role of the other factors. Thus the McNerney Task Force proposed to gain control over the spiraling costs of medical care for the poor under Medicaid—to eliminate both inefficiency and waste in the program and the inappropriate utilization of Medicaid financed services—primarily via manipulation of knowledge variables. The idea was that a more knowledgeable, hence more efficiently and effectively run program would result from the introduction of a computerized, integrated (the same system for every state) management information system. The Interstudy health maintenance strategy stressed organization as the principal lever for reform of the American health care delivery system. The Interstudy team proposed that instead of layering ever more government regulation onto the existing system of health care delivery, the federal government act to spur the growth of a new organizational form, the "health maintenance organization". Through economic incentives and disincentives built into the organizational design, the health maintenance organization was expected to function as a self-regulating market mechanism. In addition, other organizational features, most especially the principle of "vertical integration," were intended to bring the corporate rationality of the modern American business sector to bear on the medical marketplace as well. Although the McNerney Commission recommendations contained a secondary emphasis on organization (i.e., internal reorganization of the federal Medicaid bureaucracy to better align managerial structures and functions) and the Interstudy team's proposals gave similar secondary consideration to knowledge (i.e., recommending quality assurance of medical services provided in health maintenance organizations via outcome measures of a patient's health), both the Medicaid Task Force report and the Interstudy health maintenance strategy accorded little attention to showing how either societal values or power relations might affect the implementation of their reform proposals. It is for this reason that we characterized these two studies as "rationalistic" in their theoretical assumptions concerning deliberate social change.

What unanticipated consequences resulted from the relative inattention these two studies gave to power and consensus?

In the case of the McNerney Task Force inattention to political variables meant that the Task Force did not foresee and hence did not develop any strategy for overcoming state resistance to adopting the integrated Medicaid management information system, which the Task Force recommended and which HEW developed. The McNermey Task Force did not anticipate politically motivated resistance on the part of the states to implementing the Medicaid management information system because they assumed, rationalistically, that so long as the federal government bore most of the financial burden of developing, setting up, and running the management information systems, states would welcome the greater bureaucratic knowledgeability, efficiency, and long-run increases in cost effectiveness the MMIS would provide. What the Task Force left out of account was consideration of how the MMIS would affect power relations between the federal government and the states, between the states and localities (in states such as New York, where the counties retained a substantial role in both Medicaid management and financing) and between government agencies and medical care providers. The Medicaid management information system threatened the autonomy of state Medicaid programs vis-a-vis the federal government (and the autonomy of the counties in relation to New York State) because by regularly and routinely generating certain types of management information the federal agency would gain a much greater capacity to supervise both the overall managerial efficiency and effectiveness of the the state Medicaid programs as well as state compliance with various federal regulations. States would no longer be as able to hide poor performance through lack of availability of data measuring performance. By the same token the MMIS also threatened to alter the prevailing power relations between state Medicaid agencies and Medicaid providers. By giving state officials a technical capacity to regulate medical care providers, which they previously lacked, the management information system would either force state officials to take a tougher regulatory stance toward powerful vested interests or it would render much more visible the "political" sources of lax regulation and poor Medicaid management.

In the case of the Interstudy health maintenance strategy, problems stemming from insufficient attention to the interaction of organizational and consensus variables led to unanticipated consequences in terms of the viability of the Health Maintenance Organization's Assistance Act of 1973. The irony of the HMO Assistance Act is that those features (undercapitalization and overregulation) that impeded its ability effectively to promote the growth of health maintenance organizations resulted from the inability of two camps of "HMO" *supporters* to reach a consensus. Ostensibly the value conflict was over an organizational issue: Should the development of health maintenance organizations conform to a free market model or should they receive extensive government subsidy and regulation? The question of whether or not the market is a more efficient and effective mode of organization than government regulation is, however, one that cannot be answered on purely technical grounds; it is inherently normative. That is, organizational forms can only be judged more or less efficient or effective relative to some set of values. From the perspective of deliberate social change, alternative modes of organization are most appropriately viewed as alternative means of implementing societal goals, these goals in turn being defined in terms of values widely shared by the citizenry. Some organizational forms are better suited to implementing particular goals and values than others. As a result the choice of which organizational form to adopt implicitly involves a choice among societal values.

Thus in the case of HMO development, the debate over whether to opt for a market versus regulatory approach reflected a more fundamental conflict between, on the one hand, the goals of greater cost control for the middle classes who purchase private insurance and shoulder most of the costs of government programs as well as higher profits and more favorable business conditions for health maintenance organizations, and, on the other hand, the goal of promoting greater equality of access to high-quality comprehensive health care for all citizens, including the poor. Although some analysts might well argue that treating a conflict of interest between social classes or between providers and certain categories of would be consumers as if it were simply a question of choosing the more efficient mode of organization fulfills the social function of keeping a lid on potentially explosive intergroup tensions, it can also be said that this deflection of attention away from the deeper issues also prevented effective conflict resolution. Since neither the conservative nor the liberal HMO supporters wielded sufficient political power to achieve passage of the HMO legislation and shape it entirely to their preferences, they needed to confront the underlying conflict and reach an acceptable trade-off between the conservatives' concern for cost control and the liberals' concern for social justice. Although both liberal and conservative HMO proponents can be faulted for their persistent refusal to grant legitimacy to each others' values, it also seems apparent that the Interstudy researchers further muddied the waters by advocating their preferred mode of organization, that is, the "market" not simply as the most effective means of curbing medical costs but as an end to be valued in and of itself. Moreover, rather than respond to the concerns of liberal HMO supporters that a market approach would tend to exclude low-income persons from obtaining health care through health maintenance organizations, the Interstudy researchers characterized the proponents of government regulation as "prejudiced" against the market and favoring regulation for regulation's sake. Had the Interstudy researchers been more sensitive to the underlying conflict over the relative political priority to be given to cost control (best served by a private market system) versus social justice (best served by government regulation), they might conceivably have been able to formulate a government–market mix that would be far more workable than the crippling compromises that were instead written into the 1973 Health Maintenance Organization Assistance Act.

The Interstudy team also left out of account another dimension of interaction between organizational and consensus variables that has important implications for the vulnerability of government programs to financial fraud and abuse. We have seen that Interstudy's health maintenance strategy revolved around the notion of a contract between health care providers and consumers. Both parties were to be rationally motivated to live up to the terms of the contract by virtue of economic incentives built into the basic organizational design of the HMO concept. Philosophically, the underlying premises were those of 19th-century utilitarianism. As such, the Interstudy proposal failed to incorporate one of the central insights of modern sociological theory, credited to Emile Durkheim. It is that the parties to a purely economic contract can be expected to feel themselves bound to adhere to the terms of the contract only if there is a prior moral commitment to shared values.

The reason such a prior normative commitment is essential is that it is virtually impossible to design a contractual arrangement in which the maximization of economic self-interest and adherence to the terms of the contract are at all times compatible. In other words, it is frequently more economically rewarding to cheat on a contract than to live up to its terms, especially where violations of the contract are difficult, time consuming, and expensive to detect and prove. Under such circumstances the most effective check against violation of the contract is not fear of economic loss or other punishment but the inculcation of a sense of moral responsibility for the negative consequences to others that will result from one's not living up to one's contractual obligations. In health care the main means of creating such a sense of moral responsibility in physicians and other health providers has been through socialization to professional ethics. To the extent that the professional service ethic is internalized the professional will feel sufficient personal pride in applying his expertise and talents to alleviate suffering that he will subordinate economic self-interest to the client's health needs whenever the two threaten to conflict.

This is not to say one should simply assume that all health professionals have internalized and feel a strong moral commitment to such a professional service ethic. Actual practicing professionals can and do vary greatly in their degree of allegiance to such norms and the values they represent. It is worth noting, however, that many of the health maintenance organizations that later proved riddled with fraud and abuse were structured in such a way as to give the controlling power to business entrepreneurs and to limit both the freedom of action and personal responsibility of the medical professionals they hired to work for them. By not taking these factors into account and incorporating mechanisms to screen out providers deficient in service-oriented ethics, HMO advocates failed to anticipate the potential for profiteering and corruption that subsequently manifested itself in the health maintenance organizations sponsored under California's Medicaid program.

Neglecting the Rational Variables Knowledge and Organization

Thus far we have focused on examples of unexpected problems in implementation and undesired side effects of deliberate social change that are attributable to overly "rationalistic" assumptions on the theory that served to guide the reform efforts. Theories or models of deliberate social change that stress what we have termed the "political" variables, "power" and "consensus," although according little attention to the rational instrumentalities of knowledge and organization produce different but no less problematic unanticipated consequences when they are used as guides to action. One such unintended consequence, illustrated by the results of the New York State Moreland Act Commission on Nursing Homes and Related Facilities, is the substitution of symbolic reassurance for substantive reform.

To understand what is meant by "symbolic reassurance" it is useful to think of televised hearings, press conferences, and the other highly publicized reform theatrics that the Moreland

Commission—in keeping with most other investigating commissions—engaged in as the modern political equivalent of a primitive tribal ritual in which the forces of evil (read "political corruption," "special interests," etc.) are symbolically defeated by the shaman, who is allied with the forces of good (e.g., the investigating commission as representing the moral force of a democratic "People"). In primitive societies such rituals or ceremonies often serve to provide tension release or emotional catharsis for individuals and communities at the mercy of powerful natural forces (e.g., sickness, weather) of which they have little understanding or control. The reassuring sense of control and of ultimate justice the spectators gain from viewing the performance of the ritual is a kind of collective coping mechanism for handling high levels of uncertainty and unpredictability. Our purpose in comparing the highly publicized "reform theatrics" of an investigating commission to a primitive tribal ritual is not to make fun of either. Although ritual has somewhat less relative importance in modern societies, the tension release it provides is still much needed. The criminal justice system, for example, will probably always serve to fill such a need, at least in part, especially since it is difficult to imagine the total elimination of crime even in the best of societies. The problem arises when ritual and the symbolic reassurance it provides become a substitute for and indeed blocks perception of both the need and possibilities for more effective control over the sources of a problem.

Most sociologists and political scientists who analyze this consequence of symbolic politics tend to focus on the social function it is said to fulfill in maintaining and reinforcing the societal status quo (i.e., the periodic "sacrifice" of one or two nursing home profiteers may actually serve to protect most other such fast-buck operators to the extent that the public demand for justice is deflected away from structural change and focused mainly on blaming and punishing a few guilty parties). Our main concern, however, is in understanding why reformers with no apparent Machiavellian motives fail to achieve their intended goals; why, in fact, they may offer reform proposals that are inappropriate to achieving their avowed aims.

It is our contention that whatever other factors are at work, a reform effort in which symbolic reassurance both takes the place of and obscures the absence of lasting structural change is the logical outgrowth of a model of deliberate social change that places excessive emphasis on the role of consensus (e.g., the arousal of outraged public opinion) and on the moral or normative dimension of power (e.g., legal authority, legal rights) while neglecting the role of the other social levers, most especially the role of organization in providing ongoing expression for those values identified with the public interest.

Thus we have seen that the Moreland Commission focused its reform efforts on mobilizing outraged public opinion via televised hearings and on obtaining new or revised laws strengthening and clarifying the legal rights of nursing home patients and the legal authority of the state to impose penalties on fraudulent and abusive nursing home operators.

Ironically, however, the Moreland Commission's own reports repeatedly observed that financial fraud and abuse as well as poor quality care in nursing homes had become widespread in large measure because the administrative agencies charged with enforcing nursing home regulations had long been unwilling to act on the legal authority they already possessed. The Moreland Commission also knew that the reluctance of state officials to enforce the law by imposing sanctions on noncompliant nursing homes reflected in large measure the power of nursing home owners and operators as a vested interest group. This power was manifested in two main ways. First, it was manifested in political influence on and through politicians, such as state legislators and their aides, members of the governor's staff, and political party officials. Thus in addition to providing campaign contributions and other election support, major figures in the nursing homes scandals were found to have had professional and business ties with politicians that included hiring members of the legislature or their aides who were lawyers to represent them in administrative hearings before state regulatory agencies. Second, the power of the nursing home industry was expressed via court action. For example, in two major class action suits, each of which lasted several years— *Maxwell* and *Hayden Manor*—noncompliant nursing homes had showed themselves both willing and financially able to band together to block enforcement of nursing home fire safety standards via round after round of judicial appeal.

The Moreland Commission's strategy reflected its members apparent belief that only the greater power of outraged public opinion could induce the state health department to tighten its enforcement of nursing home standards. To evoke the moral indignation of the citizenry the commission held public hearings at which leading political figures were accused of shirking their duties, if not outright participation in corrupt practices. In addition, television reporters were invited to follow the commission chairman into nursing homes for a firsthand inspection of conditions. The commission expected that the public opinion mobilized in this way would force the legislature to pass the Moreland Commission's reform bills. The enactment of these new laws in turn would serve to symbolize to administrative officials a new era of public demand for tougher regulatory enforcement.

Instead, however, passage of the Moreland legislation had almost the opposite effect: It served to give the public a false sense that the new laws in and of themselves would be sufficient to prevent future nursing home abuses. What the Moreland Commission had failed to take into account was the ephemeral nature of media mobilized public opinion. Just as, according to Max Weber, "charisma" cannot be sustained indefinitely and must eventually be "routinized" or forfeit any lasting impact, so the moral force of mass public opinion roused by a crisis or scandal will be rapidly dissipated unless ongoing institutionalized expression can be found for some portion of it via political organization.

Historically, of course, many groups have organized to fight for their rights—the labor union and civil rights movements being successful cases in point. Nursing home residents are for the most part too old, too sick, too poor, and too greatly at the mercy of nursing home operators and staff to serve as a likely base for organization in their own behalf. If they were well and independent enough to organize, they probably would not need to be institutionalized. In this respect, nursing home residents are typical of the clientele, especially the institutionalized clientele, of human services organizations in general (other such groups including young children, mental patients, the retarded, and prisoners) who must depend for protection, on the one hand, on the professional ethics of those who provide services and, on the other hand, on the watchdog function of organized public interest groups (from the Children's Defense League, to the American Civil Liberties Union, to the Center for Law and Social Policy, and the various organizations sponsored by "Nader's Raiders.") To ensure that financial abuse, mistreatment of patients, and poor quality care do not reappear in nursing homes once the spotlight of public attention, temporarily focused by media exposé, has faded or shifted to some new area, it is essential to identify and organize social groups (such as senior citizens, ethnic and religious groups, civic associations, etc,) which together can create a "public interest lobby" on behalf of nursing home patients.

Finally, the recommendations of the Citizens' Board of Inquiry into Health Services for Americans concerning consumer participation in health policymaking illustrate the necessity of taking into account the interaction of knowledge with power, especially in an area such as health, in which access to expert knowledge is essential to exercise power. Where lay consumers or citizens are accorded power in the form of authority to participate directly in the decision making of government or private bureaucracies but lack the knowledge required to make full use of such authority, participation becomes pro forma and inauthentic. As with exposés of corruption that leave the systemic sources of corruption untouched and reform legislation that is enacted but not enforced, the creation of new modes of democratic participation that turn out to be inauthentic will first lead to an unrealistic sense of progress, and then to an equally false sense that meaningful reform is impossible, that the "system" will not allow it.

As we noted in Chapter One, Talcott Parsons and others have pointed out that the knowledge gap between laymen and medical professionals makes it difficult for the individual patient to evaluate the quality of care he or she is receiving in any given instance. Although we would qualify this somewhat by observing that the patient can decrease his or her dependence on the professionals' expertise and good will by becoming an informed medical consumer, the individual patient can scarcely expect to eradicate the inequality that is inherent in the doctor-patient relationship by virtue of the professional's training. As we see it, however, the Citizen's Board of Inquiry was correct in perceiving that this same relationship does not hold true between consumers and providers at the policy level. That is, the knowledge barrier to effective consumer or citizen participation in health policymaking is not as Parsons and many others would have it the individual physician's possession of professional medical knowledge and the corresponding lack of such knowledge by the individual consumer. Indeed, on the policy level, the physician's professional training in the diagnosis and treatment of illness is often of little direct relevance, although physicians may use the authority accorded them on the basis of such expertise to intimidate consumers (and, for that matter, other nonmedically trained health professionals and government officials as well). For example, a physician trained as a heart specialist does not automatically possess all or even most of the knowledge needed to determine whether or not a given hospital or community needs a new cardiac care unit. Indeed, to a considerable extent, the cardiologist's specialized training and expertise constitutes a bias, a set of blinders that tends to restrict his or her ability to consider the issue in a broadér context of competing community health needs. Much of the knowledge required for health policymaking is thus "macro" or "systems-level" knowledge concerning problems of availability, cost, and quality of resources and services required to meet the health needs of various populations.

If consumers' lack of professional medical training is not therefore the handicap to participation in health policymaking it has often been portrayed to be, neither is it sufficient to appeal to the traditional American faith in the common sense of the common man. In particular, it is important to recognize the limits as well as the value of "knowing where the shoe pinches", that is, personal, subjective experience. Personal experience is inevitably limited in scope, and, to the degree that an individual's existence is highly routinized, will tend to result in a knowledge of the world that is rather static and rigid. Certain kinds of factual data, moreover, simply cannot be known via personal experience alone. Macro or system knowledge (e.g., the five most common health problems of people living in Harlem; the major preventable causes of prenatal mortality, etc.) can only be known impressionistically, and hence with questionable reliability, via personal experience and observation alone. By the same token it follows that an individual who can be characterized by some social attribute (e.g., income, ethnicity, religion, etc.) cannot be assumed automatically, by virtue of the similar or shared personal experiences attributed to members of that group, to know most of what policymakers need to know about the health needs of this larger group. In this respect, health policymaking—despite the significant shaping influence of personal and social values as well as knowledge—is different from those policy issues, such as civil rights, that are primarily moral issues. In dealing with these kinds of issues there is a sense in which one individual's personal experiences, observations, or empathy (i.e., identification with the personal experience of others) with, say, racial injustice, are sufficient to understand the phenomenon in general.

It is important to recognize as well that even as it affects the formation of value positions and preferences, knowledge based solely on personal experience can be narrow and limiting. We saw in Chapter Five, for example, that many poor and minority health consumers express conservative value preferences that most consumer advocates believe are contrary to their true interests. Examination of the reasons for this tends to suggest that the conservative value preferences of the poor, the less educated, and minorities are often based on familiarity not ideology. If as the evidence often indicates, the conservative values of the poor on health policy issues are, in large measure, related to their limited personal experience and limited availability of knowledge beyond personal experience, then it follows that knowledge can be an important lever for deliberate social change—a factor that, far from simply reflecting class and other structurally based values, actually plays a role in shaping or overcoming them.

For all these reasons, individual consumer participants need to be better informed and educated with regard to health issues; and, in some instances, they may also require specialized training, say in aspects of public health, health law, planning, and so on, in order to participate in particular policymaking roles. It is also worth noting, however, that much of the knowledge they need is knowledge that is collected, processed, and stored by various organizational units. Indeed, it is often only organizations that possess the resources (money, personnel, computers, authority to obtain confidential data, etc.) to produce such knowledge. Thus in order to participate effectively in health policymaking, consumers need both access to the systemic knowledge generated by government agencies and professional review bodies, (such as professional standard review organizations), and they need to develop their own organizational intelligence capabilities—for example, from staff and expert consultants on call, to consumer boards or consumer organizations (or both), to consumer-oriented advocacy research.

The Decision-Making Dimension

One final guidance variable remains to be discussed. This is the decision-making or, alternatively, the goal-setting dimension in policy research and policymaking. We have kept our discussion of decision making separate from that of the other four variables, despite the high degree of interdependence that exists between decision strategy and the readings that policy researchers and policymakers seek to obtain in the other variables. The reason for this is that it is impossible for policymakers to ignore or greatly downplay the role of decision strategy in the same sense that they can the role of one of the other guidance variables, whether knowledge, organization, power, or value consensus. Although it is quite possible and indeed quite common for sociologists to study social change as if little or no conscious decision making or purposeful action were involved, it is inherent in the very nature of policy research and policymaking that choices are made and particular policies deliberately pursued. In other words, a sociologist, for example, may well wish to study the transformation of Western European societies from feudalism to capitalism without reference to decision making, since it is safe to assume that the societies in question evolved in this direction rather than chose it deliberately. In studying, however, the development of a government's or organization's policies and programs in respect to some perceived social problem, one cannot make the same assumptions. Implicit in the study of social policymaking and social regulation is the notion of one or more decision-maker–actors at large —be these government agencies, private corporations, individual officials, political lobbies or, perhaps, the active citizenry. The presumption of a decision-maker–actor or set of decision-maker–actors is especially strong when the aim of policy research is not simply to explain the origins of an existing policy but to predict and evaluate likely consequences and make action recommendations that some decision-maker–actor will hopefully take under consideration and implement.

The underlying philosophical question is, hence, the balance of "voluntarism" versus "determinism" in social and political life. That is, to what extent are social processes to be viewed as largely "ongoing" with relatively few and minor opportunities available for deliberate intervention, or, at the opposite extreme, to what extent do we assume that the social world can be molded to our preferences if we will only make a commitment to the effort required? Policy researchers and policymakers, by definition, assume some role for voluntarism or deliberate choice. As we shall see, however, they may differ considerably in how much weight they accord to such elements of conscious control in the processes of societal continuity and change.

The central criterion in our characterization of the four policy studies and their reform recommendations on the decision-making dimension has been: How "critical" were they of existing policies and the assumptions underlying those policies? We have thus characterized reform proposals on a continuum ranging from ones that differ only incrementally from existing policies to those that fundamentally critique not only existing policies but their basic underlying assumptions. An example of a highly incremental reform was the internal reorganization of the Medical Services Administration proposed by the Medicaid Task Force. Its aim was to increase the efficiency and effectiveness of Medicaid program management by creating a more rational alignment of formal organizational structures with managerial functions inside the federal Medicaid agency. At the opposite end of the continuum, the Citizens' Board of Inquiry challenged a number of fundamental premises on which our prevailing system of health services delivery and decision making is founded—most notably, the taken-for-granted primacy of professional over political authority in health policymaking and the legitimacy of unequal access to health care based on such nonneed-related criteria as wealth and social status.

The choice between comparatively incremental or fundamental reform strategies can be thought of as a two-step procedure, involving, first, a diagnosis concerning the amount and
character of change required and, second, a prognosis concerning the amount of change deliberate efforts to bring about
change can realistically be expected to accomplish. Obviously
the judgment as to the amount and kind of change needed is one
based on a mixture of empirical and normative criteria. Thus
whether or not one agrees with the findings of the Citizens'
Board of Inquiry report that "The United States has failed to
provide adequate health services to the vast majority of its
citizens" (*Heal Yourself,* p. 127) depends, in part, on an assessment of the factual evidence concerning how many Americans
are being deprived of what services with what kinds of negative
health impact, and also, in part, on how much weight one gives
to equality of access to health care as a basic criterion of a just
society, hence a value in and of itself.

It is interesting to note that in all four of the policy studies
reviewed the diagnosis seemed to point toward a need for fundamental reform. As such, the decision to opt for an incremental or fundamental reform strategy seems to have been based
mainly on the prognosis for change. Evaluating the prognosis
for deliberate social change, in turn, requires taking into account the differential malleability of the factors implicated in
change efforts. Some variables are more easily manipulated and
more precisely controlled than others. In general, however, an
incrementalist strategy assumes and requires much less malleability than fundamental reform approaches.

In the case of the Moreland Commission, for example,
there appears to have been a deeply pessimistic sense that the
main dynamics responsible for the nursing home scandals were
beyond the commission's or the legislature's decisionmaking
reach. Thus the commission saw the roots of poor quality care
and profiteering as traceable to historically evolved societal
attitudes stigmatizing old age, illness, and dependency. Since
the commission felt that it could do relatively little to reverse

such widespread and entrenched attitudes, this led naturally to the commission's own judgment that the same types of scandals would surely be repeated and that another round of public exposure and investigation would be required in 5 to 10 years.

In the case of the Medicaid Task Force, however, the researchers' perceptions of the constraints operating to limit the possibilities for more fundamental reform were much more pragmatic and short term and mainly centered around questions of proper timing with respect to the policy "decision points" that could be expected to occur in the near future, the relationship of health to welfare and other government programs, and the belief that decisions about these should be viewed from a systems perspective. Thus the members of the Medicaid Task Force believed that major overhauls would and should not be made in Medicaid or other government health programs until Congress decided whether or not to make major reforms in the welfare system (e.g., guaranteed income) which would allow efforts to increase access by the poor to medical care to be divorced from welfare and given a whole new thrust aimed more at improving the health of the poor than at providing them with a health specific income supplement. The Medicaid Task Force was also convinced that fundamental reforms in government health programs for the poor would be best considered in the context of national health insurance for all, which, like many others, they mistakenly believed to be just around the corner.

The limits in their decision-making options perceived by the Medicaid Task Force point up the important fact that deliberate social change, especially fundamental change, is costly. In purely financial terms the resources invested in an existing policy can, in the short term, never be totally recovered and reinvested in the new policy. (For example, a policy of closing hospitals in areas that are overbedded will almost certainly result in a conspicuous waste of expensive facilities that cannot readily be adapted for other purposes, even if such a policy cuts

costs in the longer run by reducing the overutilization of services.) The costs of change are not just economic, however.
There are also major psychic and social costs, as occur, for
example, when a change in policy creates, eliminates, or radically changes the character of large numbers of jobs. Thus even
if a society such as ours could definitively solve the problem of
resource scarcity, it could not tolerate lack of structure and
rootlessness that would result if every problematic situation and
every flawed social policy were totally and equally subject at
any given moment to fundamental criticism and reform. This
is one main reason why, typically, a considerable amount of
inefficiency, ineffectiveness, and dissatisfaction must build up,
before the costs of major change begin to appear lower than
those of a continuation of the status quo, and fundamental
reform approaches are given serious consideration. One such
constraint operating on the Medicaid Task Force recommendations was the fact that the political battle surrounding the enactment of Medicare and Medicaid had been a long and exhausting
one, and the program was still too new (4 years when the Task
Force was appointed) to open up to deep critical examination
those arrangements still so recently and so exhaustively negotiated.

The feasibility of deliberate social change cannot, however,
be viewed solely in either such pragmatic political terms or as
a problem of social engineering, that is, as a matter of whether
or not decision makers know how to get a handle on the main
variables and have the managerial capabilities to coordinate the
systems effects of change. Because deliberate social change
deals with people rather than with inanimate objects, it is essential to consider the moral dimension—in particular, to take into
account the needs and preferences of those individuals and
groups whose interests will be affected. Thus a particular strategic intervention might well be rejected no matter how effective
it would appear to be from the perspective of goal attainment,
either because it conflicts seriously with overarching values or

because the anticipated level of political resistance and the coercive power needed to counter resistance to it are considered too high.

For a democracy, the most problemmatic feature of deliberate social change may well be determining at what point the moral as well as the social costs of purposive action or nonaction become too high in terms of other values that are thereby neglected or violated, the alienation and resentment generated in some individuals or among some social groups, and the degree of coercive power that must be authorized to overcome the opposition and resistance of the disaffected. American political values have traditionally prescribed a low-tolerance level (even as compared to other democracies); hence, change imposed over and above the opposition of some individuals or groups is rather quickly perceived as tyrannical and illegitimate. It is an integral part of American political ideology to perceive this low tolerance for governmental action in the face of strong resistance as a safeguard existing mainly for the protection of the lone individual versus the state or of the poor and otherwise disadvantaged segments of the citizenry. Our analysis points out, however, that the maintenance of such a normative or moral aversion to utilizing and strengthening government power as a lever for social change does not always have such benevolent results. It is clear, for example, that the New York State Moreland Act Commission on Nursing Homes and Related Facilities adopted a highly incrementalist approach toward increasing the authority of the state to impose penalties on nursing homes that failed to comply with regulatory standards because the commission feared possible abuse of administrative discretion that would result in violation of nursing home owners' property rights. Critics maintain, however, that to protect the right to due process of nursing home owners faced with a cutoff of Medicaid funds or revocation of their operating licenses to the extent deemed necessary by the Moreland Commission unavoidably results in giving property rights precedence over patients' rights under the law.

If the main flaw in incrementalist strategies is an inherent conservatism, inconducive to basic societal innovations, its proponents would argue a compensating strength is that gradual, cautious modifications do not overload our societal capacity to guide the processes of change and accurately target their effects. Thus for theoretician advocates of incrementalism such as Charles Lindblom, fundamental reform is both unattainable and undesirable because it is synonymous with the impossibly demanding requirements of comprehensive planning. Eminently rationalistic, comprehensive planning is said to entail a careful and complete study of all possible courses of action and all their possible consequences, with the choice among alternatives being made on the basis of an evaluation of those consequences in the light of one's values. Comprehensive planning is also typically thought to involve an extremely detailed, step-by-step plan of implementation. Critics point out, however, that both of these requirements place impossibly high demands on the decision makers' capabilities for knowledge collection and processing—that is, their limited ability to foresee all possible consequences and to obtain the information required to evaluate them in the light of all relevant values.

Ironically, it can be argued that for this very reason comprehensive planning fits more readily into an incrementalist decision-making strategy than it does into the grand designs of those advocating fundamental reforms. That is, it is easier to survey a wide range of incremental changes in policy and to forecast accurately their likely effects. Empirically, it is possible to point to examples of comprehensive planning being used to coordinate and systemmatize a large number of incremental modifications in an existing course of action. A case in point is provided by the Medicaid Task Force, which rejected a fundamental reform proposal to disengage the administration of Medicaid from the administration of welfare and reorient the program away from income supplement toward a more direct focus on improving the health status of the poor. In its place the Task Force substituted a highly specific blueprint for reorganization of the federal Medicaid agency, aimed at making it more efficient within a larger context of "givens" which left the basic shape and thrust of the Medicaid program unchanged.

Our analysis thus leads us to question the equation some researchers make between incrementalism and decentralized decision making (either via what Lindblom calls "partisan mutual adjustment" or via the more impersonal mechanism of the economic market), on the one hand, and between fundamental decision making and comprehensive planning, on the other hand. Although in some other countries extensive planning is employed to try to achieve fundamental change (e.g., the transformation from an agrarian to an industrial economy), we would argue that comprehensive, rational planning is not, outside the context of military defense in the space race, a characteristically American approach to fundamental decision making.

In particular, neither of our two examples of fundamental reform proposals—the Interstudy health maintenance strategy and the report of the Citizen's Board of Inquiry into Health Services for Americans—exhibits the kind of concern for detailed prescription associated with the comprehensive planning model.

Thus the Interstudy health maintenance strategy's recommendations for specific governmental actions that could be taken to promote HMO development did not constitute a comprehensive plan, but rather a set of guidelines. There is a clear-cut goal—to make an "HMO" alternative to fee-for-service solo practice available to every American—but the recommendations do not exhaustively list all the steps it would take to attain that goal. The recommendations simply outline some broad policies intended to remove major obstacles to health maintenance organizations and to foster economic, social, and political conditions in which HMO development can gather momentum and continue on its own. In other words, the Interstudy approach implicitly rejects notions of total control and fine tuning of deliberate social change that are intrinsic to a comprehensive planning model. Regulatory policy is assumed to work most effectively when it seeks simply to encourage, to reshape, or to guide naturally evolving processes of societal change in desired directions. Moreover, the specific governmental actions recommended by Interstudy focus first and foremost on those spheres of action in which government has the greatest freedom to intervene and to initiate. Thus the main emphases are on removing laws hindering HMO growth and on promoting HMO development in the context of existing government programs such as Medicare and Medicaid. Insofar as the Interstudy health maintenance strategy shows great sensitivity toward the differential malleability of different aspects of the social world, as well as the need to relate deliberate, purposive change efforts to ongoing evolutionary societal processes, it can serve as an example of the decision-making strategy Amitai Etzioni terms "mixed scanning." According to this approach, which Etzioni advocates as more realistic and manageable than comprehensive planning, recommendations for fundamental reform are mainly context setting. In effect, the mixed scanning approach actually represents a synthesis—or perhaps "symbiosis" is a better term here—between incrementalism and fundamental reform since the two approaches alternate: Fundamental decision making sets goals and basic directions whereas incremental decision making both prepares for the next fundamental decision and works out the details of the last.

In marked contrast, the recommendations of the Citizen's Board of Inquiry set forth in *Heal Yourself* provide an example of a fundamental reform strategy that involves neither a comprehensive, rational planning approach nor guidelines for action, but rather the elaboration of a vision of a better society, a kind of "reachable" utopia which then serves as a rallying point for a social movement or perhaps as the platform of a political party or candidate. Although the vision of the "post reform" society, or, in this instance, health system, is portrayed in considerable detail—at least in terms of the kinds of values it would embody or give priority to—it represents the opposite of the planning approach in the sense that the concrete course of action that is to be taken to achieve the fundamental reform goals is left highly vague. Instead of being rigidly confined to a plan, decision makers are left with considerable room for flexibility and improvisation in seeking to attain overall goals. Analysis of the Citizen's Board report suggests, however, that the negative side of such a strong emphasis on goal attainment can be a crippling perfectionism. This is because the consequences of each and every concrete course of action are judged almost solely in terms of success as measured by the yardstick of the ultimate goals, rather than in terms of comparative performance relative to other available courses of action.

A great strength of such a visionary, goal-oriented approach to fundamental reform is its capacity to inspire moral commitment and in so doing to mobilize large numbers of people to overcome otherwise serious divisions to work toward collective aims. Its main weakness is that it tends to raise expectations with respect to the amount, pace, and controllability of deliberate societal change that cannot realistically be met. Moreover, the end result of repeated frustration in meeting these high expectations may be not just widespread disappointment but a corrosive cynicism.

Another problem that arises from the goal-orientation characteristic of fundamental decision making is the need to confront and deal with value conflicts and value trade-offs. Unlike incrementalist strategies that seek merely to move away from known social ills and hence make much lower demands on consensus, fundamental reforms seek to define optimum states. Proponents typically stress the need for clear goals. The difficulty is that the more clearly and explicitly policy goals are defined, the more obvious it becomes that alternative goals have been rejected. Insofar as different groups in society tend to champion or give differential support to alternative policy goals, and some groups have greater power to enforce their preferences than others, the process of defining clear goals makes latent group conflicts manifest and tends to underscore the inequality of the contestants.

Ideally, application of a comprehensive planning model would call for evaluating all the consequences of all available alternatives in the light of all relevant values to arrive at an approach that is optional in some overall sense. Yet even if such a procedure did not overburden current capacities for knowledgeable social forecasting, it begs the question that there is no purely intellectual formula for deciding how much of one value to trade-off for gains on another, since what is required is to build consensus—or at least a winning coalition from conflicting group interests and values while still ensuring a rational adjustment of means and ends. The task is a highly demanding one, politically as well as intellectually.

It is interesting to note that in neither of our two examples of fundamental reform proposals did the researchers attempt such an overall optimization of conflicting societal values. Rather both reform strategies were designed to further one set of value priorities—those of the researchers—above all others. In the case of the Interstudy health maintenance strategy the overriding concerns were economic. The Interstudy researchers presented their proposals as if the goal of cost-effectiveness in health care, in terms they defined it, were objectively self-evident. As such the Interstudy researchers refused to acknowledge the inevitably normative and political character of goal setting. Opponents of their approach were dealt with not as persons with conflicting values whose needed support and cooperation could not be gained without some accommodation to their concerns, but as people who, for some unaccountable reason, kept coming up with the wrong answer to a simple math problem no matter how many times it was explained to them. Yet the Interstudy proposal was deeply political insofar as the criteria of cost-effectiveness proposed were ones that tended to trade-off equality of access to the same health services by all Americans in order to maximize both the economic utility of the average middle-class American (as a taxpayer and as a consumer of health services) and the economic utility of health maintenance organizations.

In contrast, the report of the Citizen's Board of Inquiry into Health Services for Americans, in championing equality as the preeminent goal of fundamental health services reform, made no such effort to deny the political character of goal setting. Quite the opposite. The Citizen's Board actively embraced the notion of value conflict based on underlying group conflict. Rather than strive for reconciliation of the conflict, however, they chose to ally themselves with one side, that is, health care consumers as opposed to health care providers. If the Interstudy researchers greatly underestimated the extent of political support for equality as a value that ought to be exemplified in government initiatives such as HMO development, the Citizen's Board fell into the opposite fallacy of overestimating the priority the average health care consumer gives to equality and the degree to which consumer participation in decision making can be expected to bring about an egalitarian transformation of the American health system.

By now it must be apparent that both the incrementalist and fundamental approaches to decision-making strategy are viewed here as having major strengths and weaknesses. Often these strengths and weaknesses are complimentary. Thus incrementalism is more sensitive to the weight of history and to the constraints on change imposed by social system interchanges—in brief, to the various factors that inhibit freedom of choice in shaping society according to our individual or collective wills. Although this sensitivity to the factors that block or deflect deliberate change efforts tends to give incrementalism a conservative cast, it is also important to note that over the longer run it is extremely difficult to overcome or circumvent the kinds of constraints incrementalists are so well aware of, until their reality and strength have been acknowledged and taken into account.

Conversely, fundamental reform strategies are more sensitive to the possibilities for bringing about dramatic breaks with tradition, for transformational or revolutionary change. To perceive possibilities for fundamental decision making is also to reject an "overdetermined" view of societal processes in which human beings are reduced to passive objects that do not choose or act but simply react to the unfolding of history or the mechanical working out of laws of evolutionary social change.

Because the strengths and weaknesses of the incrementalist and fundamental reform approaches to decision making are often complimentary, it might seem well advised for policy researchers and policymakers to adopt an approach that represents some sort of synthesis. One possible synthesis is the "mixed scanning" strategy outlined earlier, in which incremental and fundamental decision-making alternate—that is, incremental decisions prepare the way for or elaborate on the fundamental decisions that set basic directions. Strictly speaking, however, at any given point in time those who seek to shape social regulation to achieve deliberate social change must choose either a relatively incremental or fundamental reform strategy. The reason for the forced choice is that fundamental reforms challenge the very assumptions that incremental strategies accept as unchangeable givens. We have suggested two main criteria for choosing between comparatively incremental versus fundamental reform strategies. These are first, the diagnosis of the problem; in particular, the character and amount of deliberate change deemed necessary to correct the problem and, second, the prognosis for change—that is, the differential malleability of the main social factors that constitute the levers by which deliberate social change is effected. Rather than favoring one single approach, either a relatively incremental or fundamental decision strategy, on general principles, we would thus argue that the question of which is appropriate is a matter for case-by-case assessment, an assessment, moreover, that is virtually always going to be subject to differences in judgment and interpretation.

CONCLUSION

The overall aim of this book has been to indicate where the levers are for guided social change. I have outlined the five main factors—knowledge, organization, power, consensus, and decision-making strategy of a theory of deliberate social change, Amitai Etzioni's "theory of societal guidance"—and endeavored to show, via analysis of four reform proposals, that failure on the part of policy researchers to pay adequate attention to a particular factor or to major interaction effects among factors can help explain not only why attempts to implement policy recommendations do not work out as expected but the particular form that unintended consequences are likely to take. Although we have used as our illustrative examples efforts to reform various aspects of American health care, we believe that this theoretical framework can be fruitfully applied to any substantive area in which policy research aims to arrive at recommendations for deliberate social change.

NOTES

Chapter 1

1. See Amitai Etzioni, *The Active Society* (New York: Free Press, 1968); and Amitai Etzioni, *Social Problems* (Englewood Cliffs, N.J.: Prentice-Hall, 1976).
2. Robert K. Merton, "The Unanticipated Consequences of Purposive Social Action," *American Sociological Review,* 1936, 1, 894–904.
3. Amitai Etzioni, *The Active Society,* pp. 3–14, pp. 60–83.
4. Amitai Etzioni, "Policy Research," *The American Sociologist* (Supplementary Issue), June 1971, 6, 8–12, p. 11.
5. Charles Lindblom, *The Intelligence of Democracy* (New York: Free Press, 1965).
6. Thomas Kuhn, *The Structure of Scientific Revolutions* (Chicago: University of Chicago Press, 1970).
7. See Talcott Parson's "Research with Human Subjects and the Professional Complex," *Daedalus,* 98(2), 330; and also *The Social System* (New York: Free Press, 1951).
8. Eliot Freidson, *Professional Dominance* (Chicago: Aldine, 1970), pp. 235–236.
9. See, for example, Robert R. Alford, *Health Care Politics, Ideological and Interest Group Barriers to Reform* (Chicago and London: University of

Chicago Press, 1975); and Howard B. Waitzken and Barbara Waterman, *The Exploitation of Illness in Capitalist Society* (Indianapolis and New York: Bobbs-Merrill, 1974).

10. Daniel Bell, *The Coming of Post Industrial Society* (New York: Free Press, 1973).
11. The first two figures are from *Health: United States 1975,* U.S. Department of Health, Education and Welfare, Public Health Service, Health Resources Administration, p. 9. The most recent statistic is from Barbara J. Culliton, "Health Care Economics: The High Cost of Getting Well," *Science,* May 26, 1978, 200(4344), 883.
12. Task Force on Medicaid and Related Programs, *Final Report,* U.S. Department of Health, Education and Welfare, 1970.
13. Paul M. Ellwood, Jr., Nancy N. Anderson, James E. Billings, Rick J. Carlson, Earl J. Hoagberg, and Walter McClure, *Medical Care,* May/June 1971, 9(3), 291–298.
14. Paul M. Ellwood, Jr., Patrick O'Donoghue, Walter McClure, Robert Holling, Rick J. Carlson, and Earl Hoagberg, *Assuring the Quality of Health Care* (Minneapolis: Interstudy, 1973).
15. The Moreland Commission's main findings as well as its draft legislation are presented in Report of the New York State Moreland Act Commission, *Long Term Care Regulation: Past Lapses, Future Prospects, A Summary Report,* April 1976.
16. The most accessible version and the one this analysis employed is the second edition, *Report of the Citizens' Board of Inquiry into Health Services for Americans, Heal Yourself* (Washington, D.C.: American Public Health Association, 1972).

CHAPTER 2

1. Karl W. Deutsch, *The Nerves of Government: Models of Political Communication and Control* (New York: Free Press, 1966), p. 77.
2. Ibid.
3. Ibid., p. 80.
4. See Amitai Etzioni, *Modern Organizations* (Englewood Cliffs, N.J.: Prentice-Hall, 1964), Ch. 3; and William L. Morrow, *Public Administration: Politics and the Political System* (New York: Random House, 1975), Ch. 2.
5. "A Report on the Health of the Nation's Health Care System," mimeograph (Papers of the Task Force on Medicaid, Departmental Archives, HEW, July 10, 1969).

6. The staff of the Senate Finance Committee reported: "In January 1967, the President's budget predicted that 48 states would have Medicaid programs in operation by July 1, 1968, and that total payments would be $2.25 billion in fiscal 1968. By January 1968, midway through the fiscal year, only 37 states had Medicaid programs in operation, but the vendor payment cost estimate for fiscal year 1968 had risen to $3.41 billion. Actual expenditures, with 37 states having Medicaid programs, were $3.54 billion." U.S. Senate Committee on Finance Staff Report, *Medicare and Medicaid: Problems, Issues and Alternatives*, 91st Congress, 1st Session (Feb. 9, 1970), p. 42.

7. Senator Leverett Saltonstall (Republican, Mass. represented this view when he said: "There was little discussion of Title 19 which certainly has proved to be the 'sleeper' in the bill. I am certain no one dreamed that within the next five years, 'Medicaid,' as the program established by that title is called, could come to dwarf Medicare." Remarks of Senator Saltonstall, Congressional Record CXII, 20267 (Aug. 22, 1966).

8. For a detailed statistical analysis of the factors that went into the rapid growth in Medicaid costs between 1967 and 1972, see John Holahan, *Financing Care for the Poor, an Urban Institute Study* (Lexington, Mass.: Heath, 1975). Holahan concluded, "Costs of a program of subsidized care for the poor need not escalate at rates approaching those under the current Medicaid program. The Medicaid experience has largely been due to the growth of public assistance generally, and not merely the predictable outcome of subsidization. The most important reason for increases in Medicaid over time has been the increases in the number of people eligible. During the 1967–1972 period new states continually entered the program and public assistance eligibility criteria were greatly liberalized. The result was an increase in the number of persons receiving public assistance and thereby becoming eligible for Medicaid." p. 111.

9. Much the same could be said about services cutbacks. During roughly the same period, Congress deferred, then repealed, the "comprehensive care" goal; it voted to transfer financing of "intermediate care" nursing homes from welfare to Medicaid, thereby adding a new, expensive category of services.

10. *Medicaid: State Programs After Two Years* (New York: Tax Foundation, Inc., 1968).

11. The commission, made up of 26 representatives from state and federal government, included Spiro Agnew (then Governor of Maryland), Ramsey Clark (then U.S. Attorney General), Senator Edmund Muskie (Democrat, Maine), (then Governor) Nelson Rockefeller (New York), and Jesse Unruh (speaker of the California Assembly). Their report,

published in Washington in September 1968, was entitled *Intergovern-mental Problems in Medicaid.*

12. U.S. Department of Health, Education and Welfare, *Report of the State Federal Task Force on the Costs of Medical Assistance and Public Assistance* (Washington, D.C.: 1968).

13. U.S. Congress, Senate, Staff of Senate Committee on Finance, *Staff Data Relating to Medicaid-Medicare Study,* Committee Print, Committee on Finance, 91st Congress, 1st Session, 1969.

14. *Summary of Medicaid State Audits by HEW Audit Agency* (HEW Audit Agency, Office of the Secretary, HEW, Aug. 26, 1969) in *Medicare and Medicaid Problems, Issues, Alternatives* (Senate Finance Committee Staff Report), p. 204.

15. Robert Stevens and Rosemary Stevens, *Welfare Medicine in America: A Case Study of Medicaid* (New York: Free Press, 1974), p. 217.

16. Stevens and Stevens, *Welfare Medicine in America,* p. 218.

17. *Task Force on Medicaid and Related Programs Interim Report,* Nov. 12, 1969, p. 9.

18. See Etzioni, *The Active Society,* Ch. 6–7.

19. Harold Wilensky, *Organizational Intelligence, Knowledge and Policy in Government and Industry* (New York: Basic Books, 1967), viii.

20. Etzioni, *The Active Society,* p. 136.

21. *Task Force on Medicaid and Related Programs Final Report,* 1970, pp. 121–122.

22. Ibid., pp. 43–46.

23. Ibid., p. 216.

24. Ibid., p. 219.

25. Ibid., p. 213.

26. Ibid., p. 214.

27. Ibid., p. 120.

28. Ibid., p. 62.

29. This recommendation was only in the *Task Force Interim Report.* See Stevens and Stevens, p. 221, p. 240.

30. *Task Force Final Report,* pp. 62–63.

31. Note that revenue sharing constitutes a still different structural arrangement, under which the federal government gives states and municipalities block grants with no strings attached.

32. These disadvantages are well set forth by James Madison in the *Federalist* No. 10. For a general discussion of federal, state, and local government in the context of modern efforts to solve social problems, see Etzioni, *Social Problems,* pp. 112–114.

33. For a perceptive discussion of the advantages and disadvantage of federalism, see Grant McConnell, *Private Power and American Democracy* (New York: Knopf, 1966, especially Ch. 4.

34. See Grant McConnell, *Private Power and American Democracy* (New York: Knopf, 1966).
35. Existing federal regulations center around process indicators. For example, states are required to perform "utilization review." This means only that they must be able to document via administrative record keeping that certain review procedures were carried out. They are not required to document that *any* financial savings resulted or that *any* medically unnecessary or inappropriate procedures were thereby eliminated.
36. *Task Force on Medicaid and Related Programs Final Report,* 1970, p. 68.
37. For a general discussion see Amitai Etzioni, *Social Problems* (Englewood Cliffs, N.J.: Prentice-Hall, 1976), pp. 108–109. For a full-scale evaluation study see H. W. Ray, *Final Report of the OEO Experiment in Educational Performance Contracting* (Columbus, Ohio: Battelle Memorial Institute, Mar. 1972).
38. And they did, too. Robert and Rosemary Stevens' *Welfare Medicine in America* provides considerable detailed documentation concerning differences among state programs. Some states took a liberal expansionist approach to Medicaid (e.g., New York, California), others a conservative, restrictive one (e.g., North Carolina). Moreover, although some states chose to administer their own programs, others contracted with Blue Cross or for-profit insurance companies to serve as fiscal intermediaries and allowed them considerable autonomy.
39. Louise B. Russell, et al., *Federal Health Spending, 1969–1974,* (Washington, D.C.: For Health Policy Studies, National Planning Association) p. 109.
40. Comptroller General of the United States, Report to the Congress, *Social Research and Development of Limited Use to National Policymakers* (April 4, 1977), p. 14.
41. Etzioni, *The Active Society,* p. 141.
42. See MSA *Forward Plan,* pp. 161–162.
43. *Task Force on Medicaid and Related Programs Final Report,* 1970, p. 66.
44. Ibid., p. 67.
45. Ibid., p. 119.
46. Personal communication.
47. "Summary of Medicaid State Audits by HEW. Audit Agency," Aug. 26, 1969, Appendix C. Senate Finance Committee Staff. Report, *Medicare and Medicaid Problems, Issues and Alternatives,* p. 237.
48. Ibid., p. 242.
49. Ibid., p. 238.
50. *Task Force on Medicaid and Related Programs Final Report,* 1970, p. 64.

51. *Medicaid 1977–1981, Major Program Issues* (Washington, D.C.: HEW, SRS, MSA, July 1975), p. 56.
52. Ibid.
53. Ibid., p. 35.
54. U.S. Department of Health Education and Welfare; Social Rehabilitation Service; Medical Services Administration, *Mars Operational Techniques; April 1973* (Washington, D.C.: National Technical Information Service), p. 2.
55. Medical Services Administration, *MMIS Development* (Washington, D.C.: April 22, 1976).
56. Office of Technology Assessment, U.S. Congress, "Computer Technology in Medical Education and Assessment" (Washington, D.C.: Government Printing Office, September 1979, p. 41.
57. New York State Temporary Commission to Revise the Social Services Law, Senator William T. Smith III, Chairman, *The Administration of Medicaid in New York State,* Interim Study Report No. 6 (Albany, N.Y.: Feb. 1975), p. 11.
58. Ibid., p. 100.
59. That is, 50% of New York Medicaid is paid for by the federal government, 25% by the state government, and 25% by local government. The introduction of MMIS would allow the state greater administrative control without, however, a correspondingly higher share of the financing load.
60. Personal communication—based on interviews with a number of federal officials.
61. The controversy centered around the federal requirement that states regularly issue "EOBs" (explanations of benefits") to all Medicaid beneficiaries. In principle these listings of services paid for were supposed to furnish protection against provider fraud since beneficiaries would be required to report any services listed that they had not in fact received. In practice, however, state officials complained that Medicaid clients misunderstood the EOBs, thought they were actually bills the clients were expected to pay, and became upset. Moreover, state officials argued that clients often did not know whether they had received certain services (such as complicated lab tests) or not; only the grossest forms of fraud could be caught this way. In short, state officials believed—and may well have been correct—that the administrative costs involved were much greater than the potential benefits to be gained. Personal communication, MSA officials.
62. Theodore J. Lowi, "American Business, Public Policy, Case Studies and Political Theory," *World Politics,* July 1964, 16, 689.
63. For an extended sociological discussion of the concepts of structural

"visibility" and "observability," see Robert K. Merton, *Social Theory and Social Structure* (New York: Free Press, 1968), pp. 373–411.

CHAPTER 3

1. U.S. Department of Health, Education and Welfare, *Towards a Comprehensive Policy for the 1970's: A White Paper* (Washington, D.C.: May 1971), p. 33.
2. Paul M. Ellwood, Jr., M.D., Nancy N. Anderson, Ph.D., James E. Billings, M. A., Rick J. Carlson, Earl J. Hoagberg, and Walter McClure, "Health Maintenance Strategy," *Medical Care,* May-June 1971, IX (3) 291.
3. Ibid., p. 295.
4. Paul Ellwood, Jr., Patrick O'Donoghue, Walter McClure, Robert Holley, Rick J. Carlson, Earl Hoagberg, *Assuring the Quality of Health Care* (Minneapolis: InterStudy, 1973), p. 1.
5. Ibid., p. 2.
6. Ibid., pp. 2–4.
7. InterStudy's quality assurance proposal as well as a summary of the conferences were published in *Assuring the Quality of Health Care.*
8. The following definitions of structural (or input), process and outcome indicators of quality of medical care are drawn from Avedis Donabedian, M.D., *A Guide to Medical Care Administration, Medical Care Appraisal—Quality Utilization* (Washington, D.C.: American Public Health Association, 1969), pp. 2–3. Appraisal of structure or input involves "the evaluation of the settings and instrumentalities available and used for the provision of care. While including the physical aspects of facilities and equipment, structural appraisal goes far beyond to encompass the characteristics of the administrative organization and the qualifications of health professionals. The term "structure' . . . also signifies the properties of the resources used to provide care and the manner in which they are organized." Assessment of process entails "the evaluation of the activities of physicians and other health professionals in the management of patients. The criterion generally used is the degree to which management of patients conforms with the standards and expectations of the respective professions." Outcome measures evaluate "end results in terms of health and satisfaction."
9. *Assuring the Quality of Health Care,* p. 27.
10. Ibid., p. 27. The reference to Fuchs is to Victor R. Fuchs, "The Basic Forces Influencing Costs of Medical Care," in *Report of the National*

Conference on Medical Costs (Washington, D.C.: HEW, June 27–28), 1967.

11. "Health Maintenance Strategy," p. 351.
12. Assuring the Quality of Health Care, p. 25.
13. "Health Maintenance Strategy," p. 292.
14. Ibid., p. 291.
15. Assuring the Quality of Health Care, p. 20.
16. Robert Alford in his book Health Care Politics, Chicago and London: (University of Chicago Press, 1975) notes that, "Market reformers believe that HMOs will restore price competition with the hospitals and will offer consumers a free choice between alternative plans. Bureaucratic reformers believe that they will integrate preventive and ambulatory care in the delivery center and, through prepayment, provide an organizational incentive to reduce costs, duplication of equipment and so forth." (p. 255)
17. Assuring the Quality of Health Care, p. 20.
18. Harry Schwartz, The Case for American Medicine (New York: David McKay, 1972), p. 216.
19. The Case for American Medicine, p. 177.
20. Ibid.
21. Walter J. McClure, "Four Points in Quality Assurance," mimeographed, January 10, 1973.
22. Assuring the Quality of Health Care, p. 28.
23. Ibid., p. 35.
24. Ibid.
25. Ibid., p. 21.
26. Ibid., p. 22.
27. New York Times, May 17, 1976.
28. Federal Trade Commission, Staff Report on the Health Maintenance Organization and Its Effects on Competition (Washington, D.C.: Bureau of Economics, July 1977), p. 11.
29. Paul Starr, "The Undelivered Health System," Public Interest, Winter 1976, 42, 74.
30. New York Times, Nov. 22, 1975.
31. Starr, "The Undelivered Health System," p. 75.
32. See Wall Street Journal, Feb. 11, 1975. Also, New York Times, May 17, 1976.
33. Stevens and Stevens, Welfare Medicine in America, p. 230.
34. See Edward M. Kennedy, In Critical Condition (New York: Simon and Schuster, 1972), p. 72.
35. Wall Street Journal, Dec. 31, 1973.

36. *American Medical News,* Feb. 25, 1974, 17, 9.
37. *New York Times,* May 13, 1976.
38. Ibid.
39. Paul Starr, "An Experiment Designed to Fail," *New Republic,* April 19, 1975.
40. *New York Times,* May 17, 1976.
41. *Medical World News,* Jan. 27, 1975, p. 54.
42. *National Journal,* Sept. 2, 1972, p. 1405.
43. Ibid.
44. Ibid.
45. "The Undelivered Health System," p. 75.
46. *New York Times,* May 17, 1976.
47. U.S. Department of Health, Education and Welfare; Social Rehabilitation Services; Medical Services Administration, *State Medicaid HMO Contracts* (Washington, D.C.: Sept. 1973).
48. Testimony from the California Auditor General's Office, represented by Gerald Hawes and Robert Christophel, before the U.S. Senate Special Committee on Aging and the U.S. House Select Committee on Aging, Oct. 28, 1975, Washington, D.C., p. 8.
49. *Los Angeles Times,* Dec. 14, 1973.
50. Hawes and Christophel Testimony, op. cit., p. 8.
51. Ibid.
52. *New York Times,* Mar. 14, 1975.
53a. *Medical World News,* July 28, 1975.
53b. *New York Times,* June 14, 1976.
54. *New York Times,* June 14, 1976.
55. Ibid.
56. *New York Times,* Dec. 13, 1976.
57. *Medical World News,* Feb. 7, 1977, p. 33.
58. Ibid.
59. Ibid.
60. *AMA News* April 25, 1977, 20, 1.
61. Assemblyman Henry Waxman, *Los Angeles Times,* Dec. 14, 1973.
62. U.S. Department of Health, Education and Welfare; Social Rehabilitation Service; Medical Services Administration, *Medicaid 1977–1981 (Forward Plan)* (Washington, D.C.: July 1975), p. 159.
63. See, for example, *Medical World News,* Sept. 20, 1976, p. 35.
64. *Los Angeles Times,* June 17, 1974.
65. Hawes and Christophel Testimony, op. cit., p. 10.
66. Amitai Etzioni and Pamela Doty, "Profit in Not-for-Profit Corporations," *Political Science Quarterly,* Fall 1976, 91(3) 433–453.

67. *New York Times,* Nov. 26, 1976.
68. Michael B. Rothfield, "Sensible Surgery for Swelling Medical Costs," *Fortune* (April 1973), abridged in *Prognosis Negative Crisis in the Health Care System,* David Kotelchuck (Ed.) (New York: Vintage, 1976), pp. 355–356, 358.
69. See, for example, David Mechanic, "Factors Affecting Receptivity to Innovations in Health Care Delivery Among Primary-Care Physicians" in *Politics, Medicine and Social Science* (New York: Wiley, 1974), pp. 69–87. Also, Stephen P. Strickland, *U.S. Health Care, What's Wrong and What's Right,* a Potomac Associates Book (New York: Universe Books, 1972), Table 21, "Doctors' Assessment of Various Kinds of Medical Practice," pp. 76–77.
70. See Talcott Parson's *The Social System* (New York: Free Press, 1951), Ch. X.
71. Ibid., p. 434.
72. Eliot Freidson, *The Profession of Medicine* (New York: Dodd, Mead, 1970), pp. 80–81, 160.
73. *New York Times,* Dec. 13, 1976.
74. See remark by Under-Secretary of Health, Education and Welfare Hale Champion before the Group Health Association of America, Bonaventure Hotel, Los Angeles, California, June 20, 1977.
75. *American Medical News,* April 25, 1977, 20, 1.
76. *New York Times,* Jan. 27, 1978.
77. *Group Health News,* Sept. 1977, 18, 1.
78. "HEW Accelerates HMO Support Efforts," *Washington Developments,* Nov. 14, 1977, 6, 4.

CHAPTER 4

1. Moreland Act Commission, *Long Term Care Regulation: Past Lapses and Future Prospects, A Summary Report* (April 1976), p. 3.
2. Ibid., p. 2.
3. Ibid, pp. 71–87.
4. Ibid., p. 10.
5. Ibid., pp. 71–87.
6. Ibid.
7. The commission's proposed "fair rental" formula provides a case in point. Although the commission claimed this new method would reduce "unconscionable profits" of nursing home owners by at least $10 million

per year, critics saw little real change. Morton P. Hyman, an officer of the State Public Health Council told the *New York Times* that his committee on Medicaid reimbursement would recommend that the council not adopt the Moreland proposal which he said "appears to perpetuate certain serious abuses and disadvantages of the pre-March 1975 rules." According to Hyman, the formula "would afford property owners unwarranted profits and would substantially increase the cost of Medicaid reimbursement to the state, without any attendant benefits to the public." *New York Times,* Jan. 15, 1976.

8. *New York Times,* Feb. 27, 1975.

9. *New York Times,* April 12, 1975.

10. Amitai Etzioni, Alfred Kahn, and Sheila Kamerman, "Public Management of Health and Home Care for the Aged and Disabled" ("Alternatives to Nursing Homes"), A Position Paper, (New York City: Jan. 1975), Center for Policy Rearch, p. 4.

11. Moreland Act Commission, Long Term Care Regulations: Past Lapses and Future Prospects, a summary Report (April 1976) p. 73.

12. See New York State Moreland Act Commission, *Regulating Nursing Home Care: The Paper Tigers* (Oct. 1975) Section IV: "The *Maxwell* and *Hayden Manor* Cases," pp. 69–85.

13. Quote from the testimony of Acting Health Commissioner Robert Whalen in the *Report on Nursing Homes and Health Related Facilities in New York State* by the Temporary State Commission on Living Costs and the Economy, Assemblyman Andrew Stein, Chairman (April 1975), p. 331.

14. Lee Dembart, "Nursing Homes in New York Had Friends in High Places," *New York Times,* 1975.

15. *New York Times,* June 2, 1975.

16. *New York Times,* July 16, 1975; Aug. 25, 1975; Aug. 29, 1975.

17. *New York Times,* July 8, 1975; June 13, 1975.

18. *New York Times,* May 19, 1976; May 20, 1976.

19. *New York Times,* June 26, 1975.

20. *New York Times,* July 11, 1975.

21. *New York Times,* May 30, 1976.

22. *New York Times,* June 13, 1975.

23. *New York Times,* May 17, 1975.

24. *New York Times,* May 30, 1976. An informal survey of New York City public interest lawyers specializing on problems of the elderly indicates no suits had been filed as of 1979.

25. "Analysis of the Moreland Act Commission Legislative Proposals," memo to Assemblyman Andrew Stein.

26. Temporary State Commission on Living Costs and the Economy, *Report*

on *Nursing Homes and Health Related Facilities in New York State,* p. 157.

27. See David Mechanic, *Politics, Medicine and Social Science,* Ch. XIV, "The Right to Treatment: Judicial Action and Social Change," (New York: Wiley, 1974), pp. 227–248.

28. Moreland Commission, Report No. 1, pp. 4–6, 10, pp. 51–68.

29. Ibid., pp. 51–68.

30. See "What To Do About the Nursing Homes: An Interview with Amitai Etzioni," A Staff Report, *Juris Doctor* (Sept. 1976).

31. Moreland Commission, Report No. 1, *The Paper Tigers,* p. 10.

32. Moreland Commission, *Summary Report,* p. 13.

33. The state of Connecticut had, in fact, established such a "point system" for interpreting and utilizing the results of state nursing home licensing inspections. Connecticut officials claimed considerable success in motivating nursing homes to meet and even to exceed quality standards. See Franklin M. Foote, "Progress in Nursing Home Care," *Journal of the American Medical Association,* Oct. 23, 1967, Vol. 202, reprinted in Senate Long Term Care Subcommittee, Nursing Home Care in the United States Failure in Public Policy, Supporting Paper #1, Oct. 1974, pp. 229–233.

34. Moreland Commission Report No. 1, *The Paper Tigers,* p. 31.

35. Ibid, p. 32.

36. Moreland Commission *Summary Report,* Appendix A, pp. 89–155.

37. Ibid., p. 95.

38. Ibid.

39. Ibid., p. 107.

40. Ibid., pp. 106, 110–111.

41. Ibid.

42. Ibid., pp. 122–123.

43. Ibid., pp. 152–155.

44. See *New York Times,* Oct. 10, 1974.

45. *New York Times,* Feb. 27, 1975.

46. *New York Times,* April 12, 1975.

47. *New York Times,* May 17, 1975.

48. Ibid.

49. *New York Times,* June 13, 1975.

50. *New York Times,* June 11, 1975.

51. *New York Times,* April 12, 1975.

52. Moreland Commission Report No. 1, *The Paper Tigers,* pp. 86–113.

53. Ibid., p. 42.

54. *New York Times,* Mar. 7, 1976.

55. *New York Times,* May 20, 1976.

56. See Murray Edelman, *The Symbolic Uses of Politics* (Urbana: University of Illinois Press, 1964) and *Politics As Symbolic Action: Mass Arousal and Quiescence* (Chicago: Markham Publishing, 1971).
57. Robert Alford, *Health Care Politics: Ideological and Interest Group Barriers to Reform* (Chicago: University of Chicago Press, 1975), p. 249.

CHAPTER 5

1. Gabriel Almond and Sidney Verba, *The Civic Culture* (Boston: Little, Brown, 1965).
2. See Donna Shalala, *Neighborhood Governance: Issues and Proposals* (New York: The American Jewish Committee, 1971); and Alan Altshuler, *Community Control* (Indianapolis: Bobbs-Merrill, 1970).
3. See Daniel Patrick Moynihan, *Maximum Feasible Misunderstanding* (New York: Free Press, 1970), Ch. 3, especially pp. 56–57 where Moynihan documents the parallels between the 1961 Mobilization for Youth proposal to the community action title of the 1964 Economic Opportunity Act. See also Peter Marris and Martin Rein, *Dilemmas of Social Reform: Poverty and Community Action in the United States* (New York: Atherton Press, 1967).
4. Daniel P. Moynihan, *Maximum Feasible Misunderstanding,* pp. iiv–iv.
5. See, for example, Allen Booz, Public Administrative Services, *Citizen Participation in the Model Cities Program,* prepared for the Department of Housing and Urban Development, Washington, D.C., June 30, 1971, and Community Change, Inc. and Public Sector, Inc., *A Study of Consumer Participation in the Administrative Processes in Various Levels of HSMHA's Service Projects. Final Report,* prepared under contract HSM 110–71–135 for the Office of Program Planning and Evaluation, Health Services and Mental Health Administration Public Health Service, HEW, Sausalito, Calif., June 20, 1972.
6. See Barbara and John Ehrenreich, *The American Health Empire: Power, Profits and Politics* (New York: Vintage, 1971).
7. Ibid., p. vii.
8. See Barry Ensminger, *The $8 Billion Hospital Bed Overrun* (Washington, D.C.: Public Citizens' Health Research Group, 1975).
9. The other members of the Citizens' Board were: Stephen Becker, author, Katonah, N.Y.; the Hon. Joe Bernal, State Senator, San Antonio, Texas; Roberta Bessetti, Supervisor, Combined Nursing Services of Minneapolis, Minneapolis, Minnesota; Gerald Besson, M.D., Physician, Sunnyvale, California; George F. Burket, Jr., M.D., Physician,

Kingman, Texas; the Hon. Richard Fitzsimmons, Minnesota State
Legislature, Warren, Minnesota; H. Jack Geiger, M.D., Department
of Community Health and Social Medicare School of Medicine, Tufts
University, Boston, Mass.: Robert Haggerty, M.D., Professor and
Chairman, Department of Pediatrics, School of Medicine and Den-
tistry, University of Rochester; Sanford Kravitz, Ph.D., Dean, School
of Social Welfare, State University of New York, Stony Brook, Long
Island, New York; Harry Lipscomb, M.D., Xerox Center for Health
Care Research, Baylor College of Medicine, Houston, Texas; C. Clem-
ent Lucas, M.D., Special Assistant to the Administrator for Youth
Affairs, Health Services and Mental Health Administration, HEW,
Rockville, Md.; Einar Mohn, International Director, Western Conference of Teamsters, Burlingame, Calif.; Rodney Powell, M.D., Department of Pediatrics, School of Medicine, University of Minnesota; John
D. Rockefeller IV, Secretary of State, Charleston, West Virginia; Mil-
ton Senn, M.D., Professor of Pediatrics, School of Medicine, Yale
University, New Haven, Conn.
10. The Citizens' Board of Inquiry into Health Services for Americans,
    Heal Yourself (Washington, D.C.: American Public Health Associa-
    tion, 1972), Forward, 2nd ed.
11. Ibid., special page.
12. Ibid., p. 26.
13. Ibid.
14. Ibid., pp. 26–27.
15. Ibid., p. 27.
16. Ibid., p. 28.
17. Ibid.
18. Ibid., p. 29.
19. Ibid., p. 25.
20. Ibid., p. 28.
21. Ibid., p. 36.
22. Ibid., pp. 38–39.
23. Ibid., p. 40.
24. Ibid.
25. Ibid. p. 47.
26. Ibid., p. 31.
27. Ibid.
28. Ibid.
29. Ibid.
30. Ibid., p. 129.
31. Ibid., p. 81.
32. Ibid., p. 132

33. Ibid., p. 132.
34. Ibid., 131.
35. Ibid., pp. 130–131.
36. Ibid., p. 131.
37. Ibid.,
38. Ibid., p. 127.
39. Ibid., p. 56.
40. Ibid., p. 111.
41. Robert K. Yin, William A. Lucas, Peter L. Szanton, and J. Andrew Spindler, *Citizen Organization: Increasing Client Control Over Services,* prepared for the Department of Health, Education and Welfare (Washington, D.C.: Rand Corporation, April, 1973).
42. Ibid., p. 30.
43. Ibid.
44. Ibid., pp. 56–57.
45. Laurelyn Veatch, "Community Boards in Search of Authority," *The Hastings Center Report,* October 1975, 5,(5) 25.
46. Gerald Sparer, et. al., "Consumer Participation in OEO-Assisted Neighborhood Health Centers," *American Journal Public Health,* June 1970, 60(6), 1094–1095.
47. Community Change, Inc. and Public Sector, Inc., "A Study of Consumer Participation in the Administration Procession Various Levels of HSMHA's Service Projects." Sausalito, Calif. June 20, 1972 (mimeo).
48. U.S., Congress, Senate, *Medicare and Medicaid Problems, Issues and Alternatives,* Senate Finance Committee Report 1970, p. 134.
49. Yin, *et. al., Citizen Organization,* p. 93.
50. Ibid.
51. Medical Services Administration, "Role at a State Medical Care Advisory Committee," *Medical Assistance Manual of Social and Rehabilitation Service,* Manual No. 2–30–00 (March, 1971).
52. Robert Stevens and Rosemary Stevens, *Welfare Medicine in America* (New York: Free Press, 1974), p. 250.
53. Ibid., p. 258.
54. See Edward W. Lehman, *Coordinating Health Care* (Beverly Hills, Calif.: Sage, 1975).
55. Citizens' Board of Inquiry, *Heal Yourself,* p. 68.
56. Comptroller General of the United States, "Comprehensive Health Planning As Carried Out By State and Areawide Agencies in Three States" (Washington, D.C.: April 13, 1974), p. 21.
57. Ibid., pp. 25–31.
58. Ibid., p. 24.

59. U.S. Department of Health, Education and Welfare, *Project Summary, Board and Staff Composition of Health Planning Agencies,* (Washington, D.C.: HEW, Public Health Service, Health Resources Administration, Office of Health Resources Opportunity).
60. Robert R. Alford, *Health Care Politics, Ideological and Interest Group Barriers to Reform* (Chicago: University of Chicago Press, 1975), p. 17.
61. Stephen Beaver and Martin Sorin, *Interorganizational Links in Community Participation* (Washington, D.C.: Center for Policy Research, June 1975).
62. Ibid., p. 30.
63. Ibid., p. 28.
64. Ibid., pp. 47–49.
65. Ibid., pp. 173–185.
66. Ibid., p. 182.
67. Ibid., pp. 181–183.
68. Ibid., pp. 185.
69. Ibid., p. 182.
70. Ibid., p. 117.
71. Ibid., pp. 68–69.
72. Ibid., p. 69.
73. Ibid., p. 82.
74. Ibid., p. 87.
75. Ibid., pp. 154–157.
76. Ibid., p. 157.
77. Ibid., p. 152. (See radicalism scale.)
78. Ibid., p. 199.
79. Ibid., p. 91.
80. Ibid., p. 134.
81. Ibid., pp. 78–79.
82. Ibid., p. 135.
83. Ibid.
84. Ibid., p. 99.
85. Ibid., p. 200.
86. Ibid., p. 154.
87. Ibid., p. 50.
88. Ibid.
89. See Stephen P. Strickland, *U.S. Health Care, What's Wrong, What's Right* (New York: Universe, A Potomac Associates Book, 1972).
90. Ibid., p. 35.
91. Ibid., p. 33.
92. Ibid.

93. Ibid., p. 35.
94. Ibid., p. 128.
95. Ibid., p. 75.
96. Ibid., p. 75.
97. Ibid., p. 78.
98. Ibid., p. 102.
99. Ibid., p. 49.
100. Ibid., p. 52.
101. Ibid., p. 54.
102. Ibid., p. 52.
103. Ibid., p. 105.
104. Ibid., p. 101.
105. Ibid., p. 104.
106. Ibid., pp. 56–64.
107. Ibid., p. 62.
108. Ibid.
109. Citizens' Board of Inquiry, *Heal Yourself,* p. 134.
110. Ibid., p. 139.
111. Ibid., p. 140.
112. Ibid., p. 112.
113. Lowell Bellin, et al. "Phase One of Consumer Participation in Policies of 22 Voluntary Hospitals in New York City," *American Journal of Public Health,* October 1972, 62(10), 373.
114. Laurelyn Veatch, "Community Boards in Search of Authority," p. 28.
115. Ibid., p. 29.
116. Consumer Commission on the Accreditation of Health Services, Inc., "The Development of A Consumer Health Network," *Health Perspectives,* July–Oct., 1977, IV(4) and (5).
117. Ibid.
118. Citizens' Board of Inquiry, *Heal Yourself,* p. 59.
119. Ibid.
120. Harry P. Cain II, Ph.D. and Frances V. Dearman, "The Federal Perspective," *American Health Care Association Journal,* July, 1977, reprinted by the U.S. HEW; PHS; HRA, 3(4).
121. Edmund Ricci, Bardin Nelson and Robert Pecarchik, "The Consumer Movement in Health Care," Paper presented at the annual meetings of the American Sociological Association (Montreal, Canada 1974), p. 15.
122. Ibid., p. 20.
123. Ibid., p. 18.
124. Ibid., pp. 18–19.

125. Citizens' Board of Inquiry, *Heal Yourself,* p. 131.
126. Steven Beaver and Martin Sorin, Center for Policy Research, "Interorganizational Links in Community Participation," pp. 198–201.
127. Moreland Report No. 3, p. 39.
128. Ibid., p. 42.
129. Ibid.
130. Ibid., p. 3.
131. Ibid.
132. Lowell Bellin, et al., "Phase One of Consumer Participation in Policies of 22 Voluntary Hospitals in New York City," *American Journal of Public Health,* (October 1972), 62(10), 1371.
133. Yin, et. al., *Citizen Organization,* p. 66.
134. Ibid., p. 68.
135. Beaver and Sorin, "Interorganizational Links in Community Participation," p. 195.
136. Ibid., pp. 195–196.
137. Ibid., p. 196.
138. Ibid.
139. Beaver and Sorin, "Interorganizational Links in Community Participation," p. 60.
140. See Stephen Strickland, *U.S. Health Care: What's Wrong and What's Right* (New York: A Potomac Associates Book, Universe Books, 1972), p. 36.
141. Grant McConnell, *Private Power and American Democracy* (New York; Knopf, 1966), p. 29.
142. Ibid., p. 362.
143. William L. Morrow, *Public Administration, Politics and the Political System* (New York: Random House, 1975), pp. 189–190.
144. Consumer Commission on the Accreditation of Health Services, "The Development of a Consumer Health Network," p. 3.
145. Ibid., p. 2.
146. *The New York Times,* June 29, 1975.
147. Consumer Commission on the Accreditation of Health Services, "The Development of a Consumer Health Network," p. 2.
148. Yin, et. al., pp. 63–64.
149. Paul E. Peterson, "Forms of Representation: Participation of the Poor in the Community Action Program," *American Political Science Review,* June 1970, 64, 291–507.
150. Consumer Commission on the Accreditation of Health Services, "The Development of a Consumer Health Network," p. 9.

INDEX

Abram, Morris B., 124, 136, 138, 154, 159–60
Accountability, 46–47
of consumer representatives, 218, 220
Advisory Commission on Intergovernmental Relations, 32
Advocacy research, 167
Alford, Robert, 160
American Enterprise Institute, 167
American Jewish Congress, 142
American Medical Association (AMA), 99, 100, 204
American Public Health Association, 169
Aronowitz, 139
Assuring the Quality of Health Care, 27
Authority relations in bureaucracy, hierarchical vs. feudal, 48–54

Bazelon, David, 167
Bell, Daniel, 25
Bergman, Bernard, 134, 136, 220–21
Berle, Peter A. A., 124
Besson, Dr., 207
Bond, Julian, 168
Breslow, Lester, 168
Brown, Jerry, 104–6
Bureaucracy
hierarchical vs. feudal authority relations in, 48–54
vs. market, 82–84
Weberian model of, 30
Bureaucratic feudalism, 48, 49, 58, 60
Burke, Richard, 98
Burke, William, 105

Cain, Harry, 214
Califano, Joseph, 121